Money in the
Multinational
Enterprise

BASIC BOOKS

IN

The Harvard Multinational Enterprise Series

EDITED BY RAYMOND VERNON

Sovereignty at Bay: The Multinational Spread of U.S. Enterprises
RAYMOND VERNON

Managing the Multinational Enterprise
JOHN M. STOPFORD and LOUIS T. WELLS, JR.

Money in the Multinational Enterprise: A Study of Financial Policy
SIDNEY M. ROBBINS and ROBERT B. STOBAUGH

Scientists and Salesmen: The Multinational Spread of the U.S. Pharmaceutical Industry (forthcoming)
LAWRENCE H. WORTZEL

Money in the Multinational Enterprise

A Study of Financial Policy

SIDNEY M. ROBBINS and
ROBERT B. STOBAUGH

With a simulation model constructed by
Daniel M. Schydlowsky

Basic Books, Inc., Publishers / New York

© 1973 by Basic Books, Inc.
Library of Congress Catalog Card Number: 73-76366
SBN 465-04715-7
Manufactured in the United States of America

74   75   76   10   9   8   7   6   5   4   3   2

To
Anne and Beverly

PREFACE

Over the past seven years under the aegis of the Multinational Enterprise Study at Harvard Business School, extensive studies have been conducted to obtain a better understanding of the U.S.-based multinational enterprises. This volume is the third in a series of books, coordinated by Professor Raymond Vernon, that present the main findings of the Multinational Enterprise Study.

This book has been a long time in the making. At times on this journey we were inclined to agree with George Orwell that "writing a book is a horrible, exhausting struggle, like a long bout of some painful illness." But not often. Usually we were in accord with the spirit of a recent newspaper headline, "Timbuktu—getting there was most of the fun." And the individuals we encountered along the way were to a large extent responsible for this fun.

We received generous help in the form of long, frank interviews with executives of multinational enterprises as well as officials of governments, international institutions, banks, and accounting firms. While our agreements with them call for anonymity, others who provided help did not require this proscription.

Daniel Schydlowsky occupies a rather special and unusual relationship with respect to this book, a relationship which is reflected on its title page. His work on the book was in the status of a principal researcher, a colleague, and a partner associated with us. By agreement, however, his contribution was concentrated on conceptualizing and executing the simulation model. The actual presentation of the model in the book and the relation of the model to the rest of the book were entirely at our choice and discretion. Therefore, while the credit for the model lies with Schydlowsky, the responsibility for the use of its output is ours alone.

This is not the first time that we have had the privilege of working with Professor Raymond Vernon. As before, we benefited enormously from his unusual ability to provide intellectual guidance that both bolstered our research efforts when they faltered and opened challenging new vistas to explore. It is a constant source of wonder that a person can give so much of his time to others and yet produce so much himself.

Max Hall, allowing his inquiring mind to dig deeply into the subject matter, reviewed the manuscript with his usual painstaking care. Whatever complacency we may have had from our early drafts was banished by the number of times that his seemingly naive questions exposed weak elements in our ideas. We gladly accepted this trade-off of shaken composure for a better book.

William Lance's initiative and thoroughness, combined with his complete reliability, constituted an open invitation for us to rely heavily on him—and we did. During his time with us, which spanned his days from his senior year at Harvard College to his graduation from Harvard Law School, he served on many different fronts. He was our principal research assistant and, among other things, conducted many of the interviews with executives of multinational enterprises, assisted in developing the computer analyses of the interviews, organized the results, and participated in discussions leading to the evolution of our theories.

Joan Curhan assumed the burden of recruiting personnel, handling funds, and making arrangements with the participating companies. To this austere administrative area, she brought a welcome combination of efficiency, tact, and charm.

Yair Aharoni, now Professor at Institut pour l'Etude des Méthodes de Direction de l'Entreprise, helped get the project underway. Later various members of the Harvard Business School faculty provided advice—especially Rita Rodriguez on the final manuscript, Arthur Schleifer, Jr., on all phases of statistical testing, Robert Hayes on factor analysis, and Edgar Barrett on accounting.

William Zeltonoga read the thousands of pages of interviews, coded the results, and carried out an extensive literature search. Jerry Zivan helped develop the framework for and, with Donald Herner, supervised the collection of financial data from published sources. James Vaupel prepared the computer program to evaluate this information. George Middleton and Manya Sesnovich ran the program and, along with Piero Telesio and Jules Pogrow, helped interpret the results of the multinational-enterprise model and analyzed published financial statements and governmental data. Piero Telesio also assisted in preparing Tables A–2 and A–3 and, with Gary Hodel, analyzed the unpublished financial statements of the companies studied.

Robert Carlson conducted interviews in Turkey. Jean-Marie Bonnet obtained unpublished statistics from the French government and used this information, as well as published data, to compare U.S. subsidiaries in France with domestic French companies. John Rudey provided the data on Eurobond operations and suggested hypotheses to test. Amos Sapir did the study of the cost of hedging. We are indebted to Hasan Bilgid for the material on Turkey, which he based to a large extent on Turkish-language sources.

William Gifford of the law firm of Ivan, Phillips and Barker advised on legal aspects, especially taxation.

Kathy Harlan was our cheerful, administrative factotum. She did most of the typing of the early drafts, ran the logistic regression analyses of the interviews, and served as a research assistant on all phases of the project.

Madelyn Wisnia typed the last several drafts as well as the final manuscript; her willingness to work nights and weekends to meet seemingly impossible deadlines made our work much easier than it would otherwise have been.

Joan Rabinow helped considerably in the typing of drafts. Also, various students on the Harvard College Work-Study Program did typing or clerical work.

Our ideas were sharpened by presentations and discussions with a number of groups. These included the Joint Economic Subcommittee of Congress, International Economic Policy Study Group of House Republicans, Financial Management Seminar at Centre d'Etudes Industrielles, International Finance Seminar at Brookings Institute, Petroleum Managers' Seminar at Northwestern University, Annual Meeting of Association for Education in International Business, International Law Society, various Harvard Business School alumni programs, several student-faculty seminars at Harvard Business School, and our classes at Columbia and Harvard Business School.

We owe a vote of thanks to the Ford Foundation, which provided the mainstay of our financial support. Also, we are indebted to the Associates of the Harvard Business School, the American Cyanamid Company Faculty Grant, and the Endowment for Research Fund of the Division of Research of Harvard Business School for generous supplementary funding.

This listing of acknowledgements is a scant way of showing the gratitude we feel to our associates. We hope they find merit in the book we now offer.

SIDNEY M. ROBBINS
ROBERT B. STOBAUGH

Boston, 1973

CONTENTS

FIGURES

TABLES

Money in the Multinational Enterprise

ONE / Introduction:
The Financial System

Several years ago an American firm told the story of "a single working day in the company's life" from the time the sun rises over an oil field on Kharg Island in the Persian Gulf until it lights up the sky above a manufacturing plant in Bombay, India. This account, suggestive of the pages of Kipling, appeared in an annual report of International Business Machines to mark the fact that the number of countries served had passed one hundred.[1]

The spread of U.S. firms into distant lands has often been described, sometimes in terms of the broad economic scene, sometimes in terms of the individual company. In this book our concern is with the company, and, more specifically, with its financial practices and policies.

The aim is to throw new light on the methods that U.S. firms use—and might use—to resolve the financial problems they encounter abroad. To that end we collected massive evidence through interviews and the study of confidential records. But such evidence alone does not point the way toward the most profitable financial policies. So we went further and employed a model of a multinational enterprise that could be manipulated to show the outcomes of alternative courses of action.

But first a preliminary look at the emerging multinational scene.

U.S. Foreign Direct Investment

Not all multinational enterprises are based in the United States. Many are controlled from other countries, including the United Kingdom, Canada, the Netherlands, France, Italy, Germany, Belgium, Sweden, and Japan. But this study of financial affairs is confined to enterprises controlled by U.S. firms.

Why have those firms chosen to create organizations in foreign countries? The question is important to any discussion of the financial function, for the original purpose of the investment should play a prominent part in evaluating the performance of a foreign subsidiary. The question of motivation also comes up in a broader context when the national and interna-

3

tional consequences of foreign investment are debated, and it is often answered in a superficial manner with too much emphasis on a single factor, such as the lower cost of labor or the need to overcome tariff barriers against U.S.-manufactured goods. Those and many other factors do influence investment decisions, but our conclusion is that the most prevalent motive, underlying the others, has been the desire to meet a competitive threat. In manufacturing, the threat is usually to an established export market; the U.S. investor is trying to maintain his place in the world market, at times against other U.S. investors and at times against European, Japanese, or other foreign competition—something he feels he cannot accomplish without foreign affiliates and more foreign affiliates. In extractive industries the fiercest urge is to prevent competitors from getting ahead in access to raw materials. All multinational enterprises, whether engaged in manufacturing or the exploitation of raw materials, have a common desire to reduce risks and to acquire knowledge about new markets and new sources.[2]

Foreign affiliates may be subsidiaries, organized abroad as separate corporations, or they may be branches, which are legally an integral part of the U.S. parent corporation or one of its domestic subsidiaries. The corporate form, which limits the enterprise's liability for the subsidiaries' activities, ordinarily is preferred for foreign manufacturing operations. Indeed, 96 percent of the income received from foreign affiliates by manufacturing firms in 1966 came as dividends from corporations.[3]

Because of the crudeness of the underlying data, published information regarding the size and growth of U.S. investments abroad can do little more than indicate orders of magnitude and general trends.[4] But any way you look at it, the magnitudes are large. According to the estimates shown in Table 1–1, U.S. companies at the end of 1970 controlled foreign affiliates (subsidiaries as well as branches) having total assets of about $134 billion. The share actually held by U.S. entities was $78 billion, which is the so-called *book value* of U.S. foreign direct investment. (The $134 billion estimate of total assets includes the share of the foreign operations financed with funds obtained from foreigners as well as from U.S. direct investors.) Of this $78 billion book value, some 90 percent was about equally distributed among three major geographic areas—Europe, Canada, and the less developed countries (LDC) as a group. A little over one-half of the LDC investments were in the Latin American countries. The dollar figures showing both a geographic and industry distribution are shown in Table 1–2.

Ownership in manufacturing industries is the major form of U.S. investment in most of the countries of the world, with a book value of $32.2 bil-

TABLE 1–1

*Estimated Balance Sheet of Foreign Direct Investment
of U.S. Enterprises, December 31, 1970
(In Billions of Dollars)*

Assets		Liabilities and Equity		
Current	62	U.S. entities' share a (Book value of U.S. foreign direct investment)		78
Fixed	60			
		Liabilities to U.S. entities	21	
		Equity owned by U.S. entities	57	
Other	12			
		Foreigners' share		56
		Short-term liabilities	34	
		Long-term liabilities	16	
		Equity	6	
TOTAL ASSETS	134	Total liabilities and equity		134

Sources: Estimated by authors from data obtained by Office of Business Economics (OBE) and reported in R. David Belli and Julius N. Friedlin, "U.S. Direct Investments Abroad in 1970," *Survey of Current Business* (October 1971): 26–38; and Office of Foreign Direct Investment (OFDI) and reported in "Foreign Affiliate Financial Survey, 1967–1968," July 2, 1970. The estimate on the balance sheet of $78 billion as the "U.S. entities' share" is from OBE data in the *Survey of Current Business,* and the other estimates were based on relationships reported by the OFDI.

a "U.S. entities' share" is book value of total U.S. foreign direct investment, which is defined by the Office of Business Economics for balance of payments statistics as the U.S. parents' share of the equity and debt of foreign business organizations whose voting stock is owned: at least 10 percent by a U.S. entity and its U.S. affiliates; or at least 25 percent by a U.S. entity, its U.S. affiliates, and its foreign affiliates; or at least 50 percent by U.S. entities when no single U.S. entity owns as much as 10 percent. It also includes the home office account in foreign branches and the equivalent ownership interest in other unincorporated foreign affiliates. Further, it includes outstanding long-term debt placed by the affiliates with the public and with nonbanking institutional investors in the United States. The table covers both manufacturing and nonmanufacturing. For further details, see U.S. Department of Commerce, Office of Business Economics, *U.S. Direct Investment Abroad, 1966, Part 1: Balance of Payments Data* (Washington: Superintendent of Documents, 1971), pp. 2, 3, and 15.

TABLE 1–2

Book Values of Foreign Direct Investment of U.S. Enterprises, by Industry and Area, 1970 [a] (In Billions of Dollars)

Area	Manu-facturing	Petroleum	Mining and Smelting	Other [b]	Total
Canada	10.1	4.8	3.0	4.9	22.8
Europe, total	13.7	5.5	0.1	5.2	24.5
European Economic					
Community	(7.1)	(2.5)	—	(2.0)	(11.7)
Germany	(2.8)	(1.2)	[c]	(0.6)	(4.6)
France	(1.9)	(0.3)	—	(0.4)	(2.6)
Italy	(0.8)	(0.5)	[c]	(0.2)	(1.5)
Others	(1.6)	(0.5)	(0.1)	(0.9)	(3.0)
United Kingdom	(5.0)	(1.9)	—	(1.2)	(8.0)
Other Western Europe	(1.6)	(1.1)	(0.1)	(2.0)	(4.8)
Less developed countries	5.5	8.4	2.5	5.1	21.4
Latin America and other					
Western Hemisphere	(4.6)	(3.9)	(2.0)	(4.1)	(14.7) [d]
Venezuela	(0.5)	(1.7)	[c]	(0.5)	(2.7)
Brazil	(1.2)	(0.1)	(0.1)	(0.3)	(1.8)
Mexico	(1.2)	—	(0.1)	(0.4)	(1.8)
Argentina	(0.8)	[c]	[c]	(0.5)	(1.3)
Others	(0.9)	(2.1)	(1.8)	(2.4)	(7.1)
Other less developed					
countries	(0.9)	(4.5)	(0.5)	(1.0)	(6.7)
Australia, New Zealand, and					
South Africa	2.2	0.9	0.6	0.6	4.3
Japan	0.8	0.5	—	0.2	1.5
International, unallocated	—	1.7	—	1.9	3.6
TOTAL OF ALL FOREIGN COUNTRIES	32.2	21.8	6.1	17.9	78.1

Source: Survey of Current Business (October 1971): 32–33.

Notes: Dash means less than $50 million. Because of rounding, some columns and rows do not total exactly.

[a] See Table 1–1 for definition of U.S. foreign direct investment.

[b] Includes agriculture, transportation, public utilities, trade.

[c] Combined in "other" industries. As a result, "petroleum" and "other" investments do not add to column totals.

[d] $12.2 billion, or about 80 percent of this total, is Latin America. The remainder includes all of the Western Hemisphere except Canada and the nineteen Latin-American republics.

lion in 1970. Moreover, the importance of manufacturing is understated, perhaps by $8 billion or so, because foreign direct investments listed in the petroleum industry and the mining and smelting industry also include some manufacturing facilities.[5] Ownership in the petroleum industry totaled $21.8 billion worldwide in 1970 and was ahead of manufacturing investment in the less developed countries as a whole. Canada has been the scene of investments in every major sector, although manufacturing is the most important.

A look into history shows that the growth of American foreign direct investment has been interrupted only by war or serious business recessions. In the latter part of the nineteenth century the United States began to export capital in significant amounts, and by 1897 had a book value of about $600 million in direct investments abroad. From that time, the recorded growth of U.S. foreign direct investment was 9 percent a year, on the average, until the outbreak of World War I.[6] Thereafter, from 1914 to 1950, the combination of two world wars and a depression slowed the growth to a mere 4 percent annually. But this average conceals sharp variations. The 7 percent rate attained in the 1920's dropped to less than 1 percent in the 1930's. This drop in the growth rate was due mainly to a shrinkage in investment in Latin America, which in turn was traceable to write-downs of values caused by depreciation of exchange rates, sales of assets, and nationalization of properties. Before the 1940's had passed, the investment rate began to climb again, and during the 1950's and 1960's, as many big American firms began to develop multinational interests, the annual growth rate rose once more, to 10 percent. Translated into absolute terms, the figures are dramatic, with an expansion between 1950 and 1970 of $66 billion, or some five times the book value added between 1897 and 1950. Figures 1–1 and 1–2 show the growth from 1929 to 1970 for the major geographic areas and the major industries.

Geography played an important role in the pattern of this growth, particularly during the initial period when transportation and communication were inefficient. The earlier investments were for the most part in neighboring countries. Investments in railways and natural resources predominated, and manufacturing accounted for only 15 percent of the stock of foreign direct investment in 1897. Thereafter the interest in manufacturing grew, and by 1929 it was firmly established as the leading industrial sector, with public utilities in second place. Nevertheless, the geographical spread was still limited. Even as late as 1929, almost three-fourths of all foreign investment was concentrated in the Western Hemisphere, primarily Canada, Mexico, and the West Indies.

FIGURE 1–1

Book Value of Foreign Direct Investment of U.S. Enterprises by Major Geographic Areas, 1929–1970

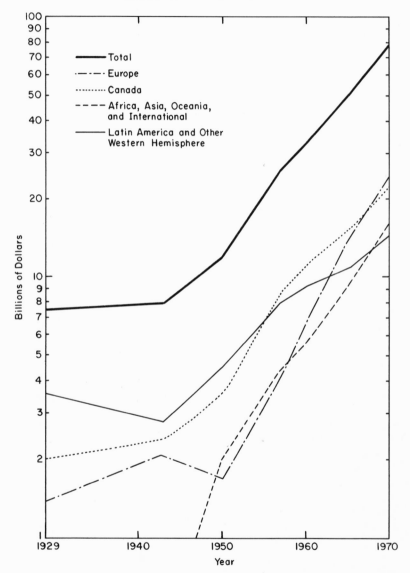

After World War II, the investments in all industrial sectors took an upward course, but the tremendous need for energy stimulated a particular interest in petroleum, which brought a heavy investment in the Middle East and a renaissance of investment activity in Latin America. As a re-

FIGURE 1–2

Book Value of Foreign Direct Investment of U.S. Enterprises by Major Industries, 1929–1970

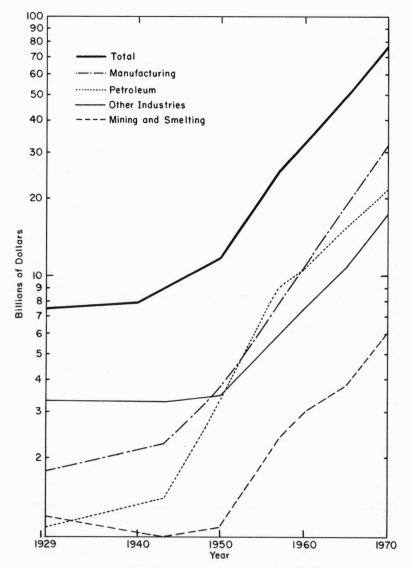

sult, during the 1950's petroleum passed manufacturing for the industrial lead. In the late 1950's, however, the petroleum industry's share of total U.S. foreign direct investment reached its peak. Although petroleum's absolute growth continued thereafter, its share of the total declined steadily, an investment in manufacturing facilities grew rapidly. Products that had been developed for the high-income U.S. market began to find increasing demand abroad, especially in Europe.[7] This demand, combined with the greater economies of scale achievable because of the European Economic Community and the European Free Trade Association, resulted in an enormous growth of U.S.-owned manufacturing facilities in Europe. By 1960 manufacturing had regained its position of leading sector, and its share continued to increase during the 1960's, primarily because of the continued emphasis on Europe, where manufacturing predominated. The book value of U.S. direct investment in Europe, less than $2 billion in 1950, grew fourteenfold by 1970.

The Idea of a Multinational System

The rapid growth of U.S. foreign direct investment might lead one to surmise that many U.S. companies have gone abroad. The reverse is true. Only a handful of companies have invested overseas to any significant degree. In 1966, the latest year for which figures on controlled foreign companies are available, out of almost 1,500,000 active corporations that filed U.S. tax returns in 1966 only 3,700 owned more than 50 percent of the stock in a foreign subsidiary.[8] Together, these 3,700 enterprises controlled almost 20,000 foreign subsidiaries and operated some 3,000 branches.[9] Approximately 75 percent of the foreign corporations were linked directly with their U.S. parents, the others being controlled indirectly through other subsidiaries.

There is no commonly accepted definition of a multinational enterprise, and not all of these 2,600 U.S. firms meet our notion of a "multinational enterprise." In a broad sense, the term could be stretched to embrace any firm that has overseas ties—even the control of a single unit. Our analysis, however, indicates that the size and spread of foreign operations contribute importantly to the tactics employed in seeking the benefits of multinationality. Accordingly, we employed these two elements—size and distribution—as the major criteria for our definition of a multinational enterprise for purposes of this study. From the *Fortune* lists of the 500 largest U.S. industrial firms in 1963 and 1964, we selected those which controlled manufacturing subsidiaries in six or more foreign countries in 1965 or before. As practically all the major U.S.-controlled raw material producers were included by these criteria, our list of companies contains the manufacturing and extractive enterprises that are generally thought of as multinational.[10]

There are 187 of these firms. Because of their huge dimensions they accounted in 1966 for about one-third of the total sales of U.S. manufacturing enterprises, about one-half of U.S. manufactured exports, and perhaps three-fourths of all U.S. foreign direct investment in manufacturing. In general, the 187 enterprises are quite profitable, make great use of scientists and engineers, and have high advertising expenditures. They have something like 8,000 foreign subsidiaries and 1,000 foreign branches. Some 40 percent of these 9,000 affiliates are engaged in manufacturing and the remainder in extraction, finance, and other activities.[11] About nine-tenths of the 187 enterprises have manufacturing units in at least four of the following five regions: Canada, Europe, other developed countries, Latin America, and other less developed countries.[12]

Viewed from abroad, the 187 U.S. multinational enterprises are a mighty force, and, in fact, the "value added" by these giants—the difference between the value of the goods they produce and the value of the items they buy—exceeds the gross national product of most countries. On the other hand, when the foreign subsidiaries are considered only in the context of the countries where they operate, their relative dimensions shrink, and they ordinarily account for a small share of the total manufacturing product—perhaps 6 percent in Western Europe and 15 or 20 percent in Latin America. An exception is Canada, where U.S. firms control about 60 percent of the manufacturing output. These percentages, however, understate the real importance of the U.S. multinational enterprises, for in most countries they dominate many of the "advanced" industries, such as computers, and in certain countries they dominate important manufacturing industries, such as ball-bearings, carbon black, petroleum products, telegraph and telephone equipment, automobiles, and tractors. Furthermore, in some countries the extractive industries are controlled largely by U.S. firms.

Among the principal attributes of a multinational enterprise are (1) it commands a common pool of resources and (2) it is capable of responding to a common strategy. Indeed, a recurring theme of the chapters that follow is that a multinational enterprise is a *system* and that it performs best when the opportunities growing out of that system are fully understood.

For purposes of financial policy, the system can be viewed as a network of operating units linked to one another by the movement of money. As a first step in describing the network, let us examine typical financing patterns, starting with the simplest pattern and moving to situations of more complexity. Figure 1–3 has three segments, labeled *A, B,* and *C*.

Segment *A* of the chart portrays a U.S. domestic corporation obtaining

FIGURE 1–3

Typical Financing Patterns of a U.S. Domestic Corporation Compared with Those of a U.S. Multinational Enterprise

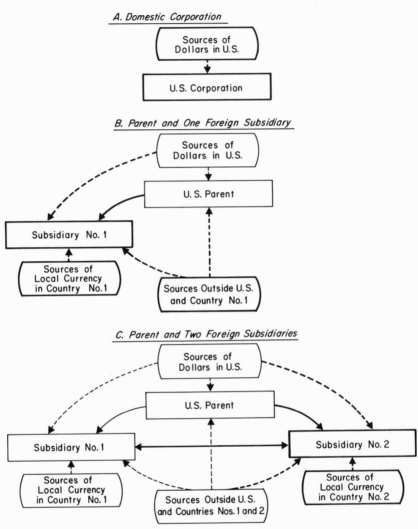

--- financial flows outside multinational enterprise system
—— financial flows within multinational enterprise system

dollars from local financing sources. In this transaction the only national laws to which the corporation is subject are those of the U.S. government and only the U.S. money market is involved.

Segment *B* shows the financing of one foreign operating unit, which we designate as foreign subsidiary *B,* operating in country *B.* This subsidiary can obtain funds from its U.S. parent, other sources in the United States, sources in country *B,* and sources in other countries. The funds are denominated in dollars, the currency of country *B,* or currencies of other countries. The dollars, in turn, can be either from sources within the United States or sources from outside the United States. In this financial arrangement, consideration must be given to the laws of different countries, the status of different money markets, and the relationships of different currencies.

Segment *C* indicates the additional complexity incurred when the second subsidiary, designated as subsidiary *C,* is added to the system. In addition to the usual problems of dealing with another set of taxes and laws, different sources of funds, and another currency, the subsidiaries can now provide each other with funds. This new dimension increases the financing opportunities. Given the fact that each connection shown on this sketch represents many different possibilities of equity and debt, it is clear that a multinational enterprise with a large number of subsidiaries operating in diverse foreign environments has many alternatives.

To structure financing programs for a given subsidiary requires decisions not only as to where the funds should be raised but also, if raised outside the local country, what method should be used in transferring them into that country. There are many methods of moving funds from unit to unit; for example, one unit can provide funds to another by granting a loan, paying interest on a loan, or granting credit on accounts receivable by deferring the collection of accounts due. These methods are used not only to finance a subsidiary but also to perform other financial tasks, such as withdrawing funds from a subsidiary to the parent firm. We conceive of the financial network as being linked together by the different methods of transferring funds.

Figure 1–4 illustrates some of the ways of effecting these shifts which represent the financial links of a system. The enterprise in this exhibit consists of a parent, *A,* and two subsidiaries, *B* and *C.* The arrows represent commonly used financial means by which funds can be shuttled at the discretion of the manager. Thus, subsidiary *B* can move funds to *A* by such mechanisms as dividends; payments for goods purchased from *A;* interest on loans or on accounts payable; and fees for services or know-how. In the opposite direction, the parent can provide funds to *B* through loans or by deferring collection of fees, royalties, and receivables owed by the subsidiary that have fallen due.

The direction of some of these flows can be reversed, as occurs for example when *B* moves funds to *A* by repaying a loan. In the illustration,

FIGURE 1–4

Typical Financial Links in a Multinational Enterprise

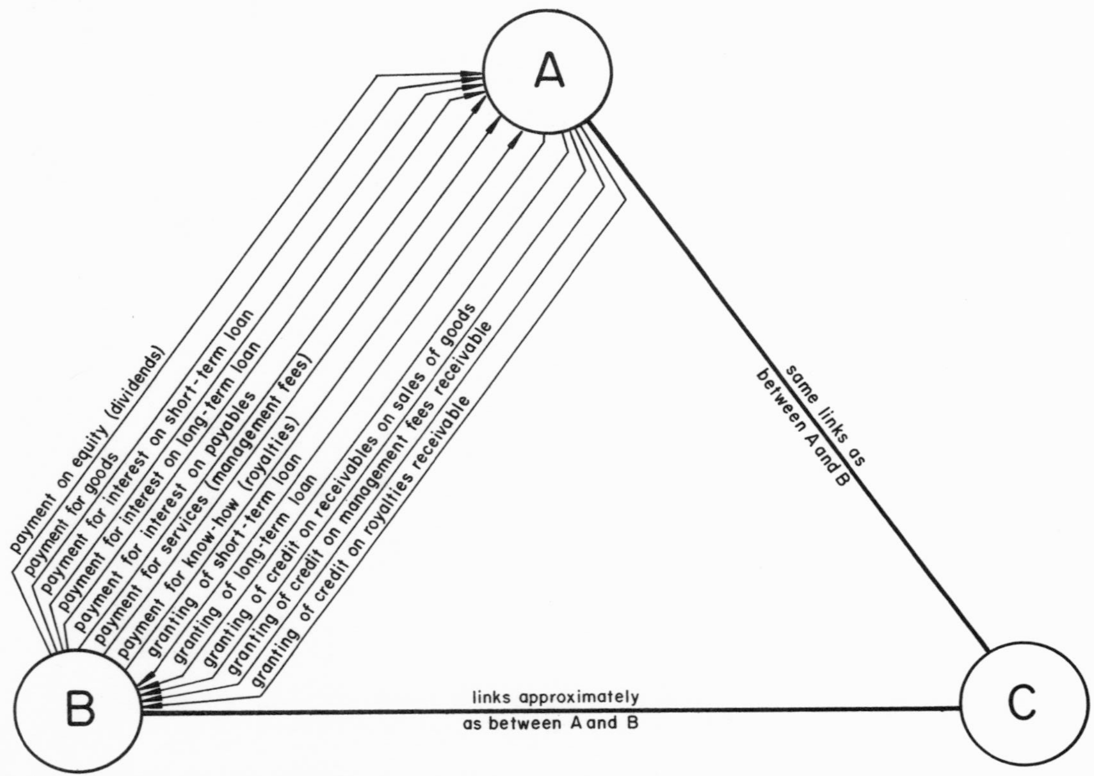
A
B
C
payment on equity (dividends)
payment for goods
payment for interest on short-term loan
payment for interest on long-term loan
payment for interest on payables
payment for services (management fees)
payment for know-how (royalties)
granting of short-term loan
granting of long-term loan
granting of credit on receivables on sales of goods
granting of credit on management fees receivable
granting of credit on royalties receivable
same links as
between A and B
links approximately
as between A and B

subsidiaries *B* and *C* occupy the same position with respect to the parent and therefore the links between *A* and *C* are the same as those between *A* and *B*. The links between subsidiaries differ somewhat from the links between the parent and the subsidiaries because typically the subsidiaries would not own equity in one another.

To be sure, the world is not so simple as this. For one thing, the financial links cannot be used without limits, which, for instance, may be set by governments. The distribution of dividends may be restricted to a certain percentage of net worth. Payments for goods may be affected by the efforts of revenue agents and customs officials to limit the freedom to set prices in intercompany transactions. In other instances the practices of the financial community of limiting the balance sheet ratios influence the limits within which financial links can be employed.

Nevertheless, much discretion in the use of the financial links typically remains. But the application of this discretion is loaded with difficulties because of the complexities encountered. For example, certain benefits may be magnified by using one unit as a conduit through which to move funds to another. Suppose the enterprise in Figure 1–4 has some funds that it wishes to invest short-term. Further, assume that subsidiary *C* can place money in the national financial markets of its home country at higher rates after taxes than can either the parent or subsidiary *B* in their respective national markets. If the enterprise wishes to maximize the consolidated profits of the system, the optimal strategy is to move funds from *A* to *C* and from *B* to *C* for investment in *C*'s money market. If for some reason the enterprise desired to move more funds from *A* to *C* than can be effected through the financial links connecting these two units, then the manager may be able to shift the excess funds from *A* to *B* and then from *B* to *C*. However, certain complications may make the obvious solution undesirable. For example, if a devaluation in the country of subsidiary *C* is expected, then the opposite strategy might be followed; that is, funds might be moved out of subsidiary *C* rather than into it.

Further complicating the choice of financial links and the direction of flow is the fact that enterprises often can earn more profits by coordinating the use of financial links rather than by just using the links individually. The following situation illustrates such a possibility. Governments often require a parent firm, in selling goods to a subsidiary, to charge "arm's-length" prices—that is, the prices that would be charged if the two corporations were unrelated. But suppose the goods are unstandardized articles for which an arm's-length price is difficult to determine, so that the parent has some leeway in setting the price without violating the governmental requirements. In such a case, customs duties would be reduced by setting the

FIGURE 1–5

The Effect of Number of Units in the System on the Number of Intercompany Financial Links

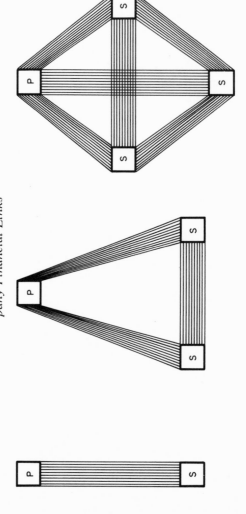

One Parent
One Subsidiary
Ten Financial Links

One Parent
Two Subsidiaries
Thirty Financial Links

One Parent
Three Subsidiaries
Sixty Financial Links

price as low as the manager has discretion to do. The profits built up in the subsidiary as a result of these low prices could be withdrawn from the subsidiary in the form of royalties. It is possible that the tax rates in the subsidiary's country and the parent's country and the level of customs duty in the subsidiary's country are such that the overall enterprise would earn a net profit by such coordinated actions as compared with the alternative of not pricing low and not withdrawing funds by means of royalties.

Coordinated arrangements of this sort increase in complexity as an enterprise grows. Figure 1–5 shows this in simple form for a system in which each unit is connected with the other by ten different types of financial links. A system with a parent and two subsidiaries has three times as many intercompany links as a system with a parent and one subsidiary. A parent with three subsidiaries has *six* times as many interconnecting links as a parent with one subsidiary. And a system with twenty-five units (a parent and twenty-four subsidiaries) and ten different types of links between each pair of units would have 3,000 intercompany financial links. The number of alternative solutions for the entire system would run into the trillions. Clearly, this complexity makes it unlikely that the enterprise could achieve an optimal solution covering all financial actions. Still, one feels the need to obtain a sense of the consequences of various financial policies.

An Analytical Approach

A formidable obstacle to anyone who aspires to analyze the financial practices of multinational enterprises is the veil of corporate reticence. Such reticence on the part of managers is understandable. Yet the veil had to be pierced. Our own experience as officers in, and consultants to, a few global organizations was indispensable, but the universe of international business is too immense and diverse to be embraced by on-the-job experience. Despite the common characteristics of the 187 companies in our group—relative bigness, engagement in manufacturing, and control over subsidiaries operating in at least six countries—these giants are extremely different in structure, products, and policies. And the reader, in order to grasp and assess our findings, is entitled to an account of our methods.

For one thing, we interviewed the financial officers of thirty-nine enterprises. These firms were selected from the list of 187 so as to provide a cross-section of all the industries in which U.S. foreign direct investment is concentrated, including petroleum refining and the manufacture of transportation equipment, electrical machinery, chemicals and allied products,

nonelectrical machinery, rubber and plastics, primary and fabricated metals, paper, and food. Within each industry we included firms of different
sizes. The number of enterprises per industry was decided on the basis of
the total foreign investment of the industry and the number and diversity
of multinational firms in it.

The interviews were conducted both within and outside the United
States. They ranged from one day to several weeks, depending on the importance of the company and the amount of material that company executives were willing to make available. To safeguard confidentiality, the
names of the thirty-nine companies are not disclosed. The responses, analyzed by statistical routines on computers, constituted the basis for determining the degree to which a financial practice was generally followed. An
example of the tabulated results of these analyses together with a statistical
measure of their significance is presented in Appendix A. Statements of
the officials interviewed are quoted in the text where they seem appropriate.

A number of the companies permitted access to their unpublished financial records. These were analyzed as a check on the interviews and to provide illustrations of various financial transactions.

In order to gain insight into the operations of multinational enterprises
from sources other than the enterprises themselves, a number of shorter interviews were held—both in the United States and abroad—with other institutions, such as investment banks, commercial banks, law firms, accounting firms, governments, and international organizations.

All this interviewing and study of documents would have been
insufficient without a means of determining the consequences of alternative
financial policies. For this purpose we used a computer model of a multinational enterprise system. Operations cover four consecutive years. The
hypothetical enterprise has foreign sales of $200 million the first year,
gradually expanding to $320 million in the fourth year. A real-life enter-
prise of this magnitude would have quite a few units—say a dozen or so
—but, for convenience the model has only three units: company A, the
parent, located in a developed country designated as country A; subsidiary
B, also located in a developed country, designated as country B; and subsidiary C, located in a less developed country, C.

The structure of the model is expressed by some 400 linear equations
that include all the financial links between units of the system and all financial connections between each unit of the system and the outside world.
Links between units of the system are those that were shown in Figure
1–4, and the financial connections between each unit of the system and the
outside world are typical of those existing in the real world. The equations

FIGURE 1–6

Inputs and Outputs of Information. Computer Model of a Multinational Enterprise

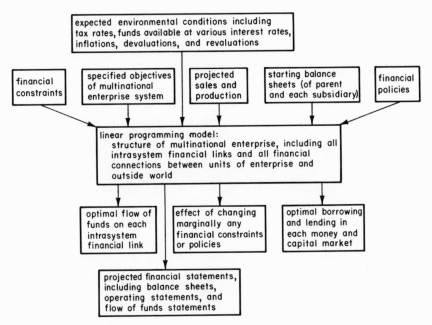

can be solved on a computer by using the conventional procedures of linear programming; the solution indicates the financial policies that will meet a given objective, which must be specified by the operator of the model. In our solutions we employed various objectives, the most commonly used of which was to "obtain the maximum amount of consolidated profits after taxes for the system over the whole four-year period." * The solution offered by the model indicates the set of financial policies that will meet the desired objective.

Certain factors must be specified in the model. Although it is technically possible to change one or more of these specified variables after each solution of the model, we did not do so. Instead, we imposed factors in accordance with conditions commonly observed during our extensive field investigations and left them unchanged during the course of our evaluations. For purposes of our analysis, we specified balance sheets existing at the

---

* A computer analysis indicated that this objective resulted in a solution that was indistinguishable from the solution which meets the objective to "maximize the present value of the wealth of the shareholders of the enterprise" when any reasonable present value is placed on future dividends.

beginning of year 1 for each unit in the system, the quantity of production and sales of the units (including sales to one another and to the public) for each of the four years, and financial constraints imposed by institutions, governments, or customs. Also, we set forth the conditions for the three different economic environments in which the units of the system operate. The relationship between the model and information inputs and outputs is shown in Figure 1–6, and more detailed information about the model is presented in Appendix B.

Models, being much simpler than reality, have to be interpreted with a certain delicacy and care. Yet they can improve understanding of the complex reality in which business is actually conducted. At times the multinational enterprise model confirmed the actions observed in the real world, but at other times it indicated an optimal solution that was different from the practice observed. Sometimes, too, it provided unexpected results, and the reasons for the indicated strategy had to be ferreted out step-by-step.

A financial manager interested in relating this analysis more specifically to his own company can expand the equations in Appendix B to apply the constraints and environments typical of his own enterprise. The expanded model can then be used in his planning activities to test various financial policies. But our primary purpose in introducing the computer model is not to persuade corporations to adopt it but to make our own analysis of the financial function more useful to the reader.

TWO / What's Different about Operating Abroad

Many of the opportunities and problems encountered by multinational enterprises are also encountered by firms operating solely within the United States. Whether operating all around the world or only on U.S. soil, a company may wrestle with interesting (and troublesome) variations in markets, wage rates, material costs, and cultural factors. Similarly, within large domestic firms as well as global enterprises, delays and misunderstandings arise from the need of the parent to deal with affiliated companies across great distances.

Nevertheless, once a firm's operations leap across national boundaries, the firm does encounter factors that are unique to international business. And the factor that most clearly distinguishes multinational from domestic finance is the need to do business in more than one currency. Exchange-rate risk is endemic to international business and is related to all major financial decisions encountered in multinational enterprises. Managers find themselves obliged to learn what this risk is and how to protect against it.

The Concept of Exchange Loss

The rate at which one currency can be exchanged for another is not chiseled in granite. It can be varied by governmental edict or left to the forces of the market, depending on national needs. Under the system of fixed exchange rates small changes are still permissible and large changes are experienced at the time of an occasional devaluation or revaluation of a currency; floating rates permit flexibility in relationships.

One problem faced by the manager when dealing in more than one currency is whether to attempt to exploit currency fluctuations day-by-day. It is possible, for example, to try routinely to gauge the optimum time to purchase currencies. However, because of the small range over which currency values typically fluctuate in routine variations, any gains or losses due to such operations are not likely to be of major importance to a multinational enterprise.

In contrast, major changes in the relative values of currencies that occur

21

during a devaluation or revaluation can have an important effect on the financial position of the parent and any of its subsidiaries. Indeed, references to currency risk as "the single greatest problem in doing business abroad" * or "the risk that poses the greatest difficulty" are common among the financial officers of multinational enterprises. Although in recent years some important foreign currencies have been revalued upward in terms of the dollar, the risk most often faced by managers of U.S. multinational enterprises in the past has been that of devaluation of other currencies. When an enterprise has subsidiaries operating where currencies are weak—that is, in danger of devaluation—exchange protection may loom as a paramount consideration. In commenting on this subject, the manager of overseas financing of a large motor car company said, "In Latin America, currency risk permeates almost everything we do. It's uppermost in your mind in how you deal with any other company."

Not all authors use the same nomenclature to describe losses and gains caused by variations in the rates of exchange of currencies.[1] For clarity in exposition, we use two categories of losses and gains: *conversion* and *translation*. "Conversion" describes exchange losses or gains that result when one currency must be changed or "converted" into another currency in order to settle outstanding liabilities. "Translation" describes exchange losses or gains that result when a financial statement expressed in one currency is "translated" so as to be expressed in another currency; in translation, one currency is not actually exchanged for another.

CONVERSION

A conversion loss or gain takes place when a liability or asset payable in a currency other than that in which a unit operates is settled at an exchange rate different from that existing at the time the liability or asset was recorded on the unit's books. For instance, if a subsidiary borrows $100 and converts the loan into 100 units of local currency (LC), it will lose money if the LC is devalued while the loan is outstanding. Once the LC is devalued, more local currency than was obtained from the loan is needed to repay the loan. If, for example, after the devaluation, LC 150 is required to repay the $100, then the transaction would entail a loss of LC 50. Conversion losses are not restricted to multinational enterprises. They may take place wherever an obligation for future payment exists between entities operating with different currencies.

A conversion *loss* typically is recorded at the time a devaluation or revaluation takes place, even though the settlement of the transaction may

* Unless otherwise specified, all quotations in this book are from our interviews.

take place later; whereas a conversion *gain* typically is not recorded until the transaction is completed and the gain actually realized. However, following the 1971 turmoil in the international monetary system, the Accounting Principles Board of the American Institute of Certified Public Accountants went counter to the long-standing philosophical opposition on the part of the accounting profession to the deferral of "losses" and tentatively agreed that firms could delay the reporting of conversion losses on *long-term* debts in foreign currencies until such time as they were realized.[2] Other than this concern with the time of recording, there is relatively little controversy surrounding conversion losses or gains. Although a conversion loss of a foreign subsidiary is not recorded on the parent's books, the fact that the loss reduces the subsidiary's profit and net worth eventually affects the enterprise's consolidated statement.

TRANSLATION

A translation loss or gain is not a result of any payment; rather it is the result of the restatement of the subsidiary's worth in terms of the parent's currency. Thus, a translation loss or gain occurs when a devaluation or revaluation affects the recorded worth of the subsidiary in terms of the parent's currency.

One way to measure translation losses and gains is to consider how a devaluation or revaluation affects the "present value" of the subsidiary, that is, the discounted value of the future stream of cash to be obtained from the subsidiary. These effects on cash flow are of two main types: (1) the consequent changes in revenues and costs and (2) the consequent changes in the level of working capital needed to support sales. These changes in cash flows must be discounted back to present value at the new rate of exchange. In order to estimate a change in the present value of a subsidiary caused by changes in currency values, therefore, estimates of future revenues and costs of the subsidiary are necessary. It is not surprising therefore that the accounting profession measures exchange loss or gain by a second yardstick, namely, the change in the dollar value of a specified set of a subsidiary's assets and liabilities, often current assets and current liabilities.

The recording of a translation loss comes in the consolidation of the subsidiary's books with the parent's financial statement. Following is a simple illustration of a translation loss. On the day prior to devaluation the local subsidiary holds LC 100 in cash at an exchange rate of LC 1 = $1; this is translated as $100 onto the consolidated balance sheet. On the day after devaluation of the local currency to LC 2 = $1, the local subsidiary still holds LC 100 in cash—there has been no change in the subsidiary's books. However, LC 100 is translated into the consolidated books as $50; thus, the consolidated balance sheet shows a decline in cash of $50. On the other hand, if a subsidiary has liabilities in local currency and a devaluation of the local currency occurs, these liabilities would decline when translated into dollar terms.

In practice, translating foreign subsidiary statements into dollars is rather complex, and the measurement of translation losses depends on the precise standards used. Accounting policies in this area differ considerably.

The Accounting Principles Board of the American Institute of Certified Public Accountants (AICPA) has recommended the "current-account" method, in which a distinction is made between current and long-term accounts. According to this method, current assets and liabilities are translated at the rate of exchange prevailing on the date of the balance sheet ("current exchange rates") and fixed assets and long-term liabilities are translated at the rate existing at the time that the asset was acquired or liability incurred ("historical exchange rates").[3] In this method, net assets exposed to a loss on devaluation would be equal to the current assets (including inventories) that are expressed in devalued currencies, minus the current liabilities that are expressed in devalued currencies.

On the other hand, the National Association of Accountants, a professional body of corporate accountants, recommends the "financial-account" method. This method distinguishes between financial items—such as cash, accounts receivable, and long-term and short-term debt—and nonmonetary or physical items such as inventories and fixed assets. It recommends the use of current exchange rates for the financial items and historical exchange rates for the physical items.[4] By this method, net assets exposed to a loss on devaluation would be equal to cash and marketable securities held in the devalued currencies, accounts receivable denominated in devalued currencies, and long-term financial assets denominated in devalued currencies *minus* liabilities, long or short, owed in devalued currencies.

Numerous other approaches have been recommended to obtain a result that more nearly represents the "true" dollar value of the tangible assets and liabilities. A typical example is the recommendation that inventories whose value remains constant in *dollar* terms be translated at historical exchange rates while inventories whose value remains constant in terms of *local currency* be translated at current exchange rates.[5]

The definition used for net exposed assets not only determines the amount of assets defined as being at risk, but also often affects the means of protecting against currency devaluations. The scale on the thermometer, in short, is capable of generating responses in the patient. For example, a manager who defines his risk in terms of the current-account method might increase his local short-term borrowings and place them in fixed assets or withdraw them from the subsidiary. On the other hand, if a manager defines exposure by the financial-account method, he has added alternatives to eliminate the risk, such as buying inventories or financing the subsidiary by borrowing locally on a long-term basis.

Translation losses are generally charged against current operations, whereas the recommendations of the American Institute of Certified Public Accountants are that translation *gains* be carried to a suspense account, except to the extent that they are used to offset current or prior losses. Most multinational enterprises follow these recommendations.

Regardless of which accounting definition is used, the accountant's measurement of devaluation losses and gains is objective in the sense that two accountants using the same standards would get the same results. But the process has a fundamental flaw in that it deviates from economic values. The economic effect of a devaluation or revaluation on a subsidiary's value is difficult to foresee without a detailed examination of the elements affecting both the income statement and the balance sheet. Yet, when a devaluation occurs, accounting methods, concentrating as they do on the changes in values of various types of assets and liabilities of the subsidiary, usually result in the reporting of a loss in the consolidated statements of the parent, even if no actual loss has occurred or is to be expected.

Devaluation, for instance, may cause domestic prices to rise in a pattern that increases a subsidiary's profit margins on domestic sales, or may cause an increase in a subsidiary's profits from exports by causing increases in export volume, profit margins, or both. Furthermore, profits of other members of the enterprise system might rise because of their increased transactions with the subsidiary in the country with the devalued currency. A variety of examples of this could be cited; an obvious one is the gain in sales and profits of another enterprise member because of the use of lower-cost components acquired from the subsidiary in the country with the devalued currency.[6]

Regardless of the possible economic outcome, executives typically use accounting principles rather than economic principles to measure the effects of devaluation or revaluation. For if accounting principles are not used to derive the financial statements, then certified public accountants will not grant their seal of approval to such statements; and this seal of approval is needed for reports to stockholders.

Since accounting principles are used to measure the effects of a devaluation or revaluation, it follows that when managers adopt protective measures they are trying to minimize accounting losses rather than economic losses. True, some executives realize that only by chance does the economic gain or loss equal the gain or loss reported by accountants, but they still feel the need to minimize those reported losses because of their possible effect on the market price of the stock. For these executives feel that players in the stock market look upon accounting losses as economic losses. But other executives genuinely believe that the accounting rules measure the economic losses, which obviously should be minimized.

The Cost of Money

Money does not cost the same in all countries, and that fact enables the financial manager of a multinational enterprise to borrow in countries with low interest rates and use the funds in countries with high ones.

To be sure, the same option is available to purely domestic U.S. companies, but in fact most of them obtain the bulk of their funds from within the United States; and within the United States the money-market centers are connected through an elaborate communications network that has largely eliminated sharp variations in interest rates among different regions of the country. Worldwide money markets, on the other hand, are more insulated from each other because communications are not as effective and economic differences between countries are stronger. For example, in April 1971, the prime rate for short-term bank credits was 5.5 percent in the United States, 6 percent in Japan, 7 percent in France and the United Kingdom, 16 percent in Argentina, and 24 percent in Indonesia.[7]

Certain considerations tend to tip the decisions of financial managers in favor of local borrowing, irrespective of interest-rate differences. Apprehension of weakness of a local currency is one of the most important of these considerations. Another is the maintenance of artificially low interest rates maintained by the local government, and still another is the desire to maintain local financing ties for business reasons. Referring to these points, an official of a multinational enterprise said in 1967: "We try to obtain the lowest cost financing that we can; but in the United Kingdom we borrow locally to protect against devaluation rather than because of low interest rates. In those countries that are not subject to near-term devaluation, local interest rates usually are the most important consideration. Sometimes government incentives provide low-cost money even if the general level of interest rates in the country are high. In Italy, for example, we got very low-cost money because we were willing to build a plant in an economically disadvantaged area and employ a lot of people. Another exception to our policy of using the lowest-cost money is the case in which we borrow locally just so the banks will have a lending account with us."

Anxious to avoid incurring losses through changes in exchange rates, some financial managers simply ignore the possibility of exploiting interest-rate differentials by moving money across boundaries. They may thereby miss some possibilities of reducing the overall cost of borrowing, but visible losses will not be incurred and a lot of planning and calculating complexities will be avoided. "We're in the manufacturing not the banking business!" some finance officials assert. In other cases, companies recognize the potential of savings through differences in borrowing costs and plan to undertake such activities—but not quite yet. Along these lines, an official of a large machinery company remarked, "I think you could say that we intend to do an increasing volume of cross-border borrowing, seeking funds at the lowest cost. We have not done much of it up to the present time."

But many managements are actively taking advantage of differences in the cost of money.

Avoiding Double Taxation

Foreign branches and foreign subsidiaries of U.S. corporations pay taxes on their income to the governments of the countries in which they operate. U.S. corporations are subject to U.S. income tax on income wherever it is earned; and this applies to their foreign branches. But if the U.S. corporation creates a subsidiary—a separate corporation—the U.S. parent usually is regarded as not having received "income" on the earnings of the subsidiary until the parent receives a dividend (exceptions to this rule are discussed later). When U.S. taxes are due on the income from foreign branches or on a dividend from a foreign subsidiary, the general rule is that the parent's tax liability to the U.S. government is reduced by the amount of income tax paid abroad by the branch or subsidiary on the same revenue. Therefore, if the foreign income tax rates are equal to or higher than those in the United States, no U.S. tax is supposed to be required. On the other hand, if the effective foreign rates are lower than those in the United States, some U.S. tax will be payable.[8]

Thus, in principle, the tax liability of an enterprise with foreign income is simple. But in practice the determination of that liability triggers a complex chain of computations and decisions. For example, the relevant profits and taxes for each foreign branch and foreign corporation for which a tax credit is claimed must be determined. Chains of relations between foreign subsidiaries must be worked out. A foreign subsidiary, for instance, may, in turn, have stock of other foreign subsidiaries and receive dividends from them. When such ownership is 50 percent or more, then a determination must be made of the amount of tax deemed to have been paid by the subsidiary directly owned by the U.S. parent. Moreover, there are numerous exceptions to the general principles. For example, dividends paid to foreign subsidiaries by a subsidiary in a less developed country and reinvested in another less developed country are not normally subject to U.S. taxes. There are special rules for various categories of income earned abroad, including the income of foreign personal-holding companies, foreign-based sales and service companies, trading operations in the Western Hemisphere that generate income from countries outside the United States, and operations in less developed countries.[9]

To obtain the full benefit of the foreign tax credit, managers of the parent corporation must be aware not only of the U.S. tax laws that apply to the foreign income received in the United States, but also of the tax laws of each of the foreign countries in which subsidiaries are located. And they must be familiar with tax treaties between the United States and these countries that may affect the amount of payments. All this knowledge must be applied to reach decisions on financial policies. An official of a large chemical company made this typical remark: "We have a philosophy of playing all the tax angles to the hilt, and we manipulate our financial situation to obtain the most tax savings."

As American business spreads, more and more U.S. corporations are in a position to claim a foreign tax credit. From 1954 to 1962, the number rose by two-thirds. Still the actual count was not large, reaching 5,266 in 1962, and most of them were large enterprises.[10] During that period, 600 U.S. corporations with assets of $50 million or more accounted for over 90 percent of the total foreign tax credits claimed. Because of the size of the firms involved, the dollar value of the total credit was substantial, amounting to $1.6 billion in 1962. This was about 12 percent of the total tax liability—United States plus foreign—of all U.S. corporations claiming foreign credit. In specific industries the proportion was much higher than 12 percent. For the crude petroleum and natural gas companies as a group, the comparable figure was 90 percent.

Taxation has an important influence on multinational financial policies in a number of other ways not likely to be experienced by a domestic firm. Taxes may have a bearing on the structure of capitalization created for a foreign subsidiary. Equally important, tax considerations often determine the form of remittances from a subsidiary. Then there is the matter of subpart F of the Revenue Act of 1962. This provision makes the U.S. parent liable for taxes on certain undistributed income, such as dividends and interest, received by a holding company in other foreign countries. But the U.S. tax on this "subpart F income" is eliminated if the holding company makes a sufficient "minimum distribution" to the U.S. parent.[11]

The effects of tax provisions such as these are considerable. Take the case of one of the leading U.S. chemical companies. Because of the rapid growth of its overseas operations, the company prefers that most foreign earnings be retained abroad for expansion. The dividend policies of its foreign subsidiaries are directed to the double aim of (1) obtaining the needed funds in the various foreign subsidiaries and (2) permitting large enough flows to the U.S. parent to minimize U.S. taxes on "subpart F income." To achieve this dual purpose requires the integration of the dividend payments of the subsidiaries into an overall plan that takes into consideration varying local profits, tax rates, and company needs. In effect, therefore, taxation is the consideration that determines overseas dividend policies. As one headquarters official noted, the tax people at headquarters generally "have the last word."

The Influence of the Local Environment

A foreign subsidiary often copies the financial practices of locally owned concerns and, indeed, in certain cases, may have to do so in order to survive.

For instance, a U.S.-owned subsidiary, in order to keep up with competitors, may be obliged to provide payment terms to its customers that are far longer than would be tolerated at home. It is common for terms in foreign countries to run 90 or 120 days or even longer, compared with 30 or 60 days in the United States. At times, the multinational enterprise has been able to turn the prevailing foreign terms to its own advantage. For example, the treasurer of one subsidiary revealed: "By having foreign sources of funds, we've been able to pay our bills on a 30-day basis. By doing this, we have driven down the costs of material that we purchase."

Most American firms assert the need to behave as "good citizens" in their operations abroad. Indeed, their observations of local regulations is apt to be more punctilious than that of their local competitors. This may generate a problem of its own, as in the case of a U.S. subsidiary in Italy that refused to adopt the local custom, which was to declare a lower income tax than it expected to pay and then bargain through an Italian agent with the Italian government to arrive at a satisfactory solution. At times the overseas subsidiary may find it expedient to conform to local practice rather than to resist. In such cases, the subsidiary may not feel it necessary to inform headquarters' management of the arrangements. Nevertheless, headquarters may not be entirely oblivious of such matters; U.S. auditors have come across accounts entitled "supplemental allowances" in Italy and Latin America, suggesting the possibility that these disbursements may have afforded some help in the tax negotiations that are quite common in those areas.

Employment practices for production workers in some foreign countries result in larger inventories than those carried for U.S. operations. The controller of a large multinational enterprise explained: "The Japanese put a great amount of emphasis on maintaining production regardless of sales variations. In the States if sales go down, we shut down the plant; but in Japan, they never shut down a plant."

The list of financial practices encountered abroad that are different from those in the United States could be extended at length. Examples: relying on short-term borrowing to finance long-term assets; and adjusting working capital needs to cater for the "float" that arises in delayed bank clearings. Furthermore, certain practices used sparingly in the United States are used more extensively abroad. For example, the discounting of receivables is not very popular in the United States, but is widely used in some foreign countries, especially when low discount rates are available for receivables generated from export sales. In each instance someone in the enterprise must decide whether to conform to local practice or to depart from it.

Another environmental difference between operating abroad and operating at home is found in the nature of the financial institutions from which companies obtain funds. These institutions, notably the local banks, will be discussed in Chapter 4, "Financing Foreign Affiliates." Although foreign practices and institutions can be troublesome to the financial manager of a multinational firm, he has opportunities to combine sources and forms of financing—opportunities either not available to or not likely to be used extensively by the domestic manager.

The great variety of economic conditions abroad can bring more difficulties than the strangeness of foreign practices and institutions. The financial manager of a multinational enterprise may be confronted at the same time with bewildering extremes: a business boom in Brazil and a recession in England; easy money conditions in Germany and a tight money market in France; ample investment opportunities but limited funds in Japan; limited investment opportunities but ample funds in India. The panorama is so large and changes occur so swiftly that the financial manager needs extraordinary agility to keep abreast of developments.

THE ACCOUNTING MAZE

Operating in a number of countries, the multinational enterprise is exposed to the vagaries of many different accounting systems. The record keeping of each subsidiary must conform to the accepted practice, commercial code, and tax laws of its host country. In addition, if the subsidiary's financial reports are consolidated within the multinational system, the subsidiary's record keeping must conform to the system's overall policies.[12] Although the subject of international accounting practices is worthy of a separate study, financial managers, whether or not accountants by profession, must be aware of the major problems. And one is the problem of reconciling the accounting practices of the different countries with standards in the United States.

Scores of differences exist with respect to such things as fixing the rate and periods of depreciation, establishing reserves that can be deducted from profit, creating bad-debt allowances, funding retirement plans, valuing inventories, classifying expenses, and writing up the value of assets. These variations sometimes cause fundamental difficulties. As an illustration, one accountant of a multinational enterprise thought that the firm's consolidated net worth was overstated because an allowance for a compulsory retirement plan had not been deducted from the earnings of a large subsidiary. He pointed out that such deductions are not required in the country where the subsidiary is located, but are normal accounting practice in the United States. Accordingly, he felt that in order to offset possible pressure for increased dividend payments from stockholders and to provide full disclosure, there ought to be a footnote in the consolidated statement indicating that the annual earnings and the retained earnings account were overstated.

To get around such difficulties, some enterprises eventually adjust their foreign statements to American reporting practices. This "solution" sometimes introduces new difficulties. When a large number of adjustments have to be made in the books of foreign subsidiaries, the subsidiaries often cannot find local accountants who understand the instruction manual issued from headquarters. One headquarters' official of a multinational enterprise embarking upon consolidation of the statements of the foreign subsidiaries remarked: "All of our figures have to dovetail with the system at headquarters. Unfortunately, our local people in some countries are not ready to handle this consolidation. For example, our Turkish subsidiary had at least twenty-four misclassifications under the new reporting system, and I had to visit Turkey to track down and find out why and how the misclassifications were made."

THE PROBLEM OF THE FOREIGN PARTNER

The advantages and disadvantages of a multinational enterprise's taking one or more foreign partners in a subsidiary have been discussed extensively elsewhere.[13] A local partner can provide the joint venture with knowledge of the local economy, politics, and customs; quick entry into the foreign country; access to markets; and resources such as capital, management skills, and raw materials. On the other hand, foreign partners cause problems to multinational enterprises by restricting their freedom to manage. Three problems in particular affect the financial manager:

1. Payment of dividends. This is a common ground for conflict, which arises for various reasons. The American parent, for instance, may prefer to withdraw cash from its subsidiaries by methods that do not result in U.S. tax liability; the payment by the subsidiary of its intercompany accounts is an example. This, of course, affords no immediate benefits to local shareholders.

Often, foreign shareholders tend to prefer dividends early in the life of the subsidiary and to have these maintained on a regular basis. On the other hand, the American parent, considering its investment a long-term one and wishing to minimize foreign-cash outlays, is likely to lean in the direction of deferring the subsidiary's dividends until it is more mature.

2. Export sales. The question of exports, of course, affects plant expansions and capital budgeting. The foreign partner often desires to expand local production in order to sell in the export market, but the parent may prefer to serve the export market from another subsidiary.

3. Prices set on the goods traded between the joint venture and the other units within the multinational enterprise. The presence of the foreign partner restricts the enterprise's use of intrasystem transfer pricing as a means of transferring funds or cutting taxes.

There are still other areas of conflict. For example, differences of opinion between the parent and the foreign partner have risen over methods of financing. Some subsidiaries employ banks because of the family relations of the local partners, and, for the same reason, have taken long-term loans even though short-term arrangements appeared to be more satisfactory. Likewise, joint ventures have purchased goods and services from firms controlled by the foreign partner at prices that seemed to the U.S. parent to be unduly high.

Freedom of action may be threatened even when the parent owns a majority of stock. An official of an American subsidiary in Turkey, for example, described an incident in which he was the only member of the Board of Directors to vote against a proposal to pay dividends. Because he represented the two-thirds interest of the parent, the proposal was rejected. The local shareholders reacted angrily to this defeat, saying, "Why do we have to have this meeting anyway? Let Mr. ——— decide all by himself since whatever he says outvotes the rest of us." (*Note:* the decision was reversed and a dividend was paid.)

THE CARROT-AND-STICK POLICIES OF GOVERNMENTS

The multinational enterprise must deal with a national government in each country where it operates. These governments, as sovereign powers, enact and enforce laws that cover a wide range of activities. Generally, such laws are intended to foster economic growth, increase the government's revenues, and improve the balance of payments.

A number of other studies have dealt specifically with this subject. They show that local laws affecting the multinational enterprise are ordinarily the outgrowth of a long history of economic and political developments topped by the existing government's interpretation of its current needs. Turkey provides a good illustration of these relationships. That country's experiences in formulating rules for foreign investment cannot fairly be called "typical" but they are perhaps as nearly typical as those of any other country.

As early as the eighteenth century, Turkey granted special treatment known as "capitulations" to foreign enterprises, enabling them to operate in Turkey but remain subject to the trade laws of their own countries.[14] As the Ottoman Empire declined, the foreign investors used the capitulations to entrench their economic position at the expense of local competitors— and exported their profits.[15] After World War I the newly formed Republic of Turkey terminated the capitulations, which still bore the overtones of a semicolonial era. But the reluctance or inability of local private sources to arrange for the necessary finances resulted in the State's buying out the foreign companies.[16] Immediately after World War II the Turkish government moved back in the other direction: it reduced government participation in economic activity and again encouraged foreign investment.[17] But the volume of foreign investment was disappointing to the government; so in July 1967 a Foreign Capital Division, composed of full-time personnel, was created to implement the law encouraging foreign investors.

Despite this Turkish official position, the ghosts of past suspicions still hover over both the content and administration of legislation affecting foreign companies. These doubts are illustrated by the difficulties that continue to harass U.S. subsidiaries in Turkey.

Turkey controls the movement of funds into and out of the country. According to law, requests for original investment and expansion must be carefully reviewed to direct foreign capital and technology into areas "where Turkish enterprises cannot go in as a result of lack of technical knowledge and experience and inadequate capital." Once a foreign investor has been admitted, he may remit earnings accruing from his foreign capital base after appropriate deductions have been made. This law has been administered with a firm hand, and the American subsidiaries in Turkey have found that decisions vary in accordance with the government's judgment as to its current needs. Thus, an appliance manufacturer stated that it was denied an enlargement of its capital base; on the other hand, the tire companies were readily allowed to expand their operations.

Closely related to the controls on funds are the controls on imports and exports. Through an extensive quota system, imports are regulated in accordance with the needs of the economy and the availability of foreign currency. Companies have complained bitterly that the varying standards and the crawling administrative machinery have severely aggravated the problem of maintaining well-balanced inventories. Some American subsidiaries have said they must keep more than six months' supplies whereas only two would be necessary in the United States.

As for exports, a firm cannot export from Turkey until it receives a letter of credit indicating that the money for the goods is available at internationally competitive prices; the Turkish Central Bank obtains the foreign currency and pays the exporter in lira. The export control laws have not yet seriously affected the American firms in Turkey, which primarily serve the local market. But the effect will likely grow because the government now often requires that a foreign firm commit itself to export part of its output.

The Turkish government attempts to control the price of imports, exports, and local sales. Prices of imports of Italian pharmaceuticals, Japanese tires, and Persian Gulf petroleum all have been used by the government as "reference points" to force down import prices on the applicable commodities. Such controls limit the freedom of intercompany pricing between the Turkish subsidiary and the other units within a multinational enterprise system. The government once persuaded the tire industry to accept a requested price cut by threatening to allow an additional foreign entry into the market.

There are special tax problems in Turkey, just as there are in many other countries. Corporate income taxes are somewhat similar to American ones, but two taxes in Turkey differ substantially from those in the United States. One is the payment of a stamp tax on a great variety of business transactions; the second is the high customs duty and attendant deposit that must be left with the government from the day a request is made

to import goods until the goods are cleared through customs. Although ex-
emptions and installment payments are possible, slow-moving bureaucratic machinery prevents easy modifications.

Turkey is by no means the world's rockiest soil for the cultivation of
multinational enterprises. We have used that country in order to lend spec-
ificity to problems widely found.

One result of local government rules is that the managers of multinational enterprises are engaged continuously in international bargaining for
improved local business terms. In Colombia, for example, a consumer
goods company had suffered a profit squeeze because of price controls on
the sale of consumer goods without similar controls on imports of raw materials. When an official of the firm was asked what was being done about
this condition, he tersely responded, "Fighting like hell with the government officials and keeping at them constantly for an increase in the price
level."

Not that American firms at home don't fight with government officials,
too. But, in the operation of global business, national governments create a
super challenge—if only because there are so many of them.

Thus the milieu of the multinational enterprise abounds with financial
variety—a rich diversity of currencies, interest rates, tax laws, local practices, lending institutions, accounting systems, forms of corporate organization, and governmental pressures. It is not surprising to find that multinational firms differ in their financial strategies. Even so, those firms can be
gathered into broad groups according to the ways in which they exercise
the financial function.

THREE / Evolution of the Financial Function

The development of a financial system by a multinational enterprise is evolutionary in nature. The evolution follows a predictable pattern as the firm's foreign business grows. By studying how firms organize to control their worldwide financial activities, one can discern three phases in the evolution. These phases, of course, are a gross simplification of the process; nevertheless they are distinct from one another in quite recognizable ways.[1]

Phase 1: Ignoring the System's Potential

Early in an enterprise's overseas expansion, executives in headquarters know little about the special problems of international business; and in many cases, according to a study by the National Industrial Conference Board (NICB), they "do not believe that the function of international financial management requires specialized attention."[2]

Typically in such enterprises there is a small staff in headquarters—sometimes only one man—dealing with international financial problems. At this first stage, which we call Phase 1, the minuscule staff has neither the time to manage closely the financial problems of the foreign subsidiaries nor the experience to issue decision rules to the subsidiaries. The size of the enterprise's foreign business is small relative to domestic operations and small in absolute terms. Accordingly, the executives directing the enterprise feel that they cannot afford a large central staff to direct the financial aspects of their international activities. As a result, even though the financial system in such an enterprise is sufficiently simple to allow a large percentage of the financial links to be operated in a coordinated manner, the lack of foreign experience, the small scale of foreign operations, and the relative unimportance of foreign operations combine to prevent the enterprise from doing so.

Because the financial staff at headquarters is limited, the financial managers of the foreign subsidiaries operate during this early phase without close direction from the parent. The operating pattern is one in which each subsidiary tends to operate independently—"every tub on its own bottom." Little use is made of the intercompany financial links. Thus, managers of the subsidiaries operate in such a way as to improve subsidiary performance, but they may do so at the expense of the total profits of the system. Although the subsidiary managers are concerned with the parent's overall interests, they are not about to serve those interests if it hurts their own performance. The activities of financial staffs in such an enterprise are depicted in Figure 3–1.

The multinational enterprises in Phase 1 are relatively small, at least by comparison with other firms that make up the 187 multinational enter-

FIGURE 3–1

Phase 1 of Financial Development of a Multinational Enterprise

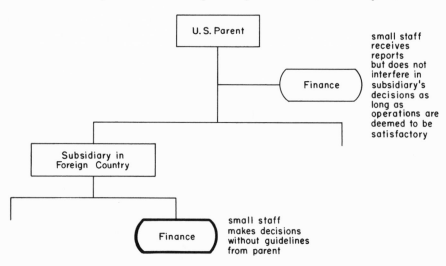

prises in our study. The interrelationship between size and the policy approach just summarized is indicated by the behavior of a group of ninety firms referred to here as "Small" multinational enterprises (having foreign operations with sales of less than $100 million in 1969). Although the correlation between the size of firm and the phase of financial development is not perfect, we judge that 90 percent of these ninety Small multinational enterprises were in Phase 1 of their financial development, the remainder being in one of the other two phases. The total sales of the foreign affiliates of the Small enterprises interviewed by us ranged from a low of $20 million to a high of $100 million; and these foreign sales typically represented from 10 to 20 percent of the enterprise's total worldwide sales. The number of foreign countries in which these enterprises manufactured typically ranged from six to twelve. In 1969 the total sales of the foreign affiliates (branches and subsidiaries) of the ninety Small firms in our universe of 187 multinational enterprises were $5 billion.[3]

Phase 2: Exploiting the System's Potential

As the enterprise's foreign business grows, managers in the parent enterprise tend to learn from experience that international financial management is different from domestic financial management. Concurrently, a cadre of experienced financial managers is being developed in the subsidiaries. As more subsidiaries are established and begin dealing with one another, the expanding number of intercompany financial connections offers some obvious profit opportunities. The growth rate in foreign business typically outstrips that in the domestic sector, and the resulting increase in relative importance of the foreign business encourages closer control from headquarters. At the same time, the increased size of the foreign commitment is large enough to justify supporting a group of financial specialists in headquarters.

Still another factor influences the decision to set up a central financial staff. As the foreign business grows, the likelihood that it will be consolidated in the periodic reports to shareholders also grows. Accordingly, the parent finds itself obliged to concern itself with the impact of consolidation, especially when devaluations and revaluations are involved.*

Despite the increasing utility of setting up a central staff, some type of shock to headquarters is often required before the decision is made. This shock, for example, may come as a result of severe losses from overseas operations or displeasure by executives in the parent's headquarters with actions taken by overseas managers. In these cases, as long as foreign sales are relatively small, headquarters may react merely by replacing the overseas management. On the other hand, when the foreign business has begun to achieve the necessary critical size, the reaction of headquarters to a disconcerting incident is likely to be a decision to set up a strong central staff to direct the financial aspects of foreign operations. At this point the enter-

* However, the significance of consolidation to reported earnings was diminished after 1971 as companies followed the provisions of the Accounting Principles Board of the AICPA set forth in Opinion No. 18, "The Equity Method of Accounting for Investments in Common Stock." According to this Opinion, which was effective in 1972, the parent must recognize in its own statements the earnings or losses in equity of nonconsolidated subsidiaries over which the parent company exerts a significant influence.

prise enters what we call Phase 2 in the evolution of the financial system and its organization and control.

Even after the strong central staff is set up, it takes some time to get foreign operations under tight control. An official of one firm described this process, "We established controls initially in Latin America, with the result that a major management overhaul was executed. We then took a year to develop a system applicable to the Continent, where no major trouble spots were disclosed. Finally we proceeded to the United Kingdom, where a need was revealed to strengthen the depth and caliber of middle management."

FIGURE 3–2

Phase 2 of Financial Development of a Multinational Enterprise

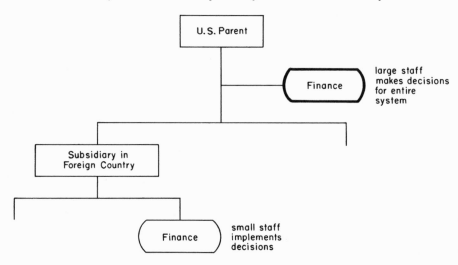

For multinational enterprises in Phase 2 of their financial development, the central staff makes most financial decisions of importance and issues frequent orders to subsidiaries. The hallmark of such an enterprise is the "system optimization" viewpoint of this central staff. The activities of the financial staff in a Phase 2 multinational enterprise are depicted in Figure 3–2.

It would be misleading to identify precisely the level of foreign business that engenders a transition from Phase 1 to Phase 2, but the correlation between financial development and size continues as a firm grows. Our analysis indicates that by the time the foreign operations of the enterprise attain $100 million in aggregate sales, the transition generally has been made. In our group of 187 enterprises there are 75 that had foreign operations with total sales between $100 million and $500 million in 1969; we call these "Medium" multinational enterprises. And we judge that about 80 percent of these Medium enterprises were in Phase 2 of their financial development. The sales of the foreign affiliates of these firms usually represented 15 to 30 percent of the total world sales of the enterprise, and each enterprise manufactured in some ten to twenty countries. In 1969 the total sales of the foreign affiliates of the Medium enterprises were about $16 billion.[4]

A corporate finance officer had this to say about the transition to the centralized control that we call Phase 2 of financial development: "It used to be 'everybody out for a pass,' with no thought of team work. The fellow on the spot would handle the financing with a minimum of guidance. We wouldn't let him go hog-wild, but whether he got the best deal and did the right thing, we didn't know. From now on, hopefully, we'll know, and we'll have more control."

A more detailed statement of what "control" means is indicated by the treasurer of another Phase 2 firm: "Even where we have sophisticated local management, both long-term and short-term financing is determined in San Francisco and not just left to the discretion of the local management. We work very closely with our financial managers and we expect them to follow very closely our policies and procedures. We consult with them, but when something critical comes up, we'll send out a cable directing them that immediately they are to hedge such and such. But generally speaking, we have an opportunity to review the subject with them, suggest what we propose to do, and then give them a chance to react to it. I mean as a matter of courtesy, if nothing else. And, many times, they can contribute in a very worthwhile way to whatever our plans may be." There is little doubt who is in the driver's seat in this organization. The treasurer summarized as follows: "I don't like to say that our companies don't have any leeway. They are part of our team and we like to use their brains just like they were sitting right here; and we try to operate on this basis. But someone along the line has to say 'this is what we do,' and that's San Francisco."

Phase 3: Compromising with Complexity

Eventually, the management group at headquarters is faced with a dilemma. On the one hand, the factors of experience, scale of foreign operations, and relative importance of foreign operations encourage them to keep tight control over foreign financial decisions. On the other hand, the greater number of financial options resulting from an increase in the number of subsidiaries makes it impossible for the headquarters' group to make a separate decision on each financial transaction between affiliates in the enterprise. An indication of the complexity involved is illustrated by some of the Phase 3 multinational enterprises that we studied in depth. One such enterprise consisted of a U.S. parent, two U.S. subsidiary corporations, thirteen foreign branches, and 101 foreign corporations, organized on three tiers of ownership. Another firm that we studied is one of the largest of the Phase 3 enterprises. This firm consisted of some 500 sepa-

FIGURE 3–3

Phase 3 of Financial Development of a Multinational Enterprise

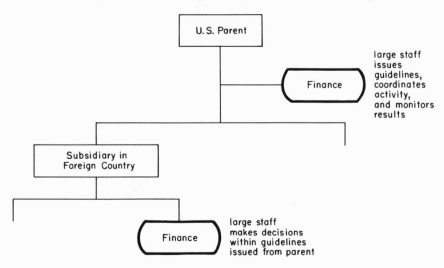

rate corporations, both domestic and foreign, and one executive of this enterprise told us that there was a change in the legal structure of the enterprise's organization on the average of once a week.

On first observation, the dilemma faced by management in the Phase 3 enterprises, that is, the dilemma of wishing to keep tight control over foreign operations but having difficulty in doing so because of the complexity, seems to be resolved in a simple way—by headquarters delegating more authority to the subsidiaries. In fact, the resolution is more complex. The headquarters' group believes that because of its substantial amount of accumulated experience, it knows how financial management should be conducted. Hence, the authority granted to the subsidiaries is accompanied by a "rule book" issued by headquarters. The headquarters' staff then spends its time revising the rule book and reviewing only the major financial decisions of the subsidiaries and the results of the subsidiaries' operations. Decisions on implementation within these guidelines in the rule book are left to local management. Figure 3–3 shows the activities of the financial staffs in Phase 3 enterprises. The managers of the Phase 3 enterprise are aware of the desirability of minimizing costs to the overall system but are resigned to the fact that they cannot hope to exploit every opportunity offered by their options in the field of financial policy.

However, make no mistake about it—even though these large enterprises seemingly are decentralized, their worldwide network of units and intercompany links are in fact controlled indirectly by their rule books, or "bibles" from headquarters. The "bibles" are in the form of standard procedures, sometimes consisting of several volumes, that specify such items as the limits of local borrowing, standard terms of payment on intercompany accounts, and standard rates for management fees.

Dow Chemical Company, in the National Industrial Conference Board's study of international financial management, describes its own transition from what we call Phase 2 to Phase 3 in these terms:

"In the past, it was this company's policy that even within the approved financial plans, *each instance* of short-term borrowing required the approval of the corporate financial unit. Because many of the company's foreign subsidiaries, as well as the regional financial management, have acquired considerable financial experience and have shown their ability to handle short-term financing successfully, the parent company has moved away from the "each instance" type of controls over borrowing. Rather the corporate financial unit performs a coordinating function when needs for short-term funds go beyond the routine credit line arrangements established for working capital financing.[5]

Another development that is related to the increase in complexity that results in the move from Phase 2 to Phase 3 financial strategy is the creation of regional financial headquarters. In general, managers in the regional offices attempt to exploit some of the opportunities for earning profits by using the financial links among subsidiaries within their geographical region. The net effect of a regional financial group is to allow more optimization and less reliance on decision rules for transactions between subsidiaries within a given region. However, in firms with regional headquarters, transactions between subsidiaries located in different regions tend to be controlled by the rule book.

In contrast with the step from Phase 1 to Phase 2, which is a recognizable alteration taken during a relatively short period of time, the transition from Phase 2 to Phase 3 is not so clear-cut. It comes about slowly as the headquarters' staff formulates guidelines on various financial policy tools one by one and returns responsibility for direct action to the subsidiaries. Though the exact level of foreign business at which the transition takes place cannot be defined precisely, it appears from our interviews to be about $500 million in sales of foreign operations.

This is also the point at which, in our terminology, an enterprise passes from Medium to Large. Among the 187 multinational enterprises, 22 were in the over-$500 million, or Large, category. And we judge that over 90 percent of them are in Phase 3 of their financial development. Some of the largest Phase 3 enterprises have foreign sales in the billions of dollars. In the Phase 3 firms we studied, foreign sales often represent a third or more of total world sales. Most of these firms manufacture in more than twenty foreign countries. In 1969 the aggregate sales of the foreign affiliates of the 22 Large enterprises approximated $40 billion.[6]

More about System Optimization

Thus we estimate that there are about 100 U.S. enterprises that have a Phase 2 or 3 financial policy and therefore actively and deliberately pursue a strategy that takes into account system optimization, either by issuing many direct orders from headquarters or by issuing a set of system rules. This is only 2 percent of U.S. firms with foreign direct investment. But these relatively few enterprises account for 70 percent of U.S. foreign direct investment in manufacturing, petroleum, and mining and smelting.[7]

The evolution of the financial function from Phase 1 to Phase 3 is depicted in Figure 3–4. This chart does not show quantitative measures of any variable. Rather, it is an impressionistic diagram suggesting the interrelations of emphasis on system, form of orders from headquarters, and size of foreign business.*

Of course, neither the amount of foreign sales nor any other measure of overseas size or experience fully determines the financial behavior of a multinational enterprise. Firms of identical size and experience often behave differently. Enterprises sometimes have reasons for preferring joint ventures over wholly owned subsidiaries. And enterprises sometimes are obliged to make a choice among the things they want to stress. High-technology firms, for example, may adopt a basic corporate strategy of focusing the firm's resources on the introduction of new products. Hence, management skill, a resource that is not unlimited, may be allocated

---

* The peak shown for "direct orders from headquarters" is consistent with the logistic regression analysis shown in Appendix A.

FIGURE 3–4

An Impressionistic View of the Development of Financial Policy

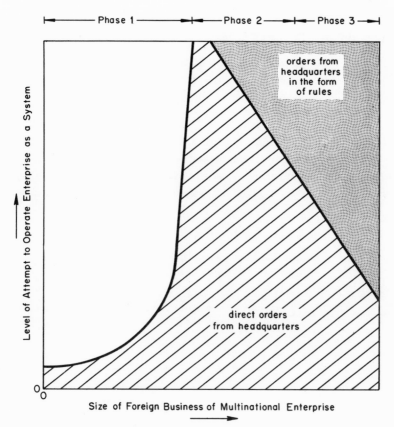

mainly to product introduction.[8] On the other hand, some firms that spend a low percentage of sales revenue on research and development have a basic strategy of cost minimization and thus prefer to allocate management time to reduce costs. A firm concentrating on new product introduction would be less concerned about saving a fraction of a percentage point in financial charges than would a firm primarily concerned with cost reduction. Thus, a multinational enterprise with a large share of joint ventures or with a high-technology level would tend to operate its worldwide system more nearly on an arm's-length basis than would other enterprises.*

The fact remains, however, that the major factors affecting financial

* Examples of statistical results showing the relation of ownership patterns and technology level to financial practices are included with the other statistical results of interviews in Appendix A.

strategy are foreign experience and size of foreign operations. That is why, as we discuss financial practices in later chapters, we will distinguish among Small, Medium, and Large multinational enterprises corresponding roughly to our three phases and classified by annual sales of the foreign units as already described:

> Small—less than $100 million
> Medium—from $100 to $500 million
> Large—over $500 million

Despite what we have said about "system optimization" in the Medium and Large enterprises, their managers, lacking perfect knowledge and living with financial complexities, actually are miles away from achieving an optimal financial policy. In contrast, our computer model, with perfect knowledge of its operations and environment—even including the timing

FIGURE 3–5

Intercompany Fund Flows in Year 1 as Multinational Enterprise Model Maximizes Consolidated Profits after Taxes (In Millions of Dollars)

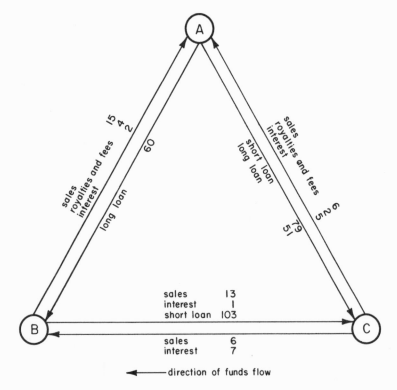

and extent of currency devaluations—can achieve an optimum for its limited multinational system.

It may be remembered that the computer model, as described at the end of Chapter 1, consists of three hypothetical companies, *A, B,* and *C,* and that *A* is the parent and *B* and *C* its two foreign subsidiaries. The model is programmed for four years of operations. Foreign sales are $200 million in the first year and rise to $320 in the fourth. These magnitudes are typical of a Medium enterprise in Phase 2 of financial evolution.

We fed into the model the problem of achieving for the enterprise an optimal financial policy, defined as the highest consolidated profits (after taxes) over the four-year period. The results are instructive: the solution entailed many financial links among *A, B,* and *C.* The intercompany fund flows in the first year are shown in Figure 3–5. The nature of such transactions and the circumstances that dictate their selection in both the real world and the model will be discussed in the chapters that follow. The main point here is that the profitability of the enterprise would have been impaired if it had been deprived of any of the tools in its financial kit. For example, if we as managers of the computer model had issued a rule suppressing intercompany short-term lending and requiring standard terms on all sales from one subsidiary to the other, consolidated profits after taxes over the four years would have been 5.5 percent less—$445 million instead of $471 million.

This exercise in simulation does not furnish a blueprint for maximizing profits in any specific real-life multinational enterprise. But it does throw additional light on how and why Medium and Large enterprises in Phases 2 and 3 try to exploit the potential not just of subsidiaries separately but of subsidiaries performing as a system.

FOUR / Financing Foreign Affiliates

A need for capital may arise at any stage in the life of a foreign affiliate, calling for decisions on how the funds can best be provided. But the problem appears in its sharpest outline at the time of gestation, before the parent firm delivers itself of the infant. Let us suppose, therefore, that a U.S.-controlled enterprise has decided to manufacture in country X. Accepting this decision as given, because it is primarily strategic rather than financial in nature, let us examine the financial ways and means of getting started.

The parent may already have a nonmanufacturing affiliate in country X, engaged perhaps in sales or finance; and in this case the parent may wish to have the existing organization expand its scope by building a factory. If the enterprise has no affiliate it must either acquire one or create one; and for this purpose, as we mentioned in Chapter 1, the parent is likely to prefer a subsidiary incorporated under the laws of the host country. Acquisition of a going corporation can be accomplished by buying part or all of the stock. If the subsidiary is to be started from scratch, the enterprise will go about it by hiring a lawyer in country X who will take out incorporation papers granting authority to issue a certain number of shares at a certain price. These shares are unlikely to be offered to the public; very few subsidiaries of this sort are publicly owned, though they may have one or more owners besides the U.S. parent. Typically, the parent firm puts up the necessary funds to own all the stock and appoints a board of directors and a slate of executive officers. The directors and officers may be either nationals of country X, the United States, or some other country. Then the new entity, in its corporate personality, sets about building the plant.

All this is fairly elementary as multinational business goes. But the financial decisions are scarcely simple.

For one thing, the capital supplied by the parent does not have to be wholly cash. Whether the subsidiary is being acquired or created, some of the capital can be equipment. Many a firm has invested in manufacturing abroad by putting up used machinery, which may have become a bit out-of-date in the highly mechanized domestic scene. Capital can also take the form of intermediate goods to be processed by the subsidiary. Or it can take the form of know-how, which can be exchanged for stock. In the early

49

1950's, for example, a U.S. firm could acquire half a company in Japan by furnishing the technical knowledge and management skills that were necessary for success. This is no longer true, but technology still plays an active part in foreign investment.

Compared with cash, though, these noncash items are not of major importance in the global aggregate. The investing of the multinational enterprise usually takes the form of cash. But under what terms, and by whom sent? The parent is by no means the only feasible source of capital for its subsidiary, especially as time goes on. Funds can be transferred in various ways from other subsidiaries within the enterprise, as will be discussed later in this chapter. The subsidiary can get cash from outside the system, notably from banks in country X. Moreover, after the subsidiary begins operations, it acquires two new sources—its own retained earnings and credit from suppliers who supply raw materials.

But this is getting slightly ahead of the story. The parent firm, establishing a subsidiary in country X, as described before, faces large questions in providing the original cash. The funds to build the plant and operate the local corporation fall into two main categories.

One category is the money that goes for the ownership of the stock. The other is credit. A simple illustration: If the stock issue is one million shares, each valued at one mark (or franc, or guilder, or peso), the parent may put up one million marks in equity and immediately supply the subsidiary with another four million marks in a long-term loan.

The appropriate ratio between equity and loans is one of the crucial decisions that an enterprise must make in its international operations. It is a continuing decision—or series of decisions—demanding all the expertise and wisdom that financial managers can bring to bear.

Equity and Credit

Most multinational enterprises lend money to foreign subsidiaries,* but the parent does this not as a normal lender, but as an owner investing in a business. The most common reason advanced for this practice is the flexibility afforded by loans in bringing funds back to the United States. Repatriation is a vital issue in the international area, and a wider latitude exists for doing so by means of interest or principal rather than by dividends or equity. For one thing, dividend payments and reductions in capital stock are characteristically more closely controlled by governmental regulations

* Appendix A contains statistical evidence supporting various statements in the text.

than are principal and interest payments. Furthermore, a reduction in equity capital, unless done to meet host-government goals designed to increase local participation, could be construed as indicating plans to leave the country. As the financial vice president of one corporation stated: "In almost every part of the world it's legally more difficult to return funds to shareholders through a reduction of capital stock than it is to pay off a loan; so, if you have any prospects of converting the operations from a 'cash requirer' to a 'cash generator' over time, it's very handy to have on the books of the subsidiary some debt that it can repay as a means of getting funds into New York."

Because of this apprehension about governmental controls on dividend and equity payments, the multinational firm makes a particular effort to limit the size of its equity commitment in a country whose currency is considered to be weak. Large enterprises are less cautious about this than Small ones, primarily because the geographic dispersion and financial strength of the Large enterprise provide some protection against the uncertainties of individual commitments.

Furthermore, should additional equity be desired in a subsidiary at a later date, it is relatively easy to convert an existing loan into equity, and this is often done in practice. For example, in one case a French subsidiary of a U.S. enterprise had to convert its loans from the parent into equity because of a negative net worth.

Another reason for the use of internal loans to finance an overseas subsidiary is the possibility of reducing taxes. Although all multinational enterprises are interested in saving taxes, the managers of Small enterprises tend to put special emphasis on such savings in the initial financing because their limited headquarters staff concentrates on specific subgoals, and the "taxes paid" item is especially relevant at this point in the development of a financial policy.

The possibility of a tax saving arises because: (1) interest paid by subsidiaries usually is deductible in the host country whereas dividend payments are not; and (2) the repayment of a subsidiary loan, unlike the payment of dividends or retirement of subsidiary stock, ordinarily will not constitute taxable income to the parent. Given certain plausible assumptions about dividend policy and the base for calculating the foreign tax credit, it is possible that the enterprise will save taxes by using a loan when the foreign tax rate is either above or below that of the United States or when a devaluation is expected in the host country.*

The great usefulness of loans as a means of transferring funds from one

* These cases are discussed in a statistical working paper available from the authors.

unit in a system to another is illustrated by the frequency with which the model elected to use this form of transfer when it was programmed to maximize the system's profits. For example, in year 1 the parent, *A*, loaned the subsidiaries a total of $190 million, as shown in Figure 4–1, making long-term loans of $60 million to subsidiary *B* and $51 million to subsidiary *C*, plus a $79 million short-term loan also to subsidiary *C*. The short-term loan proved to be a flexible financial tool, for subsidiary *C* avoided a conversion exchange loss on this loan by repaying the entire $79 million immediately prior to the devaluation of country *C*'s currency in year 2. In contrast, both subsidiaries made only their fixed schedule of payments on the long-term loans, thereby leaving substantial outstanding balances on which they each suffered a conversion loss.

FIGURE 4–1

Making and Repayment of Loans between Parent and Subsidiaries. Optimal Financial Policy, Multinational Enterprise Model for Years 1 and 2 (*In Millions of Dollars*)

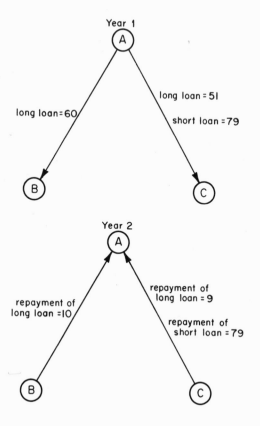

Many firms do not operate their corporate systems with the same flexibility illustrated in the model with respect to short-term loans. Rather, these companies tend to regard their loans to subsidiaries as business arrangements that should not be modified to reflect changing conditions. The Large enterprise typically has its loans with a fixed repayment schedule; the parent in the Small enterprise, on the other hand, preferring to minimize its long-term commitments to subsidiaries, primarily uses short-term loans with an informal understanding that the loans will be renewed for several years. The Medium firms prefer to use flexible terms for their loans because they more frequently use loans to move funds than do the other types of enterprises.

A parent can provide credit to a subsidiary not only by making loans but also by delaying the collection of accounts owed by the subsidiary for goods and services received from the parent. Compared with loans, these intrasystem, or intercompany, accounts have one major disadvantage: the amount of credit that can be granted is limited by the quantity of goods and services sold. Furthermore, at times the length of the credit terms is limited by governments. As one headquarters' official explained, "We had financed the working capital of our Italian subsidiary by not collecting on imports from the United States for over two years. But Italy has a regulation that you are not supposed to have payables over one year, so to avoid bankruptcy our Italian subsidiary had to reduce its payables down to one year." Figure 4–2, depicting the model's use of intercompany accounts between the parent and the two subsidiaries, illustrates the point that the amount of funds that can be moved by granting credit on intercompany accounts is relatively small compared with the sums moved by granting loans. The largest sum shifted between the parent and either subsidiary through intercompany accounts in any one year was $4.8 million between A and C in years 3 and 4, whereas Figure 4–1 showed that $130 million moved from A to C by intercompany loans in year 1. However, within the constraints of availability, most parents do use intercompany accounts in financing subsidiaries, for they have certain advantages over loans.

First, intercompany accounts are easier to use, for no formal note is needed and the amount of credit can be regulated up or down by shortening or lengthening the terms on the accounts. Governments do not always allow such freedom with loans. For example, one official reported that his firm's policy of keeping the terms of all loans on a demand basis could not be rigorously followed because a number of countries insisted that a loan be for a particular period of time, and other countries permitted repayments only in accordance with a fixed schedule registered with exchange control authorities.

FIGURE 4–2

Granting Credit through Intercompany Accounts Receivable between Parent and Subsidiaries. Optimal Financial Policy, Multinational Enterprise Model for Four Years (In Millions of Dollars)

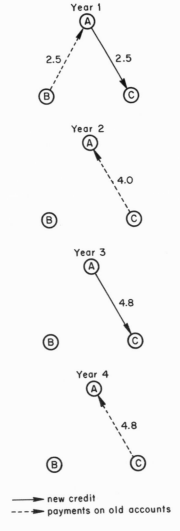

Second, when the time comes to withdraw the funds from a subsidiary, the local government is even less likely to interfere with payments on intercompany accounts than on loans.

Third, intercompany accounts have another advantage over loans in that Section 482 of the U.S. Government's Internal Revenue Code allows intercompany accounts up to six months' duration to be interest-free if the enterprise so decides.[1] In contrast, interest must be charged on all intercompany loans, for the Internal Revenue Service (IRS) can impute a tax if the lack of an interest charge reduces U.S. taxes lower than they would otherwise be.

The model illustrates the benefits that a system can obtain when a parent finances a subsidiary that needs funds by deferring payments the subsidiary owes for goods and services and by waiving interest on the debt. As shown in Figure 4–2, *A* collects its receivables from *B* in year 1 but does not collect them from *C*. This has the effect of permitting *C* to keep funds that ordinarily would have been paid to *A*. An alternative is to have *C* borrow in its own financial market and pay its accounts to *A*—enabling *A* to pay off some of its own bank debt. But that would entail higher interest for the system, because *C* would pay 9 percent interest whereas *A* pays 6 percent. The system also saves taxes because *A* waives interest on the intercompany accounts owed by *C* and because *C*'s tax rate is lower than *A*'s. Here are the costs compared:

	A's Cost		*C*'s Cost		System Cost	
	Before Taxes	After Taxes	Before Taxes	After Taxes	Before Taxes	After Taxes
(1) *C* obtains funds from local bank	—	—	9%	6.3%	9%	6.3%
(2) *C* obtains funds from *A*	6%	3%	—	—	6%	3%
Net saving by alternative (2)					3%	3.3%

Intercompany loans can be combined with intercompany accounts to accomplish several financial objectives. This is illustrated by the case of Alpha, a Medium multinational enterprise whose name is here disguised. In 1965, the president of Alpha and his top financial advisors framed a series of financial arrangements that had three basic aims, as stated in a letter to us:

1. Provide a large pool of cash outside the United States for use in financing foreign affiliates.
2. Demonstrate a good performance under the U.S. Voluntary Restraints Program (that was applicable at that time to help ameliorate the country's balance-of-payment deficit by encouraging corporations to hold down their outward flows of capital and accelerate inward movements).
3. Arrange debt of a pliable nature.

To accomplish these objectives, four steps were taken, as shown in Figure 4–3.

First, the parent, Alpha United States, loaned $23 million to Alpha Canada. This met the objective of placing the money outside the United States, but such loans to Canada did not count against the firm's quota under Voluntary Restraints Program. (Sidelight: The president selected Canada as a safe place to have an account because he remembered that when the U.S. banks closed in 1933 his father was able to get money that he had in Canadian banks.)

Second, Alpha Canada loaned $23 million to Alpha International Sales, a Panama corporation.

FIGURE 4–3

Movement of Funds by Alpha Enterprise (In Millions of Dollars)

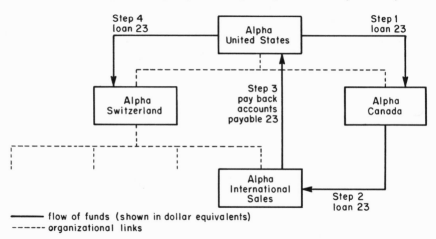

——— flow of funds (shown in dollar equivalents)
------ organizational links

Third, this sales subsidiary, a direct purchaser of goods from Alpha United States, immediately used the $23 million to reduce accounts payable to Alpha United States. This repayment provided a positive flow of funds to satisfy the Voluntary Restraints Program. The credit earned under the Restraint Program by this maneuver was used in the fourth step.

In this fourth step, the $23 million received by Alpha United States from repayments by Alpha International Sales was loaned to Alpha Switzerland in order to increase the amount of money held overseas. This loan, a short-term obligation, helped provide a pliable debt structure in which intrasystem loans could be granted and repaid with ease. Alpha United States continued to ship goods to the sales subsidiary, which could now let its accounts payable build up to six months, and the cash generated by this subsidiary could be held outside the United States. The net result of the entire series of maneuvers was that $46 million rather than $23 million was held outside the United States.

Governments have their own view of such uses of intercompany financial links; a U.S. government official commented in 1972: "Alpha's transactions not only violated the spirit of the Voluntary Program but raised questions of possible fudging of reports. Since there was no compulsory compliance during the Voluntary Program, the company's actions may not have been illegal but clearly were evasive."

Even though intercompany credit, regardless of form, has advantages over equity, enterprises are not free to use any ratio of credit to equity that they choose. For example, the host government might insist that a parent provide a certain amount of equity before the subsidiary is allowed to borrow locally.[2] Or, the local banking community might have "rules of thumb" by which they decide on a maximum allowable ratio of debt to equity. One major U.S. firm, which prefers its subsidiaries to borrow locally, reported that in the Netherlands the local investment bankers insisted on a certain ratio of capital to long-term debt before they would float a public offering of bonds.

Furthermore, as one official stated: "If we tried to minimize the equity investment in a foreign subsidiary, then when we reported our profits to the government, they would be able to show that we were getting a very high return in terms of a percentage of an equity investment. This would subject us to cries of being the exploiting American investors." There is danger from the press if subsequent dividend payments are high relative to the initial equity base.

And there is always the U.S. government. Many executives and tax lawyers believe that a ratio of debt to equity of four to one is satisfactory to the IRS: "Our government will not permit us to have too thin a capital base for a subsidiary. If you go beyond a debt-to-equity ratio of four to one, the IRS may raise questions. Our government does not have the right to say that you must take the debt into stock; but for tax purposes, they will treat it as stock—they can set up the proportions."[3]

The Large multinational enterprises, and surprisingly the Medium ones also, often use guidelines in determining the amount of equity to be provided in starting a manufacturing subsidiary. Typical examples are to let equity equal:

50 percent of total assets, or
fixed assets, or
fixed assets plus inventory, or

50 percent of fixed assets plus three months inventory plus 30 percent of normally expected accounts receivable plus one month's cash.

Such rules almost always provide for less debt and more equity than would be required by the four-to-one ratio believed by many executives to be satisfactory to the IRS. The rule of "equity equals fixed assets" usually provides for the least equity and most debt of any of the four listed above, but when it was applied to an investment in a manufacturing plant in Taiwan, the resulting ratio of intercompany debt-to-equity was 0.6 to 1, well below the four-to-one ratio believed to be satisfactory to the U.S. government and very much lower than that required by the Taiwanese government. The Taiwanese and U.S. income tax rates were such that the enterprise carried a heavier tax burden than was necessary.

In contrast, some firms have used a capital structure inordinately concentrated in debt. In one case, for example, a Small electronics firm's subsidiary located in a less developed country had the following initial capitalization:

Capital	$ 10,000
Long-term debt, owed to parent	1,550,000
Total	$1,565,000

This use of less than 1 percent equity was the most highly leveraged subsidiary on which we had information. At the time of our data collection, neither the U.S. government nor the host government had raised any questions about the financing of this subsidiary.

Still, we think the Taiwanese case is more representative of the typical U.S. multinational enterprise, for based on our interviews and an examination of the unpublished records covering several years' operations of more than fifty foreign subsidiaries owned by multinational enterprises in the three size categories, we concluded that U.S. multinational enterprises generally were using more equity than required to meet governmental regulations in starting and expanding subsidiaries. As a result, these firms were losing profits by paying more U.S. taxes than would result from alternative financing methods.

The Traditional Path

Ask managers of multinational enterprises what they expect of a newly formed subsidiary once it "gets on its feet," and many will say, "grow, grow, and grow some more, without our sending more funds from headquarters."

This behavior was captured in the early literature on international firms, perhaps most vividly by Edith Penrose in her theory of the independent growth of foreign subsidiaries [4] and E. R. Barlow and Ira T. Wender in their description of U.S. firms' gambling small sums in starting subsidiaries in hopes of large payoffs later.[5]

There is much evidence to support this pattern, for indeed most foreign subsidiaries were started with a modest sum. After the initial incubation period, retained earnings and depreciation allowances are the dominant source of funds, and these sources, when coupled with local borrowing, leave relatively little need for fresh funds from headquarters. Any original loan either is turned into equity or left until the subsidiary becomes suitably profitable to pay it off. To be sure, at times additional funds from the system are provided to the subsidiary, sometimes to provide needed capital when the subsidiary's losses have been heavy, or when there is opportunity for faster growth than retained earnings would allow.

Relatively little money is withdrawn from the subsidiary during its early years, for these are the years when the subsidiary has a ravenous appetite for funds in order to stimulate growth at rates as high as 20 to 30 percent annually for years on end. The original plant often is quite small with a narrow product line, serving the function of testing the local water as well as earning a monetary profit. If the water seems fine, other product lines are added and vertical integration commences. Finally, a subsidiary's growth rate begins to slow, and it becomes an important cash generator for the system. But this takes time, and dividends often are negligible for the first ten years or so. But when dividends do start they can be quite large compared with the original equity. A $1 million investment grows to $10 million in ten years at a 25 percent annual growth rate, and such rates are on record.

A classic case, about which much has been written, is that of General Motors-Holden's Ltd., General Motors' wholly owned subsidiary in Australia. This subsidiary was started in 1926 and had an original equity investment of A£1.75 million. Most of the earnings were reinvested until 1954, by which time the value of General Motors' equity investment in the subsidiary had grown to A£25 million. The first dividend, that of A£4.6 million in 1954, seemed reasonable to General Motors' management, who compared the dividends with the then existing equity and remembered the many years with little or no dividends. The Australian press and politicians had a field day complaining about the size of the dividend, for they had a different view: the initial dividend was larger than the original investment.[6]

Our findings differ a bit from this traditional pattern. The Small multinational enterprise most closely follows the pattern, for once headquarters makes an initial investment it is reluctant to provide additional funds. The Medium firm, on the other hand, follows the traditional pattern the least, for the parent is willing to, and often does, send in additional funds with little reluctance. The Large enterprise is more willing than the Small but less willing than the Medium to provide additional system funds for local growth. Certainly it often does just that.

Funds from Sister Subsidiaries

The fact that a subsidiary can receive credit from its sisters in addition to its parent vastly expands the possible alternatives for financing the growth of a multinational system. In specific instances, intersubsidiary credit has provided most of the funds received by a subsidiary. Yet this set of financial links has been used much less than one might imagine.

For one thing, local financial institutions may frown upon arrangements that have the effect of moving funds from them to the local subsidiary to a sister subsidiary in another country. Explained one treasurer: "If Italy needs money and our British subsidiary gives them extended terms, the British bankers will know that and will say, 'We're not going to finance the Italians. We don't mind going along with you, but this isn't a worldwide financing operation. We're trying to help the English.' It's the same in France and the same in Italy. They ask you why you want the money and let's see your balance sheet; so, any intercompany financing is pretty obvious."

But even when financial institutions do not stand in the way, there is another reason why these financial links are not used as extensively as they might be. That reason is complexity, for it is difficult for headquarters to keep track of the intricate relationships that can materialize.

Although headquarters can avoid part of the problem of complexity by not creating intersubsidiary loans, it still must deal with the many financial links that are automatically created when subsidiaries sell goods and services to one another. Subsidiary-to-subsidiary sales are not extensive in the Small enterprise, so relatively few intersubsidiary financial links exist. But to the extent that they do prevail, the subsidiaries often are free to negotiate at arm's length with one another for extended credit and the interest rates to be paid for such credit. The parent does not usually worry about the situation's getting out of hand.

Firms in the Medium and Large categories, however, face a major problem in controlling their relatively large number of intercompany accounts.

In particular, using intersubsidiary accounts to provide needed funds to a subsidiary and varying interest-rate payments to maximize profits pose a dilemma for the headquarters' staff of the Medium multinational enterprises. On the one hand, such coordinated arrangements may add to profits, but on the other hand, the overall corporate systems are such a size that it is difficult for managers in headquarters to control closely all subsidiary-to-subsidiary transactions. The resulting compromise is that relatively few Medium systems use intersubsidiary accounts as a funds-shifting mechanism; however, when such a device is used, it is controlled by headquarters for the specific purpose of minimizing system costs rather

FIGURE 4–4

Source of System Funds for New French Subsidiary, Beta Enterprise
(In Millions of Dollars)

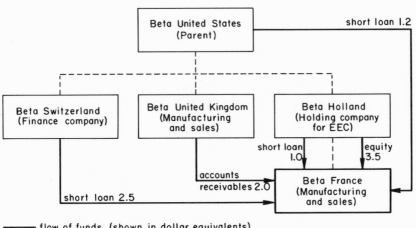

——— flow of funds (shown in dollar equivalents)
- - - - organizational links

than controlled by agreements between subsidiary managers to meet their goals, as tends to be the case of the Small, as well as of the Large, enterprises. Thus, in those situations in which intersubsidiary accounts are used for funds shifting, the Medium firms are much less likely to have a standard operating practice of charging interest on such accounts than are the Small and Large systems; instead, they charge what they consider to be optimum for the system.

Beta is our code name for a Medium enterprise that finances its foreign affiliates with a combination of equity and loans, from sister subsidiaries as well as the parent. Figure 4–4 shows the financing of Beta's French subsidiary. Of the $10.2 million provided from the enterprise's system to start this subsidiary, some 34 percent was equity, 46 percent short-term loans, and 20 percent credit on accounts receivable. Almost half the funds were provided by sister subsidiaries. The parent and its Dutch holding company, an extension of the parent, provided the remainder.

The model, too, made use of its subsidiaries to provide funds to one another. As shown in Figure 4–5, intercompany accounts were used to grant credit between *B* and *C* during each of the four years of the model's operation. Furthermore, although not shown in Figure 4–5, intersubsidiary loans also were used extensively.

FIGURE 4–5

Granting Credit through Intercompany Accounts Receivable between Subsidiaries. Optimal Financial Policy, Multinational Enterprise Model for Four Years (In Millions of Dollars)

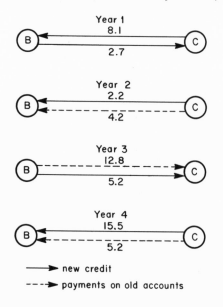

Some Medium enterprises control intersubsidiary accounts by having all such accounts go through one sales subsidiary. As an example, we quote from a letter to us from the Assistant Treasurer of Gamma (we have substituted "Gamma" for the real name of the firm): "It was Gamma policy prior to December 31, 1966, that shipments between foreign subsidiaries must go through a Gamma export company. Therefore, final destination information on foreign subsidiary intercompany shipments (excluding export companies) is not readily available." Commencing in 1967, when Gamma's foreign sales were $330 million, Gamma in its process of becoming a Large enterprise was beginning to loosen its centrally controlled reins on intercompany transactions and allow some subsidiaries to deal directly with one another.

Some Large enterprises, especially the oil companies, have gained experience in handling intersubsidiary accounts and at times use them. Also, in some Large enterprises one subsidiary treasurer may negotiate directly with another to obtain or give credit for short periods, but in general the Large firm prefers to have its subsidiaries maintain established trade terms in order to avoid the complexities; their budgets usually establish the permissible levels. As one treasurer sadly concluded, "Usually it is too complex, so we use just straight financing with an outside source."

Thus, in theory, sister subsidiaries represent a large potential in the search for an optimal pattern of financing foreign operations, but the complexity of reality greatly limits their use.

Local Borrowing

Subsidiaries of multinational enterprises do a lot of borrowing in their host countries to obtain needed funds. The overseas subsidiaries of every multinational enterprise that we interviewed use this source, whether it is only a little short-term borrowing from local banks or both short-term and long-term borrowing from a variety of sources. In fact, over one quarter of all the companies that we interviewed favor local borrowing over borrowing from outside the host country regardless of interest-rate differentials.

The stress on short-term borrowing in the foreign area suggests that current liabilities are relatively bigger in the balance sheets of the overseas units than is true of their domestic counterparts. Adequate data for such comparisons are hard to come by. But in a study that we made of the domestic and overseas operations of a number of multinational enterprises for which published information was available, we found that, over the six post-World War II years covered, current liabilities (excluding intercompany liabilities) represented 26 percent of the total liabilities and equity of the foreign subsidiaries compared with only 18 percent in the statements covering domestic activities.[7] This emphasis on local borrowing was asserted succinctly by one official in response to an inquiry regarding the policy of the enterprise: "Definitely we would like them to borrow locally as much as possible. Actually, I can't remember any case where that policy was reversed."

The most important reasons for using local sources are (1) to obtain automatic protection against devaluation of the local currency—if a devalua-

64   MONEY IN THE MULTINATIONAL ENTERPRISE

tion occurs, the debt is repaid in the devalued local currency; and (2) to obtain funds at a lower cost than is available from alternative sources.

The model confirmed that at times local borrowing is indeed the right answer. In fact, because each subsidiary could use the other subsidiary as a source or an outlet for funds, the model entered into huge local money-market ventures.

In Figure 4–6, the upper set of vertical arrows in each year show local borrowing and repayment. The lower set of vertical arrows show the net of all other sources and uses of the subsidiaries' funds; some of these nets represent the purchase, or liquidation, of short-term securities within the subsidiary's own money market. The horizontal arrows represent transactions between the subsidiaries. For example, in year 1, subsidiary *B* obtains $51 million from local borrowing, shown by the upper arrow moving down toward the subsidiary, and $52 million net of other sources and uses, shown by the lower arrow pointing upward; part of this net is from liquidating short-term securities. Subsidiary *B* lends this $103 million to subsidiary *C*, who uses it to repay $25 million in loans previously made and combines the remaining $78 million with other sources to provide funds for other uses.

FIGURE 4–6

Local Short-Term Borrowing. Optimal Financial, Multinational Enterprise Model Policy for Four Years

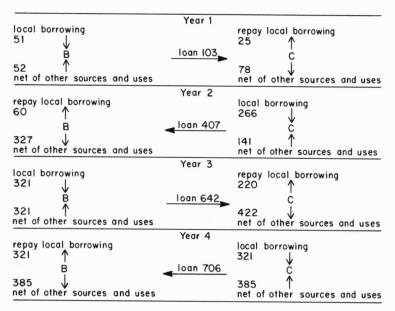

From the changing directions of the vertical arrows, we see that in years 1 and 3, subsidiary *B* borrows heavily in its own money market and liquidates short-term securities; it moves the funds to *C,* which repays outstanding loans and invests in the short-term money market. These transactions are made primarily to save interest costs. In years 2 and 4, the pattern is reversed as subsidiary *C* obtains funds locally both by borrowing and by liquidating short-term investments. *C* then moves the funds to *B,* who repays local short-term debts and invests in the local short-term market. This time, the factor motivating the financial actions is the threat of loss from devaluation of country *C*'s currency. The to-and-fro intercompany lending that takes place is illustrated by the alternating direction of the horizontal arrows from year to year.

There are other reasons why real-world firms employ local borrowing that were not programmed into the simulation model. One of these is that sometimes the debt of a subsidiary does not appear in the consolidated statement that is used as the basis of obtaining loans in the United States. Enterprises often do not consolidate the statements of subsidiaries in areas where exchange restrictions exist or seem likely, and, indeed, some Small firms do not consolidate any of their foreign operations. So if the parent has not guaranteed the loan obtained by the subsidiary, then accounting convention does not require that the amount be indicated by a footnote in the financial statement.* Thus, a high ratio of debt to equity can exist in the subsidiary without affecting the overall borrowing capacity of the multinational enterprise. On the other hand, debt contracted by a parent to supply a subsidiary with funds would, of course, appear in its financial statement and have a bearing upon its further borrowing potential. In the case of one Small multinational enterprise that made its financial records available to us, management did not know the extent of foreign borrowing because most subsidiaries were joint ventures which had not been consolidated into its annual report; in fact, the financial statements of their foreign subsidiaries had not been translated into dollars. This management judged the subsidiaries only by their payments of dividends and royalties to the parent. In the latest year for which we reviewed the records, the foreign subsidiaries had total loans of $7.3 million, of which only $600,000 were guaranteed by the parent (we did the translation into dollars).

Another reason for local borrowing is that some host countries, such as Japan, restrict the amount of funds that foreign firms can bring in, for the

---

* The rules, mentioned on page 39, adopted for 1972 affecting the reporting of losses and gains from unconsolidated subsidiaries did not affect the reporting of unguaranteed loans by subsidiaries whose operations are not included in the parent's consolidated statement.

government feels that such funds could give the subsidiary a competitive advantage over locally owned firms as well as impede the government's control over its own money market. Thus, local borrowing may become the only source of needed funds.

Finally, subsidiaries borrow locally to foster good relations with the local institutions, especially banks. As one treasurer said, "It's good business, they get to know you better and you get some standing in that community."

Banks occupy a role in many foreign countries but the lending ability of many of them is limited; so a subsidiary sometimes employs a larger number of banks than it would in the United States. One American official of a Japanese subsidiary commented: "When a tight money situation occurs as is expected at the end of this year, we have to use all available sources; and we deal with thirty banks."

Not only do multinational enterprises characteristically use banks for at least part of their subsidiaries' funds, but many depend upon them as the only outside source of funds other than trade credit. Several factors lead to this widespread use of local banks. In some countries, no choice is possible since they are the only intermediaries available. Also, in comparison with U.S. institutions, they often grant loans on a much smaller equity base. Commonly they play a key part in obtaining supplier and third country credits for the firm. Furthermore, local banks often serve as a source of long-term funds, for it is common practice in many foreign countries for a subsidiary to obtain a short-term obligation and renew it regularly as it matures. On this score, one official stated: "The bank establishes our line of credit on a one year basis, but it's renewable every year, so for practical purposes, it's long-term." While "rolling over" short-term loans is employed by all categories of firms, the Medium enterprise is less disposed to this practice than the others. As a "system optimizer," such a firm is prone to seek out the least expensive means of financing rather than to persist with existing lines indiscriminately.

The majority of the U.S. multinational firms use both locally owned banks and branches of U.S. banks in their financing operations. Maintaining ties with these two types of institutions is a sort of insurance that enables the subsidiary to "keep its fingers in both pies," as one official stated.

Each type of institution is believed by the managers of multinational enterprises to afford special advantages. Local banks sometimes have more funds available and usually provide keener insights into the customers of the subsidiary. On the other hand, the local branches of American banks at times have an advantage, as one subsidiary treasurer stated. "We are able to borrow from American branches at slightly lower than normal borrowing rates because of the associations with our parent company. The American branches, of course, remember that we have big brother over there. We are treated rather as a son of a rich father." Another advantage of American branches was indicated by the treasurer of the Philippine subsidiary of a U.S. enterprise. "In the Philippines it is quite a comfort to know that the National City people here know what is going on in the world. It is now always easy to get information and sometimes the local institutions just don't know enough." In fact, some Large firms require that their overseas subsidiaries deal with a branch included in an international banking network that can help units elsewhere in the firm's system.

When a multinational enterprise uses an American bank abroad, the banking system sometimes serves as a network that helps keep headquarters informed of the activities of its subsidiaries. The financial manager of the Japanese subsidiary of a Large enterprise noted: "If an American bank here lends us something, they will have their head office in New York tell our financial people in New York that this loan is being made." As a result of such practices, one regional treasurer in Europe said that he insisted on using European rather than American banks.

One point of contention continually arises between multinational enterprises and financial institutions—the question of whether the parent will guarantee the local borrowing done by their subsidiaries. Most parents prefer not to give such guarantees, although the size of the firm affects its preference.

We mentioned above that Small firms often have foreign subsidiaries whose financial reports are not consolidated into the parent's financial reports, so that subsidiary borrowing not guaranteed by the parent is not reported to stockholders or lenders. This fact gives the Small firm a preference for not guaranteeing its subsidiaries' loans. But there also is another reason: a desire to avoid "giving local management a crutch." "I think international companies ought to stand on their own feet. What is the use of separating the international business into separate corporations and then going along and guaranteeing their obligations?" Furthermore, "when you give a guarantee, you lose the bank as your partner in controls."

In contrast, the parent in the Medium enterprise often is willing to grant a guarantee in exchange for a minor reduction in borrowing costs—even a quarter of a percentage point—or other relatively shallow benefits. For example, by providing the guarantee, the parent may be able to avoid the inclusion of complicating covenants in the loan agreement between the subsidiary and the local bank. "We didn't mind these covenants particularly, but they did reduce our flexibility a bit. We felt that it was to our advantage to provide a guarantee and obviate the limitations."

The Large multinational enterprise often adopts a simple "no guarantee" role. In the words of one financial executive, "It is easier to avoid facing the problem of where you draw the line. If you say 'no' to everybody, you don't have to worry about justifying case by case where you're willing to say 'yes' and where you're willing to say 'no.' Furthermore, our subsidiaries are big enough so that they can get the best rates without our guarantee." This line of reasoning was reiterated many times: "It's a lot easier to say that we don't guarantee and let it go at that," and "Our policy is not to guarantee our subsidiaries' loans. We expect them to be properly capitalized so that they can borrow as an individual company. It makes you a better citizen of a country to say that you have the capital for the subsidiary to stand on its own. Also, the trouble is that if you agree to guarantee one loan, then all the banks want you to guarantee all of them."

Two other factors militate against the grant of a guarantee. One is the existence of governmental regulations. For example, if a firm guarantees a long-term debt in West Germany, the guarantee is subject to a capital tax of 2.5 percent.

The other factor militating against the parent's giving a guarantee is the presence of a foreign partner, for the parent may be amenable to providing a guarantee in proportion to its ownership of the subsidiary but may refuse completely if its share is too low. One official noted, "When it comes to associated companies, we will not guarantee more than our ownership. For the Indian subsidiary—since we only own 25 percent—we've said we just won't provide any guarantee. If they want to get bank loans, they've got to make their own arrangements."

Even if the parent does not provide a legal backing, it may provide a "moral" guarantee in the form of a letter, sometimes called a "monkey" or "Oklahoma" letter. To the parent, the moral guarantee is no more than tangible evidence of its willingness to do what it expected to do in any case, that is, to stand behind the obligations of a subsidiary to protect the reputation of the entire corporate system. To the lending institution, the "moral" commitment provides a sense of satisfaction even though no additional legal security is involved. Thus, both parties appear to gain a sense of added comfort from the arrangement. As one manager observed: "In Italy we said, 'we just don't guarantee.' The bank asked, 'Will you write a letter that implies that you stand behind it?' We did and it's a famous letter now within the company. It reads: 'It is as inconceivable to us as it would be to you that we would change our ownership or draw out our investment without first notifying you and honoring our proportion of all debts.' It made them happy, and it made us happy."

When political issues are involved, however, the parent may be reluctant to stand behind a subsidiary's debts. As an example, Raytheon management let an Italian subsidiary go into bankruptcy because of the subsidiary's political difficulties in Sicily.[8]

The multinational enterprise uses other institutions abroad in addition to banks to help in its financing. But the nature of the financial institutions often differs from those in the United States. Capital markets in foreign countries usually are limited in scope. Funds from insurance companies often are not available. On the other hand, the institutional structures of some foreign countries provide alternative sources of funds, particularly for long-term purposes; examples are special developmental banks and governmental financing to assist in establishing industrial companies in distressed areas. In addition to the financing institutions of foreign countries, funds for overseas activities may be obtained from bank subsidiaries formed under the U.S. Edge Act, which can engage in long-term financing of industrial ventures abroad. Furthermore, U.S. and international agencies such as the Export-Import Bank, Overseas Private Investment Corporation, Inter-American Development Bank, and International Finance Corporation provide long-term funds abroad.

The Large enterprise particularly is notable for its employment of a variety of financing sources, a tendency that is encouraged by its substantial requirements for funds and is supported by its specialist staffs of people, both in the home office and in the subsidiaries. Besides, the renown of the big company serves as a magnet to attract offers of financing services.

One factor limiting the use of nonbank sources is the lack of awareness displayed by some multinational firms, especially the Small ones. One official of a Small firm observed somewhat whimsically, "I probably should investigate those more than I have; we haven't done anything with them. Are there any restrictions, or does the government get into the act with you?" But even when a firm is aware of these other financial institutions, obstacles still prevent their extensive use. The quantity of funds that can be provided may be limited; the parent may be required to have more equity in the subsidiary than the parent desires; the lending agency may desire a portion of the equity or a mortgage on the properties; the lender may take advantage of its position to become an undesired managerial consultant.

In some mature countries of the western world, relatively strong capital markets exist, and even many less developed countries have taken steps to develop local markets. Ordinarily, however, most U.S. multinational enterprises prefer not to undertake a public offering of equity even if the local market could absorb the issue, for, as already mentioned, many U.S. enterprises tend to prefer wholly owned subsidiaries. Furthermore, many

of the firms willing to accept partial ownership would prefer a local partner that can provide resources such as raw materials, management, or marketing skills in addition to capital, rather than public ownership which just
provides capital.[9]

Since ownership interests are not affected by sale of bonds, multinational enterprises wishing to raise long-term funds locally are more willing
to issue bonds than to sell equity. But the use of local bonds is hampered
by the limited size of most foreign bond markets.

The subsidiary may obtain funds from outside the system or local
sources. For example, some managers believe that they get extra benefits
from borrowing from the Export-Import Bank. "If you go into a new country with a new venture and have an Ex-Im loan, I think you've got the
support of the United States behind you. I know of no case where a foreign government hasn't given foreign exchange to serve an Ex-Im Bank
loan. So to me this puts you in good shape."

One foreign-capital market deserves special mention because of its
uniqueness. This is the large international-capital market that emerged in
Europe after the imposition of U.S. controls on capital exports. The main
effect of this market was to shift procurement of funds for foreign use
from the United States to Europe. Many of the users of this market were
special financing subsidiaries of U.S. multinational enterprises, but the
market had little impact on relations between the parent and its operating
subsidiaries, for these financing subsidiaries were managed as an integral
part of the parent, with the funds disbursed by headquarters just as though
the funds had come from the United States.

The fledgling Eurobond market grew rapidly, from an estimated $1.1
billion in 1966 to $3.6 billion in 1971.[10] Earlier offerings in Europe at-
tempted to develop special currency packages such as the "unit of account," which interrelated seventeen European currencies to the price of
gold, and the "parallel loan," which was divided into different parts, each
placed in a local market and denominated in the local currency. But the
overwhelming majority of issues were placed in only one currency, usually
dollars.

Because a certain minimum scale of offerings is required to absorb the
fixed costs of distribution, the Eurobond market has been dominated by
the big multinational enterprises. Indicative of the scale involved is the
fact that extensive records collected for us for all Eurobond issues through
1968 show that the first 132 bond issues by U.S. firms on the average
amounted to $24 million each. Virtually every Large multinational enter-
prise had tapped this market, whereas less than 20 percent of the Small
firms that we interviewed had done so.

Perhaps because of the heavy concentration of big, well-known U.S. multinational enterprises in the market, an analysis by us indicates that neither the size of the enterprise nor the quality rate of the parent's bonds in the United States had much of an effect on the cost of borrowing. The variable that seemed to have the most influence was the currency in which the bonds were denominated. During the period 1965 to 1968, when the two effects of size and quality of the borrower were held constant by means of statistical analysis, we found that, compared with bonds denominated in dollars, bonds denominated in Swiss francs had an interest rate about 15 percent lower. Thus, in round numbers, if dollar bonds were selling at a level to yield 8 percent, Swiss franc bonds would sell to yield 6.8 percent.*

Concurrent with the rise of the Eurobond market, large sums of dollars which began to be held abroad in banks were loaned to various borrowers, including U.S. multinational enterprises. Although the exact size of this pool of dollars is difficult to determine precisely,[11] some estimates have placed the total at more than $50 billion. Our interviews indicated that this source of funds was widely used by all sizes of U.S. firms operating abroad.

Following the rise of the Eurobonds and Eurodollar bank loans, Euro-commercial paper made its appearance in June 1970. By mid-March 1972, the size of the market was estimated at $100 million with fifteen major U.S. companies issuing these notes.[12]

Regardless of the development of the foreign capital markets, the foreign subsidiaries of U.S. multinational enterprises will continue to obtain local funds primarily by short-term borrowing. The evidence of the simulation model highlights the value of a flexible financial policy in which subsidiaries borrow and repay as circumstances require. Short-term loans enable the enterprise to adapt quickly to new conditions.

The Statistical Picture

The results of the financing policies adopted by U.S. multinational enterprises primarily engaged in manufacturing are shown in Table 4–1 for 1969.** In that year, some 60 percent of the required funds were obtained from within the multinational enterprise, mostly from retained earnings

---

* This analysis is in a statistical working paper available from the authors.

** This table is taken from a Department of Commerce Study of the 313 largest U.S. foreign direct investors in manufacturing; we estimate that our 187 enterprises account for 90 percent of the total.

TABLE 4-1

Sources of Funds, Majority-Owned Foreign Affiliates of 313 U.S. Foreign Direct Investors Primarily Engaged in Manufacturing, 1969

			Percentage
From within multinational enterprise			60
Internally generated by affiliate		46	
Depreciation	29		
Retained earnings	17		
From parent		14	
Equity	9		
Loans	5		
From outside multinational enterprise			40
Loans		39	
Equity		2	
TOTAL			100 a

Source: U.S. Department of Commerce, Office of Foreign Direct Investments, *Foreign Affiliate Financial Survey, 1966–1969,* July 1971, p. 34.

Note: All foreign currency amounts were translated into dollar values prior to publication of source of data.

a The total of the sources of funds was $10.1 billion. Because of rounding, all columns do not total exactly.

and depreciation of the foreign units. As would be expected, the outside funds were primarily in the form of debt.

This portrayal is deceptive in that it understates the use of credit within a multinational system. Because the results of all the overseas units are lumped into a single figure, the transactions between units have been netted out. As a consequence, the data do not identify the financing assistance that one offshore unit in the same system provides to another. Another shortcoming is that it is a still-shot of a corporate world which is in a continual state of flux. The picture fails to capture the financial scurrying that often occurs within and between particular foreign units as they borrow locally, repay, shift funds to another overseas unit, and deal with the parent. We estimate that intrasystem credit outstanding at the end of 1969 for the group of manufacturing enterprises shown in Table 4-1 was about $14 billion.[13] Since much of this was short-term credit, the net loans of $0.5 billion from the parent to foreign affiliates shown in this table grossly understates the use of credit.

The simulation model can be used to show the drastic differences that can occur when the aggregate facade is broken to reveal the results of its

TABLE 4-2

Sources of Funds for Subsidiaries. Optimal Financial Policy,
Multinational Enterprise Model. Four Years (In Millions of Dollars)

	Year 1			Year 2			Year 3			Year 4		
	B	C	Total B and C	B	C	Total B and C	B	C	Total B and C	B	C	Total B and C
From within multinational enterprise	88	170	258	299	−147	152	−297	447	150	412	−392	20
Internally generated by subsidiary	22	31	53	8	51	59	28	−15	13	36	65	101
From parent	58	133	191	−10	−91	−101	−9	118	109	−7	−113	−120
From other subsidiaries	8	106	114	301	−107	194	−316	344	28	383	−344	39
From outside multinational enterprise	28	−25	3	−64	220	156	327	−219	108	−320	265	−55
Debt	28	−25	3	−64	220	156	327	−219	108	−320	265	−55
Equity	0	0	0	0	0	0	0	0	0	0	0	0

Note: Positive number is inflow to a subsidiary. Negative number is outflow from a subsidiary. In year 2, the positive flow of $301 million "from other subsidiaries" to subsidiary B primarily represents a new loan granted from C to B. The negative flow of $107 million "from other subsidiaries" to subsidiary C primarily represents a repayment by C to B of a loan previously received from B.

component units. In two out of the four years covered, the overall financing pattern of the foreign subsidiaries in the model system was like that of the foreign affiliates in the Department of Commerce report. As shown in Table 4–2, in year 2, the foreign subsidiaries in the model's system in the aggregate obtained about half their funds from sources within the subsidiaries and half from external sources ($152 million * from within and $156 million ** from outside); in year 3, the ratio was about 60:40, the same as that indicated by the Department of Commerce data in Table 4–1. But when the figures for the two subsidiaries are disaggregated, the results are strikingly different. Subsidiary B in year 2 does all its financing internally and uses a portion of these funds to liquidate some external loans; in year 3 the same subsidiary borrows heavily from external sources and applies much of these funds to reduce its intersystem accounts. This financing pattern is reversed in the case of subsidiary C.

In some respects, we believe that the model's changing panorama of events is a better facsimile of the multinational world than any aggregate data. In the model there is a constant shift between financing sources within and outside the system as each of the subsidiaries seeks the routes that make the maximum contribution to earnings. As a result, the choice of sources varies as interest-rate and currency relationships change. Moreover, in pursuing these tactics, the two subsidiaries of the model often move in different directions rather than in tandem as conditions change in the countries where they are located. Likewise, companies in the real world, albeit to a lesser extent, shift their financing policies to take into account the ebb and flow of economic tides rather than allowing their worldwide financial patterns to remain fixed.

Underlying all these variations in the financing of foreign affiliates is the parent's preparation for the day when the cash will flow in the opposite direction. The method of financing is closely geared to the eventual method of withdrawing funds.

* 299 for subsidiary B minus 147 for subsidiary C.
** 220 for subsidiary C minus 64 for subsidiary B.

FIVE / Withdrawing Funds from Abroad

A key problem that confronts the financial managers of multinational enterprises is whether, when, and how to withdraw funds from their overseas subsidiaries. This question is of particular importance to the Large enterprise that has been abroad for a long time and has a great many profitable foreign subsidiaries. Indeed, virtually all the Large multinational enterprises that we interviewed mentioned the withdrawal of funds as a major financial issue, whereas only about half of the Medium and Small enterprises did so. These smaller firms have relatively more of their foreign subsidiaries still in the early stages of growth, when the cash flow is likely to be in the other direction.

Dividends are the most common means of making remittances, but few multinational enterprises rely only on this method for the withdrawal of funds. As shown in Table 5–1, dividends from foreign manufacturing affiliates in 1966 accounted for slightly more than half the funds that the U.S. government reported were received from abroad by all U.S. foreign direct investors engaged primarily in manufacturing. The rest was royalties, management fees, income from sales affiliates, interest, and rentals.

Flows of cash to the parent also are accomplished by methods not covered separately in those statistics. The most important of these methods were discussed in the preceding chapter on financing foreign affiliates. One is the repayment of the principal of a loan. (Though the parent also receives interest on the loan, this is seldom thought of as a deliberate means of withdrawing funds.) Another is accounts receivable: the parent changes the terms of payment so as to hasten the centripetal movement of money.

The most important means of withdrawal, though, and the ones primarily discussed in this chapter, are dividends, royalties, and management fees. Another method, also discussed in this chapter, is transfer pricing: the parent raises the price that it charges subsidiaries for the sale of goods.

One way of thinking about the various ways of calling in funds is to divide them into two groups: (1) payments tied to arrangements previously made, and (2) payments of a more flexible character. The "arranged" methods have contractual implications: the payments themselves are fixed,

TABLE 5–1

*Funds Received from Foreign Operations by U.S. Foreign
Direct Investors Engaged Primarily in Manufacturing,
1966, Excluding Capital Movements and Payments
for Merchandise (In Millions of Dollars)*

	Dollar Value [a]	Percentage
Dividends [b]	895	51
Royalties	304	17
Management fees	299	17
Income from sales affiliates [c]	162	9
Interest [d]	99	6
Rentals	5	—
TOTAL	1,763	100

Source: U.S. Department of Commerce, Office of Business Economics, *U.S. Direct Investments Abroad, 1966, Part 1: Balance of Payments Data,* pp. 105, 109, 117, 120, 157, 159, 160, 175.

Notes: All income is from subsidiaries unless otherwise noted. These statistics omit flows that are considered as "capital flows" in U.S. balance of payments data, such as sale of subsidiaries' capital stock and reductions in debts or intercompany accounts owed by a foreign affiliate to the parent.

[a] Because of rounding, column does not total exactly.

[b] Includes $37 million of branch income, representing about 4 percent of the $895 million.

[c] Defined as dividends and interest from subsidiaries and branches engaged in wholesale trade of manufactures and semimanufactures.

[d] Includes $1 million of interest from branches.

such as principal (and interest), or they are fixed in terms of sales of services or goods, such as royalties and accounts receivable. Distributions in the "flexible" category, notably dividends, ordinarily may be varied more readily at the discretion of management.[1] The distinction is loose because the intimacy of contracting parties makes it easy to modify the agreements, while the overseeing eyes of governments sometimes inject rigidities into otherwise "flexible" dividend policies. It therefore is sometimes difficult to tell which withdrawal form may be adjusted more easily and with minimum repercussions. But, at least in theory and often in fact, the distinction exists and is recognized by management in developing programs of withdrawal.

One means of taking into account the differences between contractual remittances and dividends is to have the subsidiary meet the contractual requirements as they become due and to use dividends as the residual channel. For the Large firms, this method of operation provides a convenient rule-making base. Thus an official of one Large enterprise stated, "Actually, the foreign subsidiaries are expected to meet their obligations of fixed indebtedness. They're expected to pay for what they purchase, pay their research fees, and pay their export company commissions." As a result of this policy, said the official, commissions and royalties have been a much larger and more stable means of withdrawing funds than dividends.

Some Medium enterprises, on the other hand, reverse this arrangement. Their emphasis is upon minimizing taxes through the amounts of dividends paid from different countries, and once this aim is accomplished the remaining funds are used to repay loans. "Let's put it this way," observed an official. "Our tax lawyers determine what the best dividend policy is and then if there's any money left over in the subsidiaries, we apply it to paying off the loans."

The budgets of multinational enterprises indicate the total amount of funds to be withdrawn and in many cases the form of the withdrawal. The decision on the amount and form is so important that it is ordinarily made by management in headquarters,[2] although the needs of the system play a less dominant role in the final decision than do the needs of the foreign affiliate in question; this is so, especially for the Small and the Large enterprises. Granting that management generally considers some mix of methods in effecting withdrawals, very few firms consider all the possible avenues available and formulate a program to maximize the system's profits after taxes. To the extent that an overall withdrawal policy exists, it is likely to be geared to a particular subgoal such as minimizing taxes or maximizing the parent's liquidity. Forming a policy for the whole system that takes into account all relevant objectives has usually proven too complicated for the multinational enterprise to follow.

Dividends

Framing a general policy on dividends alone is not quite so formidable, but, even so, many multinational enterprises tend to play it by ear.

This is especially true of the Small firms. To be sure, they give dividends a bigger proportionate role in their withdrawals than do the Medium and Large firms. But they are less likely to have worked out any underlying principles for determining these payments. Thus, an official of a Small enterprise noted typically: "We have not really come to the point of developing an overall dividend policy. We look at each case individually." An official of another Small firm observed, "Well, actually there is no rule at all because we have found that in many cases dividends depend on local conditions, the capitalization of the subsidiary, and the total capital required. There are so many factors that there is no fixed rule applicable here." But he added that as the enterprise gained experience in working with its overseas subsidiaries, "we are beginning to think about formulating 'principles.' "

Dividend policy in Medium firms, as one might expect, is characterized by flexibility. Such firms find that foreign profits now are big enough to matter, and yet the system often is not complex enough to require rule-of-thumb procedures. With the concentration of control at a single source that is so typical of the Medium firm, the financial managers can exercise comparative flexibility in moving money through limited circuits, directing funds to the parent for its own use and for redistribution through the system.

An official of one Medium firm, which we will call "Delta," referred thus to the expanding nature of its international interests: "In recent years with the establishment of one worldwide headquarters in the United States, we now have a coordinated dividend plan that we did not have before." Delta's dividend policy provided for the integration of the flow of funds into its organizational structure and for their concentration at the U.S. parent.

In 1965, the U.S. parent owned a Canadian operating company, a United Kingdom operating and holding company which was the major foreign subsidiary in the system, a European holding company, and a holding company in Panama. The U.K., European, and Panamanian holding companies were the top units in three subsystems, each including manufacturing as well as sales subsidiaries. Within this organizational arrangement, two types of international flows of dividends occurred. One was to the U.S. parent from the foreign corporations that it owned directly—the Canadian operating company and the U.K., European, and Panamanian holding companies. The other type of dividend flow was to the holding companies from subsidiaries held by them.

As seen in Table 5–2, the foreign dividends received by the U.S. parent were equal to about 20 percent of its operating profits; these dividends were not negligible but were not enough to affect significantly the parent's own dividend policy. Most of the foreign dividends came from the U.K. subsidiary, primarily from its own operating profits rather than from dividends paid by the units below it. Part of the foreign dividends received by the U.S. parent were reinvested in foreign operations in the form of equity and loans, for each year the parent either increased its investment in its foreign holding companies or made loans directly to operating subsidiaries.

In Large firms, on the other hand, the intricacy of the network imposes a need to simplify the decision process. So the parent often introduces a rule of thumb as a guide in determining the percentage of total foreign earnings to be paid each year. Within this limitation, the dividend policy is then established, as illustrated in our interview with a headquarters' official of a Large enterprise: "One basic policy that the Chairman of the Board instituted is that we should determine the percentage that our foreign business represents of our total business; and then our foreign business should supply that percentage of the dividends paid to the parent company's shareholders. In other words, if the foreign business is 40 percent of the total business, the foreign business should pay 40 percent of the dividends. So if we're going to pay out $30 million in dividends to our stockholders, our foreign operations should remit $12 million to the parent company. But this is just a rule of thumb. We're not held to that, because

TABLE 5–2

Dividend Movements within Delta Enterprise
(*In Millions of Dollars*)

	1963	1964	1965
U.S. Parent			
Operating profit	13.4	18.5	16.2
Foreign dividends received	3.2	3.3	3.3
U.K. Subsidiary			
Operating profit	12.4	16.7	12.3
Dividends received	0.1	0.4	0.3
Dividends paid to United States	2.3	2.8	2.8

Source: Unpublished company records.

business conditions may be such that some year we might want to bring back more or some year less." When asked who determines how much each subsidiary should pay, the official replied, "We set the dividend policy for each foreign subsidiary right here in Chicago."

So dividend policy, like policy on the whole mix of withdrawals, is a facilitating framework for the hugest multinational enterprises. Within this framework sharp modifications can be made without essentially changing the basic structure. Unpublished figures that we received from a Large multinational enterprise, which we call "Epsilon," illustrate this principle. Epsilon during the period 1963 to 1965 followed a policy of paying about 50 percent of its consolidated earnings (domestic and foreign) as dividends to stockholders. It expected to receive approximately this same percentage distribution from both its domestic and foreign affiliates. As shown in

Table 5–3, these relationships were generally observed in 1963 and 1964, when the payout rate, that is, the percentage of net income paid as dividends, hovered about the 50 percent level for the consolidated operations and also the domestic and foreign operations taken separately.

In 1965, however, the payout rate from domestic operations declined to 35 percent and was offset by a rise to 58 percent in the payout rate of the foreign operations to the United States. Within the overseas category, the payout rates of most of the geographic groupings did not change very much and the primary reason for the higher foreign rate was the sharp rise in the percentage of earnings distributed by the Panama sales subsidiary. This unit's function was to purchase all exports from the U.S. parent and all foreign affiliates and re-export them to related affiliates as well as to nonrelated foreign customers. As a result of these activities, its profits

TABLE 5–3

Earnings and Dividend Payout Rates for the Domestic and Foreign Segments of Epsilon Enterprise, 1963–1965 (In Millions of Dollars Unless Otherwise Noted)

	1963	1964	1965
Consolidated			
Net income after tax	$40.3	$44.7	$53.4
Dividends	20.3	22.5	25.7
Dividend payout rate	51%	50%	48%
Domestic Operations			
Net income after tax	17.6	17.6	23.4
Dividends	8.3	8.5	8.3
Dividend payout rate	47%	48%	35%
Foreign Operations, Total			
Net income after tax	22.7	27.1	30.0
Dividends	12.0	14.0	17.4
Dividend payout rate	53%	52%	58%
Consolidated Foreign Subsidiaries, Excluding Panama Sales Companies			
Net income after tax	n.a.[a]	11.1	16.6
Dividends		5.8	6.9
Dividend payout rate		52%	42%
Panama Sales Company			
Net income after tax	n.a.[a]	16.0	13.4
Dividends		8.2	10.5
Dividend payout rate		51%	78%

Source: Unpublished company records.
[a] n.a. = not available to authors.

were about equal to those earned by the remaining fifty or so foreign affiliates.

Probing one step deeper, we find that the payout rates of different subsidiaries of Epsilon rose or fell sharply from one year to the next. Table
5–4 shows that a U.K. subsidiary lowered its payout rate from 149 percent
of earnings to 33 percent, a Spanish subsidiary raised its rate from 0 to 41
percent, and a Pakistani subsidiary zoomed from 17 to 117 percent.

TABLE 5–4

*Dividends as a Percentage of Net Income after Taxes,
Consolidated Foreign Manufacturing Subsidiaries
of Epsilon Enterprise, 1964–1965*

	1964 Percentage	1965 Percentage
United Kingdom		
subsidiary A	51	39
subsidiary B	149	33
Greece	0	0
Spain	0	41
Turkey	0	0
Italy	0	0
Netherlands	0	0 [a]
Germany		
subsidiary A	0	33
subsidiary B	0	43
France		
subsidiary A	62	57
subsidiary B	0	0
subsidiary C	0	0
Switzerland	0	0
Denmark	0	0
Sweden	0	0
TOTAL, EUROPE	40	39
Canada	0 [a]	0 [a]
Central Africa	0 [a]	0 [a]
South Africa	0 [a]	0
TOTAL, AFRICA	0 [a]	0 [a]
India	98	55
Pakistan	17	117
Australia	0	0
Japan	0	0
TOTAL, ASIA	41	49

TABLE 5–4 (*Cont'd*)

*Dividends as a Percentage of Net Income after Taxes,
Consolidated Foreign Manufacturing Subsidiaries
of Epsilon Enterprise, 1964–1965*

	1964 Percentage	1965 Percentage
Argentina	0 [a]	0 [a]
Brazil	0 [a]	0 [a]
Colombia	0 [a]	0 [a]
Mexico	0 [a]	0
Others	0 [a]	0 [a]
TOTAL, LATIN AMERICA	0 [a]	0 [a]
TOTAL, ALL SUBSIDIARIES LISTED ABOVE	52 [b]	42
TOTAL, OTHER FOREIGN SUBSIDIARIES (of which an international sales company is most important)	52	76
TOTAL, INTERNATIONAL OPERATIONS	52	58

Source: Unpublished company records.

[a] Subsidiary or geographic area operated at a loss; results are included in averages.

[b] The reason all subsidiaries averaged a 52 percent payout rate while no single geographic area had a rate this high is that some of the areas with zero payout rate had operating losses. Thus, the total earnings are less than the total earnings from the geographic areas that made a profit.

DIVIDENDS AND FINANCIAL STATEMENTS

A great many factors enter into the dividend policies of multinational firms and into their individual decisions on withdrawing funds in the form of dividends. One of these factors is the effect that dividends have on financial statements. With the considerable expansion of foreign business after World War II, companies began to consolidate their foreign operations into their published reports. General Foods did so in 1956, Colgate-Palmolive in 1957, and International Harvester in 1960. Despite the trend toward consolidation, some companies still were excluding their foreign earnings in the early 1970's. Other companies include the earnings of most foreign subsidiaries but exclude the earnings of subsidiaries in countries with unstable currencies.

In consolidation, all the earnings of a foreign subsidiary are counted regardless of the amount paid as dividends, whereas, prior to consolidation, earnings retained by the subsidiary are not counted. When Colgate-Palmolive consolidated the total earnings of its foreign subsidiaries in 1957, for the first time, the system's consolidated net income amounted to $19.9 million, or $7.81 per share; but if only the dividends received by the parent from its foreign subsidiaries had been counted, the company's earnings reported to shareholders would have been $14.4 million, or $5.60 per share. So it is easy to see that when foreign earnings are not consolidated in the company's annual report, managers are especially concerned about the influence of dividends on annual statements.* An official of a Large multinational enterprise put it this way: "Before consolidation of foreign earnings, the amount of foreign dividends played an important role in affecting the parent company's published income. Consequently, we juggled these foreign dividend payments to make the parent company's income equal to the amount that we wanted to report. After the consolidation, of course, the foreign subsidiaries don't play any role at all in this area."

DIVIDENDS AND TAXATION

Taxation affects the dividend payments of multinational companies in all categories, especially the Medium and Large firms. An official of a Small firm, when asked about the impact of taxation on dividend payments, said: "I don't think that's a prime consideration, to be honest with you. And I don't think our tax people are involved with any decision to declare or not to declare a dividend." But this firm was not typical even in the Small category. An official of a Large firm, when asked to explain the variations in his company's dividend policies from country to country, put it this way: "Particularly in the developing countries, where we have low tax rates, we like to keep our dividends low. It helps our effective tax rates. In a new subsidiary with a small capital stock, if the tax rate is low enough we might forego dividends for ten years and get loan repayments instead. In a very high-tax country, on the other hand, we try to have a very heavy payout."

The case of "Zeta" is illuminating. Zeta is our code name for a real-life Medium enterprise that emphasizes taxation in its dividend practices: "We have a philosophy of playing all the tax angles to the hilt, and we will manipulate our financial situation to obtain the most advantage in saving taxes." By means of its intrasystem pricing practices, the company concentrates profits in a few sales subsidiaries, and to withdraw funds it relies heavily on the repayment of receivables and loans that involve no tax incidence.

In one instance, before enactment of the Revenue Act of 1962, Zeta ex-

---

* However, this influence was changed in 1972. See footnote on page 39.

ecuted an elaborate series of maneuvers in order to avoid paying a U.S. tax on the income of a foreign sales affiliate. The dividend payments in these maneuvers were worked out by the company's international tax attorney. He made his recommendations to the head of the tax department and this was the only approval required.

The maneuvers grew out of the accumulation of a surplus of $30 million in Zeta's foreign sales company, which we will call Zeta Intersales. U.S. headquarters decided to move the surplus into its Swiss holding company through the payment of dividends in order to accumulate funds in that company but avoid paying the U.S. tax that would be imposed if the shift were made after the new Act took effect at the end of the parent's fiscal year; at that time the distribution would represent "foreign base income" and therefore become subject to tax as the passive income of a tax-haven company. The major impediment to the desired shift was that only $10 million of the $30 million surplus was in cash.

To accomplish this objective, a plan was executed in three rounds, as depicted in Figure 5–1. In the first round, Zeta Intersales paid an initial $10 million dividend to the holding company, Zeta Switzerland, which

FIGURE 5–1

Zeta Enterprise Flow of Funds Involving Payment of Dividends in Three Rounds (In Millions of Dollars)

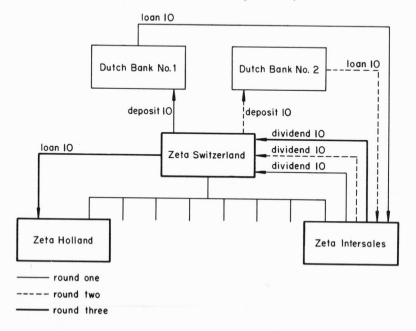

then deposited it in a Dutch bank, labeled Dutch bank No. 1 in the chart. Based upon this deposit and upon collateral in the form of trade receivables, the bank loaned $10 million to Zeta Intersales. In round two Zeta Intersales used the cash to pay a second dividend of $10 million to the Swiss holding company, which again deposited it in another Dutch bank (No. 2). Once more the deposit and trade receivables were employed to obtain a loan of $10 million for Zeta Intersales. The third $10 million was distributed as a dividend to the Swiss holding company, which this time loaned the money to the System's Dutch operating company, Zeta Holland. Looking back at the three rounds, one can see what had happened: Zeta Intersales had incurred debts of $20 million for which trade receivables served as collateral. Zeta Intersales distributed, without creating a U.S. tax liability, dividends of $30 million to the Swiss holding company which, in turn, had transferred to an operating company $10 million by means of a loan and still had $20 million on deposit at two Dutch banks.

OTHER FACTORS AFFECTING DIVIDENDS

The age of a foreign affiliate is an obvious factor, already mentioned, influencing its dividend payments. As overseas units become more firmly established, they tend to provide a greater share of their earnings to their parents. This gradual changeover is seen in the higher payout ratios and greater dollar distributions made by the older compared with the newer affiliates. Thus the combination of dividends from foreign subsidiaries and income earned by foreign branches (and deemed paid to the parent according to U.S. government statistics) was 38 percent of the combined earnings of all subsidiaries and branches not over nine years of age, compared with 73 percent for those over nine years. In dollars the difference is even more striking. The greater earnings of the older affiliates, coupled with the higher percentage of payout of earnings to the parent, resulted in the parent's receiving an average of $30,000 in income (dividends from subsidiaries and income earned by branches) from affiliates not over nine years of age, versus $346,000 from those over nine years.[3]

Another factor affecting dividends is the economic condition of the host country, especially the condition of the currency. Companies of all sizes indicate a willingness to accelerate dividend payments in cases where they anticipate a currency devaluation. The Large enterprise is particularly sensitive to this problem.*

And, of course, dividend payments are directly influenced by the various restrictions that foreign governments impose upon the freedom to

---

* The subject of exchange-rate risk has been introduced in Chapter 2, and the principal means of protecting against it will be described in Chapter 7.

move funds out of the country. For example, an official of a Large enterprise said, "Yes, we've had many occasions of that. There are two pertinent ones at present. We've constantly had to go to the exchange control in East Africa, and our allowed dividend remissions are based on our equity and our borrowing position. The same thing is true in South Africa. Also, in Brazil you have limitations related to your registered capital. In France years ago our advisers there suggested that it would be improper to declare dividends and the same thing happened in Australia and New Zealand in the past. It's not uncommon."

In order to reduce the danger of such interferences with the flow of funds, the multinational enterprise may strive to maintain a consistent dividend disbursement to demonstrate that such payments are part of an established financial program rather than an effort to flee from a weak currency. As would be expected, the Large firm, in view of its preference for following a specified policy, is especially prone to take this position. An official of such a firm commented: "In some countries we try to pay dividends every year just to get the local government or the central bank used to the idea that this is a continuing policy." An official of another Large firm went even further and asserted that his company had been willing to add to its tax liabilities in order to create the image of a subsidiary that was obliged to maintain continued dividend payments. "We are prepared to accept and in the past have accepted some tax leakage simply to maintain the principle that an operating affiliate has the responsibility to pay dividends to its stockholders, and this is not wholly an internal management question. We also wanted to make that point clear to the local monetary authorities, especially under conditions where they are flirting with the idea of acting discriminatorily towards foreign-controlled enterprises."

Another official pointed out that even if special restrictions are not feared, "Your record of paying dividends may be a contributing factor in whether you get approval next year for a dividend and how much you get. So if we can say we've done this every year for the past three, five, or ten years—it's routine—well, you stand a better chance."

Availability of funds is a conspicuous influence on dividends. When payments are frustrated by a shortage, the companies differ in their attitudes toward seeking outside financing for this purpose. The smaller firms are usually reluctant to borrow; the bigger ones, bent on the system's objectives, are usually willing to do so.

Still another consideration of importance to many parents in determining dividend payments is the ownership of the subsidiary.[4] In general, the presence of local stockholders tends to result in a more stable dividend record because in many countries shareholders expect to receive a designated percentage of the company's par value regardless of earnings. "In those areas where we have joint interests," noted an official, "we try to hold the dividend on a stable basis. We don't like to reduce dividends; so at times we'll pay more than our earnings." Such a company may well hesitate to increase dividends because of the difficulty of reducing them later if earnings decline.

The willingness of the Large firm to take into account such special circumstances in determining the distributions from foreign subsidiaries may appear at odds with its tendency to operate through general rule of thumb decisions. In practice, however, rule of thumb procedures prevail and special adjustments take a secondary place. An official of such a company, after describing the general policy of relating the subsidiaries' payout ratios to those of the parent, added: "Also, there are local factors, foreign-exchange factors, and even minority-ownership factors that still affect our payments."

Because dividend payments are shaped by such a variety of forces, the dividend payout rate of an individual subsidiary can be expected to fluctuate. Figure 5–2 summarizes payout rates for twenty-eight Canadian and

FIGURE 5–2

Dividend Payout Rates of Twenty-Eight Foreign Subsidiaries of Ten U.S.-Controlled Multinational Enterprises, 1960–1965

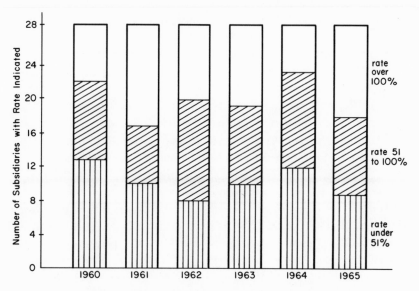

Note: Dividend payout rates are based upon unpublished records obtained from the ten multinational enterprises.

Western European subsidiaries of a group of ten multinational enterprises that made this information available to us. Payout ratios varied sharply from year to year. For example, in 1964 five subsidiaries paid out over 100 percent of earnings whereas in 1965 ten did so. Furthermore, during the six years covered, half the subsidiaries were represented at various times in all three payout ranges shown in the figure.

Royalties and Management Fees

Royalties typically are paid for use of trade names and manufacturing know-how, the latter often being covered by patents. Management fees typically are paid for management services, such as advice from headquarters. Each of these classes of fees provides about the same amount of funds for U.S. foreign direct investors, but royalties are more important in manufacturing, whereas management fees are more important in petroleum and mining.[5]

In some cases, especially when a subsidiary is young, payments for royalties and management fees are larger and more persistent than dividend disbursements. Such payments ordinarily are geared to the amount of sales or total assets, and therefore a growing subsidiary may be required to make substantial payments to the parent as the volume of its business expands. This of course is the very period when the subsidiary may be allowed to keep dividends low or even omit them in order to reinvest its earnings.

The U.S. parent of a jointly held subsidiary may look with particular favor on a royalty received from the subsidiary because the distribution does not have to be shared with its foreign partner. Thus, the general manager of the Far Eastern area of a U.S. multinational enterprise pointed out that the company's Japanese subsidiary is a joint venture, "And we're putting a damn sight more into it than our partner is. So, as compensation for this additional effort—our trademarks, and our product developments that we're giving—we are getting a royalty payment which is rightly due to us."

In some cases, the use of royalties and management fees is dictated partly by Section 482 of the U.S. Internal Revenue Code. This regulation, as mentioned in Chapter 4, requires "arm's-length" prices—prices that would be charged to an unaffiliated party—for all goods and services provided by parents to its subsidiaries and vice versa. However, as the technical know-how and management services provided by one unit of a multinational enterprise to another usually are unique items without a market value, there is no exact arm's-length price applicable to such transactions. In practice, therefore, the enterprise has a certain amount of leeway in setting the price.

A firm that attempts to set management fees on a strict arm's-length basis finds it cumbersome to work out separate arrangements with each subsidiary in the system. A simplifying alternative is to determine the total annual fee, covering the actual costs incurred for services rendered by the parent (or its management affiliate), and then to make allocations to the subsidiaries on some prescribed basis, such as sales. This method is relatively inflexible but has the advantage of being sanctioned by Section 482 of the Internal Revenue Code where it is accomplished through a "bona fide cost-sharing agreement."

Despite the relative rigidity of the management fee as a tool in effecting withdrawals, companies have at times employed it to help achieve a designated subgoal, such as minimizing taxes. For example, the firm we call Alpha used this withdrawal device for its subsidiary in Argentina, a relatively minor unit. A fee of $5,000 monthly was collected in order to withdraw funds from the country and at the same time avoid Argentina's withholding taxes on dividends. Indeed, the achievement of a tax benefit is perhaps the reason most often advanced for the discretionary use of both royalties and management fees.

Take the case of a Medium multinational enterprise which has subsidiaries in countries with widely varying tax rates, both higher and lower than in the United States. This company, emphasizing tax minimization as a subgoal, tends to consider royalty payments as the responsibility of the tax department.

The use of royalties and management fees typically brings tax advantages to the system when a subsidiary's local tax rate is higher than that of its U.S. parent. The royalties and management fees are tax-deductible locally; but if such a subsidiary remits by means of dividends, it must pay a tax on its earnings prior to the distribution. Though the parent receives a tax credit, the amount it is entitled to offset against the foreign payment is limited by the lower tax rate of the parent. Accordingly, the fee-paying subsidiary benefits to the extent of the differential between the tax rate prevailing in its country and that in the country of the parent.

When the local tax rate is the same as, or lower than, that of the United States, ordinarily total tax payments are the same for royalties and fees as for dividends. In these circumstances, the tax reduction obtained by the subsidiary if it pays a fee tends to be matched by the credit to which the parent is entitled on the foreign taxes incurred by the subsidiary if it pays a dividend. But not necessarily. Sometimes, even though the subsidiary's local tax rate is below the U.S. rate, a parent can save taxes by collecting dividends rather than royalties or fees. As an illustration, an enterprise using the overall rather than the per-country limitation in calculating its foreign tax credit may have paid so much tax to foreign governments that it has unused credits. This condition makes it possible for the parent to receive a dividend from a subsidiary in a low-tax country and pay no U.S. tax on the distribution because of the tax credit already available.*

Host governments sometimes impose barriers to the payment of royalties and management fees, just as they do against dividends. The parent may have to experiment to ascertain the maximum amount that will be permitted. In the following exchanges with an interviewer an official describes his company's reliance on royalties to move funds and his constant efforts to increase flexibility:

Interviewer. Are the royalties calculated on a standard basis?
Official. No, it varies due to historical patterns and laws within a given country. Sometimes countries limit the amount of royalties. So it varies.
Interviewer. Have you varied royalties as a deliberate tool in order to withdraw funds other than as a means to collect for know-how rendered?
Official. The whole purpose of it is to withdraw funds. And, we deliberately set it as high as we can.
Interviewer. Then in the case of two subsidiaries in two different countries, one may be paying 10 percent on sales and the other, 5 percent?
Official. Yes, but we'd be charging the 5 percent only because we couldn't get away with 10 percent in the second country.

Once agreement has been reached with a government on terms for royalties and management fees, difficulty may be experienced in seeking subsequent modifications. In this connection, an official mentioned the case of France, where obtaining an initial contract for royalties was simple, but he added: "If you modify that agreement, then it must go through all the processes. It goes through the exchange control, the taxing authorities, and everyone else along the line. And they all will take pot shots at you." To get around government restrictions, a company may resort to special devices such as raising the sales price to offset the loss of royalty revenue.

Another factor that limits the use of royalties or management fees is the financial condition of the subsidiary. Referring to this situation with regard to management fees, an official commented, "Our international management fee covers the total cost of our international operation and takes into account salary, traveling expenses, floor space, and everything along with it. This then is allocated to subsidiaries. Those subsidiaries that can pay, we bill; but those that can't pay for one reason or another, we don't bill."

* This case is discussed in a statistical working paper available from the authors.

Transfer Pricing

The multinational enterprise uses transfer pricing as a means of with-drawing funds from subsidiaries by raising prices on goods and services sold to an affiliate by other units in the system. Conversely, the enterprise also employs transfer pricing to finance an affiliate by lowering prices on goods and services sold to an affiliate by other units in the system. But the most widespread use of transfer pricing is to locate profits in an appropri-ate affiliate in order to reduce the system's total tax burden. Because of its diverse applications, transfer pricing is discussed in a number of places in this book. The subject, however, is so sensitive that it is difficult to draw unequivocal conclusions regarding variations in practice among firms. Our impression is that the influence of size is felt. In establishing intercompany prices, the big companies tend to establish uniform policies that involve standard mark-ups. Thus, an official of one large firm observed, "We use standard cost plus a 5 percent surcharge, and we do this on a regular basis. The 5 percent surcharge covers expenditures that don't find their way into the normal cost of our inventory." In a similar vein, the assistant treasurer of another Large firm noted, "We have regular intercompany billing prices and they determine the price list for everybody. We have a standard for-mula and everybody does it the same way." Nevertheless, when special reasons exist, some big companies will bend their rule-of-thumb proce-dures to adjust their transfer prices. Echoing this note, a regional official of the same Large firm whose assistant treasurer is quoted above—as in-sisting that a standard intercompany billing is used—added, "If I cannot get dividends out and my royalty rate is fixed, and I want to remit more money, then I do this on an uplift of my transfer prices."

The Medium firm tends to favor more flexible pricing procedures, which take into account the varying circumstances in the relationships between the foreign affiliates. For example, an official of such a firm remarked, "If it's purely an intercompany activity, the transfer price should not be one at which a loss is generated, and it must be a reasonable sort of a price. If the seller has purely a production plant, with no R&D [research and de-velopment] effort and no engineering effort, then the transfer price would be some type of standard cost that can be agreed to within the firm plus some rate of profit. But if they have responsibilities for R&D, continued engineering, market research, and so on, their prices should include some factor for that also. Then you can measure them as a total company." Im-plicit in this discussion of a "reasonable sort of a price" is that no comparable open-market sales exist and that some consideration is given to using transfer prices to effect fund movements aimed at the system's needs. Suggesting this attitude, the same executive concluded his remarks with a brief comment: "Certainly taxes influence what the price would be."

The Small company, relatively new in the international field, often is not in a position to worry much about intercompany pricing tactics. Its officials are more concerned with giving their subsidiaries enough elbow room to develop their operations and attain some degree of profitability. In responding to a query regarding the degree to which transfer pricing is used to shift funds, an official of a Small firm remarked, "We haven't done it because quite frankly we're not doing too well on our sales; so we haven't found a place where we can juggle the profits around to take advantage of the best tax rate."

Even if a multinational enterprise is reluctant to employ transfer pricing for the purpose of shifting profits to minimize taxes, it is likely to relax its inhibitions when the bogey of exchange difficulties is involved. One official indicated that though his company would not use transfer pricing for tax purposes, it would use this method as well as any other method available if exchange restrictions block the transfer of funds or if the company is apprehensive about a country's currency.[6]

There is no way to estimate the amount of funds that are shifted by the discretionary use of transfer pricing. Some idea of the potential involved may be gauged by comparing the volume of sales among the units of the same system with the amount of money moved through other withdrawal devices. On an aggregate basis for all U.S. foreign direct investment, a 10 percent change in the estimated $40 billion [7] of intrasystem sales by U.S. multinational enterprises in 1972 would substantially exceed all payments of royalties and management fees and would approximate the size of dividend payments.[8] Because of the various constraints imposed by governments [9] and arising within the organization of the firm, however, we believe that the use of transfer pricing is substantially below this indicated potential.

Tax Savings Versus Location of Cash

In determining the most effective means of withdrawing funds, management may have to make a tradeoff between contribution to income through tax savings and a change in the location of liquidity. The tax savings may result by avoiding a levy that otherwise would have been imposed—for example, when a parent withdraws funds by repayment of principal on a loan rather than dividends. Or, the savings may come from tax arbitrage such as occurs when a unit in a high-tax country makes a payment that is considered an expense to it and income to a unit located in a low-tax country. A change in the location of the liquidity, of course, results from every movement of funds, and the opportunities for benefit to the system come primarily from the differences among areas with respect to investment opportunities, the financing of receivables, and exchange risk.

Loans are the most effective way of providing liquidity because of the substantial size they can attain and the fact that they directly affect only the balance sheet and not the income statement. On the other hand, transfer pricing, royalties, management fees, and interest create income and liquidity shifts of the same magnitude. As an illustration, a parent-to-subsidiary loan of $100,000 reduces the cash account in the parent's balance sheet by $100,000 and increases the account of its subsidiary by the same amount but does not involve the income statement (until interest is subsequently paid). Similarly, as the subsidiary repays the loan, its cash is drawn down and that of the parent correspondingly increased. But when the subsidiary pays $5,000 as interest on the loan, the subsidiary loses both $5,000 in cash and before-tax income while the parent gains the same amount of cash and before-tax income. All these methods of moving funds are employed in the real world, but the exact amounts involved are not available. In the computer model, however, these figures are known and the extent to which the model used them between the parent and the subsidiaries to maximize net income after taxes is summarized in Table 5–5. To make the table manageable, we did not include subsidiary-to-subsidiary flows, nor did we include flows between each of the units and the outside world.

The table is intended to provide a broad perspective of the major fund movement that took place. In the table the positive figures are the transfers from subsidiaries *B* and *C* to the parent; in the first row it is indicated that in all periods cash moves from both subsidiaries to the parent as a result of arm's-length sales transactions. The negative figures are transfers from the parent to the subsidiaries, and in the second row it is indicated that the parent reduces its transfer prices,[10] thereby in effect generating a reverse movement of funds from it to the subsidiaries.

The parent and subsidiary *C* enter into substantial short-term lending arrangements because of the advantages gained by exploiting the sharp differentials between the two areas in tax and interest rates and by taking advantage of exchange-rate relationships. The tax and interest factors predominate in years 1 and 3 when the parent grants substantial amounts of

TABLE 5-5

Flow of Funds between Parent and Subsidiaries. Optimal Financial Policy,
Multinational Enterprise Model for Four Years
(In Millions of Dollars)

Item	Subsidiary B				Subsidiary C			
	First Year	Second Year	Third Year	Fourth Year	First Year	Second Year	Third Year	Fourth Year
Cash sales at arm's-length prices	16.0	17.6	19.4	21.3	10.0	11.0	12.1	13.3
Transfer pricing	−3.2	−3.5	−3.9	−4.3	−2.0	−2.2	−2.4	−2.7
Change in receivables	2.5	0.0	0.0	0.0	−2.5	4.0	−4.8	4.8
Royalties	4.0	7.8	5.0	6.0	1.7	5.5	2.0	6.7
Management fees	0.0	1.0	0.0	0.0	0.0	0.0	0.0	0.0
Interest	2.4	2.0	1.7	1.4	5.1	1.7	6.2	1.2
Short loans	0.0	0.0	0.0	0.0	−78.6	78.6	−120.5	120.5
Long loans	−60.4	10.1	8.4	7.1	−51.1	8.5	7.1	6.1
Dividends	0.0	0.0	0.0	0.0	0.0	3.8	55.3	0.0
TOTAL	−38.7	35.0	30.6	31.5	−117.4	110.9	−45.0	149.9

Positive figures are flows from subsidiaries to parent. Negative figures are flows from parent to subsidiaries.

low-interest loans to *C*. The exchange-rate factor is dominant in years 2 and 4 when *C* repays these loans, thereby shifting liquidity to the parent as a means of protecting against devaluation.

In the world of the model, the corporate tax structure renders it undesirable for *C*, whose tax rate is only 30 percent, to pay any more than the minimum allowable royalties, management fees, or interest to the parent, unless a devaluation occurs, as in years 2 and 4. On the other hand, there is incentive for *B* to make the maximum allowable value of such payments to the parent, thereby displacing taxable income from a 60 percent to a 50 percent jurisdiction. But in fact, *B* pays the minimum allowable royalties and management fees except in year 2, when devaluation occurs. This seemingly unusual behavior on *B*'s part apparently is caused by the liquidity needs of *B*.

The net flows to the parent from both subsidiaries combined, as well as from each subsidiary individually, vary substantially from year to year, as shown in Table 5–6. In years 1 and 3 there is a net outflow from the parent, whereas in years 2 and 4 the parent receives a net inflow. By contrast the profits of the two subsidiaries combined show an increase each year. Over the four-year period, net funds received by the parent, $158 million, come to 66 percent of the total income of both subsidiaries, $240 million.

TABLE 5-6

*Net Flow of Funds into Parent Compared with Subsidiary
Earnings. Optimal Financial Policy, Multinational
Enterprise Model for Four Years*
(In Millions of Dollars)

Flow of Funds	First Year	Second Year	Third Year	Fourth Year	Total
From Subsidiary *B*	−39	35	31	32	59
Subsidiary *B*'s profit after tax	15	0	20	25	60
From Subsidiary *C*	−117	111	−45	150	99
Subsidiary *C*'s profit after tax	29	52	37	62	180
Total flow of funds to parent from both subsidiaries	−156	146	−14	182	158
Total profits after tax of both subsidiaries	44	52	57	87	240

Positive figures are flows from subsidiaries to parent. Negative figures are flows from parent to subsidiaries.

As in the case of Delta, the real-life enterprise discussed earlier in this chapter, the model operated as one system so that dividend payments were tied in with other flows into an integrated financial strategy. Confronted with various ways of moving funds between the parent and subsidiary, the course chosen by the model sometimes followed odd turns. Note in Table 5–5 that in year 3, for example, the parent loaned $120.5 million to subsidiary *C,* which at the same time paid $55.3 million in dividends to the parent.* By this means the model was able to maximize system earnings while at the same time maintaining required liquidity standards. To determine why the model elects to employ this two-way movement of funds rather than any other procedure such as the obvious one of the parent's transmitting the net amount to the subsidiary requires an analysis of the effects of all possible remittance methods. Each method, in turn, sets in motion an elaborate chain of circumstances that not only involves taxes, income from money-market investments, financing costs, and exchange gains or losses but also runs into different financial constraints. Such an analysis, even in the case of this simple system, necessitates an explanation that is too extensive for inclusion in this book.

* In the real world this dividend could have been in the form of a note rather than cash, but some careful tax lawyers may be reluctant to give their blessings to this approach.

The steps taken in the model and the resulting movements of funds are designed to cope with a particular set of environmental conditions and financial considerations. Though they suggest the type of flows that may result and the benefits that can be attained, each system must operate in the light of its own circumstances and create its own measures and outcomes. The hypothetical achievements of the model, however, are replicas of the real gains possible through effective centralized planning.

SIX / Managing Current Assets

Two of the major elements of current assets—cash and accounts receivable—entered into the discussions of Chapters 4 and 5 because these assets are involved in both the financing of foreign affiliates and withdrawing funds from abroad. But there is more to managing current assets: they must be controlled so that they move efficiently through the whole working-capital cycle, that is, inventory to receivables to cash and back to inventory again. So, the stress in this chapter is on control and on probing more deeply into the handling of all the current assets including inventory.

Both multinational and domestic firms are faced with the same general question of what balances should be kept of each of the current assets—cash, accounts receivable, and inventories—relative to operating needs. This basic similarity was noted by one official: "Well, I would say the three critical problems in the management of current assets are excess cash at the local level, incorrect procedures on accounts receivables—we are not too much concerned about the terms because most of the local subsidiary companies sell on normal terms—and the size of the inventory. Those are our main considerations, but I don't think they're peculiar to overseas subsidiaries; we have the same problem in the States."

Even when efforts are made to apply uniform principles at home and abroad in handling current assets, differences creep into the methods employed. These arise in part because of local conditions, such as the long credit terms on sales that often exist overseas and the rudimentary money markets with which many foreign affiliates must cope. In part, too, differences occur because managing the current assets of a subsidiary which is performing an integrated business function requires a multitude of daily decisions that typically are within the province of the subsidiary. This makes it more difficult for the parent to control current assets than to control the financing decision or the withdrawing of funds—operations in which, usually, the decisions are less frequent, larger in magnitude, and more directly related to financial flows between the parent and affiliates.

In order to obtain some degree of consistency between foreign and U.S. practices, many parents, especially the larger ones, prepare manuals governing financial management for use throughout the system. An interviewer asked one official of a multinational enterprise, "You say that the same procedures exist from country to country?" The official replied, "Right. We issue a comptroller's manual. There are about four volumes and each is four or five inches thick. So it should provide you with the answer to any question that you might have on financial management."

Consistency with headquarters is also obtained by appointing an American, or at least an individual trained in U.S. procedures, as the financial head of the overseas operation. Typical of this policy is the following comment: "In general, every one of our locations is headed by an American. The managing director is an American and the comptroller is an American. Now, in some of the larger operations, the comptroller may have two or three more Americans under him."

The top financial man may be both competent and knowledgeable in U.S. practices but he may not find it easy to recruit a suitable staff. Along these lines, the chief financial officer of a firm's Turkish subsidiary commented: "The only difficulty we have with the local people is impressing them that our procedures must be used in keeping the books. Because they think their way is better, they like to change the procedures in the middle of the month without mentioning it to anyone." The handicaps experienced by an American firm in imposing its standards on foreign subsidiaries was also voiced by the senior partner of a large U.S. accounting firm with an office in Japan: "We've had many experiences in which someone from the U.S. parent comes over here and says, 'Here's our accounting manual and there's a big chart that says on the twentieth working day after the 31st you do this report.' The Japanese say, 'Yes.' But it happens only one month and then the Japanese forget about it, and the American comes back next year and they try it again."

Concerning these differences, headquarters' managers have voiced all shades of opinion. Some contend that the relatively large size of the U.S. operations and the resultant specialization has raised domestic standards above those in the foreign affiliates, where fewer people cover the broad range of financial functions. Others have concluded that, at least within their own organizations, working-capital management is "probably more sophisticated" than in the United States because "the cost of working capital overseas is higher" and therefore it "has tended to get more attention." Still others, shrugging off any attempt at evaluation, speak along this line: "It's awfully hard to compare the caliber of foreign and domestic asset management because of the differences encountered."

Current assets held abroad by U.S. foreign direct investors amounted to about $62 billion in 1970. Our estimate is that about $4 billion of this was in cash and marketable securities, about $26 billion in accounts receivable, and about $32 billion in inventories.[1]

Cash and Marketable Securities

Cash is an asset at rest—that is, not being used for profit. Managing cash, therefore, is directed toward converting it as speedily as possible into income-producing uses. The formulation of principles toward this end is still relatively new within the United States, and headquarters' management does not appear to have been aggressive in extending their application to overseas affiliates. Lately, though, managers have been pushed into better cash management abroad by U.S. capital controls and the recurring international monetary crises. This improved control has been facilitated by specialized computer programs. The results have been rewarding. As one manager put it, "We found cash lying around that we didn't know existed."

There are several reasons for this delay in extending good cash management principles abroad. One is a reluctance to grant blanket authority for overseas units to put their cash to work in activities outside normal business uses, such as investing in short-term money instruments. This reluctance, in turn, creates inevitable bureaucratic hurdles as explanations hurtle back and forth by wire and mail before permission is obtained. Another reason is the absence abroad of the tight interchange facilities among financial institutions that exist in the United States for moving cash swiftly from one spot to another. Still another reason for the delay is that the availability of overdrafts in many foreign countries causes headquarters to feel that cash at these locations is characteristically kept low. As some companies quaintly put it, "We operate with negative cash balances." This helps to explain the tendency of these firms to concentrate on the other elements of working capital. "When we talk about working capital in the field," an official commented, "we're not talking about cash. Accounts receivable and inventory are our big concerns."

It is hard to verify these beliefs regarding the relative amounts of cash held at home and overseas because there are no published data showing a breakdown, within the same multinational system, of the current assets of foreign affiliates compared with those of the units within the United States. Internal records were provided, however, revealing this information over a three-year period for three multinational enterprises in different size categories. Their total cash and marketable securities, measured in terms of

TABLE 6–1

*Cash and Marketable Securities at Year End, Three Multinational
Enterprises, 1963–1965, Expressed in
Number of Days of Sales*

Location of Operations	Small Multinational Enterprise			Medium Multinational Enterprise			Large Multinational Enterprise		
	1963	1964	1965	1963	1964	1965	1963	1964	1965
Canada	—	—	—	51	53	32	—	—	—
France	—	—	—	n.a.[a]	26	6	—	—	—
Germany	9	13	38	11	13	10	6	3	11
Spain	8	6	9	—	—	—	1	1	—
United Kingdom	—	—	—	7	15	9	—	—	—
Australia	3	16	13	n.a.	n.a.	0	n.a.	2	6
South Africa	—	—	—	6	10	9	—	—	—
Mexico	11	12	9	—	—	—	8	6	9
Colombia	n.a.	21	7	17	20	8	6	17	17
Argentina	3	3	n.a.	—	—	—	1	3	3
Brazil	25	34	57	34	12	98	16	23	10
TOTAL FOREIGN	8	15	17	15	24	9	8	9	12
United States	25	40	22	94	92	91	22	23	20

Source: Unpublished records of the three unidentified enterprises.
[a] n.a. = not available to authors.

days' sales, varied from country to country, but in almost every case the level in the United States was substantially above that of the foreign units. The figures appear in Table 6–1.

Yet, sophistication in the management of cash undoubtedly could bring the foreign levels even lower, thereby contributing to profits and reducing the dependence upon banks as a source of funds, a big consideration for overseas subsidiaries that operate in areas where banking facilities are limited. Accordingly, both abroad and in the United States, an important element of financial policy is the design of a program for planning cash requirements and handling its use so that a company can keep to a minimum the amount needed to sustain any given level of operations.

PLANNING THE USE OF CASH

The computer model, operating with perfect knowledge and foresight, expended cash according to a plan that was limited only by built-in constraints. One of these constraints was that each unit had to carry an amount of cash equal to at least ten days' sales. In the not-so-perfect world of reality, a company cannot plan its cash with the same degree of precision. It knows that in order to survive, it must have an inflow of cash that exceeds the outflow over the long run, but during any one period deficits may occur. The primary tool for dealing with these cash variations is the budget, which for a long time has been an integral part of the financial planning of the domestic operations of U.S. multinational enterprises. A majority of these firms now compile cash budgets for their foreign units as well. Their checkpoints for controlling cash are likely to be similar to those employed in the United States. For example, each overseas facility of one Large multinational enterprise, in preparing its cash budget, is expected to answer the following questions:

Does the projected balance of cash and of net current assets provide the necessary liquidity to meet day-to-day commitments?

Does the projected cash balance indicate an adequate minimum balance based on past experience and anticipated growth?

Have the monthly cash projections for the end of the first year been prepared?

Is the short-term loan position sound and not being used to finance investment in capital assets?

But because there often are more complexities abroad, fewer suitable personnel, less adequate record keeping, and less extensive sources of information, the projections of a manager abroad are likely to be less reliable than those of his domestic counterpart. The controller of one enterprise observed that overseas cash budgets tend to be "best guesses" rather than realistic forecasts based upon adequate evidence.

HANDLING CASH

An important way of reducing cash requirements is to cut down the time that cash remains in pipelines flowing either from the customer or between units within the firm.

One need is to shorten the time between payment of a bill by the customer and availability of the cash for spending by the firm. Toward this end, corporations operating in the United States have integrated banking relations in which selected institutions arrange for the gathering of funds and their redistribution throughout the corporate system. A firm is apt to notify its customers to forward checks to a designated post office lock box where a bank rapidly collects the checks and deposits them to the firm's account. But in many foreign countries the availability of cash is delayed by the unhurried processing of checks. One official says that "in France, there's a lot of cash in transit through the French banking system. But it isn't cash that's available to us." Moreover, in the multinational enterprise, tremendous distances may separate a unit form its customers.

Some multinational enterprises do try to improve the transfers of cash from foreign customers to their foreign subsidiaries. Witness this statement in an interview: "Before we set up a lock-box operation in Europe, we could figure on taking roughly two weeks from the time the customer made his payment to the time the money was collected by the subsidiary and transferred to us in New York. Now it's down to an average of about two days. But we're still pressing to figure out how to do this within one day or the same day. It's only been in the last five years, I would say, that the corporate treasurers have begun to appreciate the value of float. When the banking system is not sophisticated, such as in Brazil or Central America, you have an awfully hard time doing this. In Brazil, for example, we found that it would take two weeks from a customer's bank to the company's bank across the street. So we went ahead and opened up accounts at our customers' banks. Then we had our money in no more than two days."

This same firm has several Brazilian subsidiaries and a number of customers that buy from more than one of these subsidiaries. In order to speed the collection process, each subsidiary has opened an account in their customers' banks. As a result, the corporate system keeps sixty-six separate bank balances in Brazil. To pay the corporation's foreign-exchange dealer for an invoice of imported goods may require drawing checks on six different banks. This added banking complexity apparently is considered a small price to pay for the benefits achieved through swifter movements of cash.

Not only external collections but intrasystem flows need short-cutting to improve liquidity. In some enterprises the parent or some other delegated unit functions as a clearing house, so that funds associated with intrasystem transactions never move. Instead, payments are offset against each other through bookkeeping entries. This process of netting transactions in the classical clearinghouse tradition materially reduces the length and intricacy of the pipelines through which cash might otherwise have to flow.

For example, let us assume the following highly simplified hypothetical series of transactions among the units of an international petroleum company. The parent in the United States loans $500,000 to an affiliate producing oil in North Africa. The affiliate then spends the funds on operations producing oil. The oil is sold for $600,000 to a European refining subsidiary. This subsidiary, in turn, forwards it at the price of $700,000 to a European marketing subsidiary, which sells the product at $800,000 to

the public and remits the full amount to the United States. All these transactions would be recorded in the New York clearing center where they
would be simply offset against each other with a final balance of $100,000
applicable to each affiliate but kept in New York.

The use of an intrasystem clearing mechanism of this sort to reduce the
transfer of funds originating from intrasystem payments for merchandise
can reduce intrasystem flows substantially. The reduction for the four year
planning horizon of the model can be summarized as follows: Netting all
flows in the model between the two subsidiaries for the four years resulted
in eight transactions and net payments of $130 million instead of the six-
teen transactions and total payments of $229 million that would have re-
sulted without a clearing house.

The oil companies, with a considerable background in coping with complex interrelationships, have pioneered in the formulation of clearing
systems for intercompany accounts. Thus an official of a Large multinational enterprise in the oil industry said: "We operate a central dollar
clearing house out of New York so that affiliates do not have to make
transfers among themselves internationally. If Sweden buys some product
from the Dutch refinery, the Dutch refinery charges New York for the account of Sweden, and New York charges Sweden. And New York gathers
in all the debt and credit to keep this multilateral clearing mechanism on a
relatively prompt settlement basis."

This Large company's multilateral clearing system was created about
1958. Before that, transactions were settled directly, and this entailed numerous bilateral agreements, negotiations with various foreign-exchange
control boards, and constant follow-ups by New York. With cash dis-
persed, it was also necessary at times to dispatch frantic cables to effec-
tuate heavy shifts of funds. "I remember seeing a cable," noted an official,
"that came out of the treasurer in New York asking a foreign subsidiary if
they could make available £20 million next Monday to meet a maturing
U.S. bill." Under present arrangements, all excess liquidity is controlled by
the treasurer in New York.

INVESTING SURPLUS CASH

Domestic firms, by exercising better control over cash and smoothing its
movements, have been able to reduce the amount of balances needed to
conduct their business. As a result, funds formerly tied up in operations
have been freed and invested primarily in marketable securities, that is,
short-term, low-risk instruments. The U.S. financial manager now readily
buys Treasury bills, commercial paper, and bankers' acceptances. On the

other hand, neither the international manager in headquarters nor his financial managers overseas ordinarily exhibit a comparable interest in short-term investments.

Again, a major cause of the lackadaisical attitude toward foreign short-term investments is that the parent believes that overseas cash is held to a minimum through the use of overdrafts. It logically follows that there is no need to worry about excess funds that have to be invested. With the recurring insistence of a Greek chorus, this opinion appears in our interviews. Also related to this belief is the feeling that as the subsidiaries abroad are expanding, they constantly require funds. Thus an official pointed out that "these companies of ours are growing and they usually need additional funds; so generally speaking we do not find a situation where they have excess funds."

At times, however, overseas subsidiaries do manage to have funds that could be invested locally. If the local currency is not in danger of devaluation, or if governmental actions force the retention of the surplus cash in the host country, reinvesting it there becomes more attractive, especially if the rate of return is good. "So if our requirements are such that we may be needing funds in that country within the next year or two, we might just keep them there," said a manager. The form of such investments is governed in part by how soon the funds will be needed.

If they will be needed shortly, liquidity is important and investments are likely to be confined to time deposits in banks. Ordinarily, within designated limits, the parent's permission for such an investment is not required, although the parent may want to approve the banks selected. Sometimes money-market instruments such as commercial paper and short-term obligations of the local government are used, and for these investments the confirmation of headquarters is more apt to be required. Approval may be obtained on a blanket basis, as in the case of a subsidiary in Japan that received permission from headquarters as follows: "We have no objection to the Japanese subsidiary's investing in short-term government bonds with a maturity of less than one year, provided there are no adverse tax or legal implications in Japan." In other enterprises, each transaction must be approved by headquarters, although the approval may involve no more than a cable exchange between the local area and New York.

Where the funds may be excess for relatively long periods of time, less emphasis is placed on liquidity. In these cases, subsidiaries have sometimes found it expedient to invest in unusual outlets. In one instance the stock of a Japanese bank was purchased in order to provide some reciprocity to the bank for the unusually large amount of loans that it had granted. Later, when the subsidiary was given parent-company financing and no longer needed these loans, it sold the stock, after receiving permission because "possession of the shares of the bank which is also our customer has become rather unfavorable from the standpoint of trade with other customers." The subsidiary also stressed that the sale of the shares was not intended for financing purposes, but would be "reflected in our cash and marketable securities balance."

In special cases, the multinational enterprise may be willing to make investments of a very long-term nature where liquidation is difficult, and invariably headquarters' approval for such an investment is required. Such a decision might apply to funds that are immobilized because of currency restrictions. The local manager of an American subsidiary in Argentina, for example, had this problem in mind: "We are not anxious to repatriate funds to the parent because of the problem of getting foreign exchange at this time. However, being concerned about possibilities of devaluation, we looked at the possibility of buying land, gold, or whatever we could to hedge against devaluation. We decided the best thing was to invest in additional plant and equipment."

When the center of clearing operations for the intercompany accounts of a multinational firm is located in the United States, as may occur in the case of the Large enterprises, the investment of the system's excess cash is directly under the control of the U.S. headquarters and is largely confined to U.S. dollars, often in the domestic money market. An overseas official of a Large firm described his investment activity: "The international company just clears their bank account every day into the parent company's account, so that the international company then has an account receivable from the parent. All cash above the $50 or $60 million needed for the whole system for purely short-term liquidity reasons is held by the parent. This cash, up to $1 billion or more, is invested in the United States in such things as Treasury bills. The parent runs a short-term investment operation that is one of its big operations in the United States."

As a result of the U.S. restrictions on foreign direct investment, many multinational enterprises have borrowed in bond markets abroad in anticipation of future capital expansion needs. During the interim period, their finance subsidiaries that issued the bonds have held the cash abroad, typically in dollars, until required by the operating subsidiaries. Such funds, which totaled about $3.1 billion in 1971,[2] were held abroad because the return available in the Eurodollar market was higher than that in the United States. In these cases, the finance subsidiaries are extensions of the U.S. treasurer's office rather than being under the control of the foreign affiliates.

A small number of companies have financial managers who are willing to place short-term excess funds in the most remunerative outlets regardless of location. The simulation model observed this investment philosophy by exploiting the differentials in interest rates and taxes that existed between the countries where units of the hypothetical system operated. In the model, the parent can borrow at rates that range from 6 to 8 percent while subsidiary *B* must pay 7 percent and subsidiary *C* must pay 9 percent. Similarly, the parent can invest short-term at a return of 5 percent whereas subsidiary *B* can get 6 percent and subsidiary *C* can get 8 percent. So the most obvious arrangement is for the parent to borrow in country *A* at 6 percent and shift the funds to *C* for investment in country *C* at 8 percent. When taxes are taken into account, the system can even earn a net return by borrowing in country *A* at 8 percent and investing in country *C* at the same rate. In that case the after-tax cost of borrowing would be 4 percent because the parent has a 50 percent tax rate, and the after-tax investment yield would be 5.6 percent because subsidiary *C* has a 30 percent tax rate. In the environment in which the model operated, however, the higher interest rate prevailing in country *C* is correlated with the greater probability of exchange devaluation. Consequently, the model finds it profitable in years 2 and 4 to borrow in country *C* and shift to country *A*, where no devaluation occurs in either year, and to country *B* where a relatively modest devaluation takes place in year 2.

In the real world, the Medium firm is more likely than the others to seek the benefits that may come from this system-oriented point of view in its investment program. The international treasurer of such an enterprise provided an illustration of how he carried out these practices: "Let me give you an example of the kind of things we do. I see a subsidiary that is getting a little more cash than it needs. So I contact the financial director and say, 'By the way, I notice that you have got a couple of hundred thousand dollars and I know that you don't need that. Don't you think it would be advisable to get some short-term investments for a few months?' So he does. Or, for instance, there is the case of the Swiss company. They owed money to the U.S. parent and were paying interest on the debt. They had some cash piling up in Switzerland and were investing it for a pretty good return by Swiss standards, but by other standards it was very low. A second factor was that Switzerland has a very low tax rate, so the interest that the subsidiary pays us generates only a small tax deduction. And yet, when the money came over here, we had to pay Uncle Sam 48 percent of the income. So from the group point of view we would be better off to take the money in Switzerland and pay off the debt to the United States because there is a difference of about 40 percent on the tax."

Accounts Receivable

For a multinational enterprise there is an important distinction between the management of its trade accounts receivable from outside customers and its intercompany receivables.

OUTSIDE THE SYSTEM

The heart of effective management of trade receivables is to design a policy that provides for converting them to cash as soon as possible while permitting their use as a competitive tool when considered desirable. This objective is the same whether overseas or within the United States, and the steps to achieve it are broadly similar. The circumstances affecting these steps, however, are more likely to cause delays abroad than at home; and the prevalent feeling of the firms interviewed is that their foreign accounts are larger relative to sales than in the United States. Support for this belief is found in the unpublished records of the three multinational enterprises that were previously cited in connection with cash holdings. Table 6–2 shows that in each of the three enterprises, in three years, the accounts receivable in foreign affiliates almost always represented a substantially greater number of days' sales than was true of U.S. operations.

The initial steps in the management of receivables are recording an order, checking the inventory for availability, invoicing, and transmitting the invoice. Within the United States the time for these steps has been shortened through electronic accounting procedures, thereby advancing the date when payment is received and reducing the amount of receivables appearing on the books. Many overseas subsidiaries have not been able to match these automated procedures. Moreover, many subsidiaries do not find the specialized finance companies that are relied upon in the United States, and this too adds to the problem of managing receivables.

There is also the matter of local trade practices, which often provide long terms. "In some places you can sell on ninety-day terms but in other places you have to go to six months or one year. All the central office does is to instruct the local manager of the policy of not going beyond the local situation." The Small multinational enterprise, more than the bigger firms, tends to be respectful of established patterns and to follow the credit terms of the host country. "It depends on the local conditions; whatever the local terms are, we are more or less within those." The Medium and Large multinational enterprise with their greater financial resources may go even further and employ trade terms as a competitive device. An official expressed

TABLE 6–2

Accounts Receivable at Year End, Three Multinational Enterprises,
1963–1965, Expressed in Number of Days of Sales

Location of Operations	Small Multinational Enterprise			Medium Multinational Enterprise			Large Multinational Enterprise		
	1963	1964	1965	1963	1964	1965	1963	1964	1965
Canada	—	—	—	49	49	64	94	94	90
France	—	—	—	n.a.ª	159	62	n.a.	86	78
Germany	56	60	54	34	27	32	30	45	39
Spain	105	113	208	—	—	—	60	34	n.a.
United Kingdom	—	—	—	100	114	113	58	55	65
Australia	61	81	65	67	59	63	n.a.	50	59
South Africa	—	—	—	62	103	103	125	130	160
Mexico	67	64	78	n.a.	n.a.	n.a.	105	89	100
Colombia	n.a.	152	66	136	127	178	106	103	91
Argentina	74	74	n.a.	—	—	—	119	87	81
Brazil	99	77	201	193	146	250	103	59	85
TOTAL FOREIGN	64	75	66	97	106	96	88	86	95
United States	48	50	42	34	32	43	58	42	41

Source: Unpublished records of the three unidentified enterprises.

ª n.a. = not available to authors.

it this way: "We have in the United States very little credit beyond the normal terms of thirty or sixty days. Abroad we'll go to long terms—not with short-term notes but trade receivables—with maturities up to a year. We will go with a long-shot special deal with a distributor. He'll say, 'Look, if you can give me one year's credit on this, I will take 1,000 units.' 'Fine,' we say. That's like making a separate bid because we are generally going against competition on the same type of thing. Yet that would be classified as part of receivables."

Despite recognition that it is desirable for on-the-spot personnel to establish credit terms, headquarters' management is reluctant to give the subsidiaries full tether lest they move too far. Accordingly, it is common policy to require that any departures from prevailing arrangements be approved by some headquarters' group which, in the case of the Small multinational enterprise, probably will be located in the United States. For example: "The policy is fixed. If they want to change their terms for trade, they have to ask for approval in Philadelphia." For the bigger firms, authority to grant approval may be lodged with regional headquarters. Sometimes the regional management may be allowed to authorize terms up to 180 days, and headquarters in the United States must grant consent for anything beyond that limit. A variant of this practice, employed by some firms, is for the regional manager to have full authority to establish credit terms except for so-called special deals.

When funds are readily available within a country and interest rates are low, buyers are willing to borrow in order to obtain trade discounts. On the other hand, if money is tight, they may be unable to obtain bank credit or may find its cost so high that they are reluctant to take advantage of trade discounts. Said one official, "When money rates are expensive, as much as 30 percent in Argentina and 45 percent in Brazil, your customers are going to drag their payments at all times." In dealing with its customers, a subsidiary of a multinational firm often has a special advantage over its local competitors because the subsidiary can draw financing from the multinational system to carry these extended receivables.

When customers abroad do not pay promptly, charging interest on accounts receivable once they become overdue seems to be more widely used than in the United States, but primarily by the Large enterprise, whose strong competitive position puts some weight behind such a policy. The Small firm collects interest on its outside accounts much more sparingly, as one official of such an enterprise observed somewhat caustically: "It's one thing to charge and another thing to collect from the customers."

Other techniques are employed to put pressure upon negligent customers. A customer may be asked to formalize the obligation underlying a long overdue account by issuing a note against it. "Many times we get accounts receivable overdue, and we will herd them from stray accounts receivable to notes receivable," an official remarked picturesquely. Not only does the note provide tangible evidence of the debt, but it is easier to include an interest charge on it. Or, the price of the goods may be negotiated to include an allowance for the additional period involved: "If the guy has asked for extended credit beyond the normal period of ninety days, we will bump up the price of goods and include an interest charge for the extra days he has credit." As in the United States, these "pressure" devices are ordinarily handled on an individual basis.

The subsidiaries of relatively few enterprises employ credit insurance for their accounts receivable, and those subsidiaries use it sparingly. "Our subsidiaries use credit insurance on a selective basis depending on whether they're in the wholesale or retail business, depending upon the lengths and maturities of the contracts, and depending most of all upon the kind of risks you can insure against and what it costs you to insure; but they do that on a selective basis."

The last stage in the management of trade receivables is concerned with measures to collect the persistently outstanding accounts. Within the United States, firms ordinarily calculate the age of their receivables and may establish guidelines to determine at what point collection efforts should be instituted. This procedure, in turn, may follow a prescribed routine of collection letters, telephone calls, registered letters, wires, personal visits, and finally the use of collection agencies. In many places overseas, the manager may have to rely on a more personal collection arrangement. Conditions vary tremendously. "You sell a machine in the Congo and it goes into the bush. You have to send somebody up to collect. You don't wait for somebody in the Congo to write you a check."

In enterprises that have working-capital budgets for their subsidiaries, headquarters exercises additional control over the accounts receivable by including such data in the budgets. For example, one Large firm has an asset-management category in its operating plan which incorporates data on the number of days a subsidiary expects its receivables to be outstanding. These figures are discussed with headquarters' management, and once agreement is reached they become the subsidiary's projected goals. After the budget period, results are compared with expectations and local management is queried on substantial excesses.

In addition, headquarters in some firms checks the trend of outstanding receivables and asks the subsidiaries to explain movements that are considered unsatisfactory. As an illustration, another Large enterprise provides a series of guidelines in order to evaluate the operating plan of its foreign subsidiaries as a group. Included is the question, "Does the accounts-receivable balance show a declining trend in terms of monthly billings outstanding?" The importance of trends was emphasized by a headquarters' manager of still another firm who noted that management could establish some degree of control by calling for reduction in the amount of receivables outstanding, whereas it could not readily strike comparisons among subsidiaries in different countries because of variations in local practices. The same thing was explained by the treasurer of a subsidiary in Germany: "We're fairly autonomous in managing accounts receivable; because conditions vary so much from country to country, it's difficult for New York to function. However, what they do is say, 'I want you to get your accounts receivable down by 10 percent this year. Now if you can't achieve this, tell me why you can't.' This is the type of control they wield. The 10 percent figure is something someone pulled out of a hat, but it's sometimes achievable and we have to come up with a program of 'how' if we will, or 'why' if we can't."

INSIDE THE SYSTEM

Since intercompany receivables represent an important financial link for moving funds between the units of a multinational system, these receivables are in a different category from those of the nonrelated trade customers. For outside accounts, where marketing considerations usually dominate, a firm may be willing to grant long terms for competitive reasons, but ordinarily is reluctant to do so lest it lead to bad paying habits on the part of customers. For intercompany accounts, as discussed in Chapter 4, a firm may place nominal terms of credit that are uniform throughout the system; but, at the same time, it will have a more liberal attitude toward extending the payment date because this decision is tied into the common strategy for moving funds within the system.

Inventories

As in the case of accounts receivable, the typical financial manager feels that his enterprise has more difficulty in controlling inventory abroad and that the ratio of inventories to sales is greater overseas than in the United States. That inventories are higher abroad, especially in countries far away from the United States, is at least partially confirmed by the data in Table 6–3 for the same three enterprises already cited in connection with cash and receivables. With the exception of the Medium enterprise in 1963, inventories in foreign subsidiaries were almost always well above those in the U.S. operations. (The reader should note that this exhibit is in terms of percentage of annual sales rather than number of days' sales, as the latter measure is misleading for inventories because inventories are not all finished goods but also include raw materials and work in process.)

Managers abroad are inclined to employ the same control techniques that are used in the United States. Thus, the financial officer of one subsidiary pointed out, "We brought the broad principles of inventory management with us, but the implementation varies from subsidiary to subsidiary, depending on the special problems encountered." The diversity of special problems encountered abroad is reflected in the fact that no single problem was identified as most important by a majority of the enterprises where we conducted interviews.

In many cases inventories are imported and must travel across an ocean. This necessity to use ocean transportation was the problem cited most often—by almost half of the enterprises—as a contributing cause of the larger ratios of inventories abroad. The inventories purchased from outside

TABLE 6–3

Inventories at Year End, Three Multinational Enterprises, 1963–1965, Expressed as a Percentage of Annual Sales

Location of Operations	Small Multinational Enterprise			Medium Multinational Enterprise			Large Multinational Enterprise		
	1963	1964	1965	1963	1964	1965	1963	1964	1965
Canada	—	—	—	21	25	26	31	21	32
France	—	—	—	n.a.[a]	22	35	n.a.	20	25
Germany	20	18	18	18	14	17	35	27	24
Spain	83	96	52	—	—	—	33	30	n.a.
United Kingdom	—	—	—	11	15	17	34	29	26
Australia	25	22	28	21	19	30	n.a.	58	50
South Africa	—	—	—	14	26	30	45	76	96
Mexico	13	18	13	—	—	—	89	69	41
Colombia	n.a.	18	41	13	40	37	46	35	16
Argentina	28	26	n.a.	—	—	—	61	38	45
Brazil	29	19	35	16	18	32	31	37	20
TOTAL FOREIGN	22	21	17	13	17	21	42	37	37
United States	14	14	11	25	18	19	17	17	15

Source: Unpublished records of the three unidentified enterprises.

[a] n.a. = not available to authors.

the multinational system and inventories moved within the system are often on shipboard for long periods of time. These goods in transit are commonly included in the subsidiary's inventories and therefore substantially inflate these levels, a factor noted by an officer of a subsidiary: "You look at our balance sheet and you'll say, 'Gee, their inventory is higher overseas.' But this is because we take into our inventory figures the 'in-transits,' which in many cases double the inventory figure."

Another official made some comparisons with land shipments in the United States: "In the States, a part may be made one day in a manufacturing plant and delivered to an assembly plant twenty-four hours later. Shortly after that it's in the finished item, sold and billed to the dealer. In an overseas location—let's say Peru—that imports components from the States, you've got to allow thirty days just for the stuff to be processed for shipment and on the water. Then when it's in the port, clearance requires another two weeks, and then it's two weeks from the port up to the plant."

Not only is more time needed to deliver the inventories, but there is greater uncertainty. Delays may be incurred as shipments follow prescribed water routes and cargoes are transferred from one vessel to another. In one case "the goods move from a factory in New Jersey to the boat to be shipped to Bermuda, where they stay from a week to a month before another boat carries them to Australia, and this journey may take two months. And, of course, ocean shipments are delayed because of storms." In the less developed countries even land transportation may create special difficulties.

Next to ocean transportation, the factor mentioned most often as causing problems in managing inventories abroad is governmental policies, especially the import restrictions of some host governments. In some cases allocation decrees determine what goods can be imported, and when. And slow-moving administrative machinery can create tedious delays in gaining necessary approvals. An executive declared that "in Mexico because of local restrictions we had to import a year's supply of inventories at one time, because the Mexican government said that the borders would be closed pretty soon." He added that in Singapore possible curtailment in shipments of air conditioners led to such heavy advance ordering that for the next two years the market was completely saturated because the warehouses were full of air conditioners.

The need to obtain allocations of hard currency to bring in goods from other countries is another element in the higher levels of inventory abroad. From an interview: "In some countries where dollars to pay for imported raw materials are difficult to obtain, you try to build as large an inventory of raw material as you can." An official of another company put the import-licensing and exchange-allocation problems together as he noted, "We've got problems of import control in lots of places—Colombia, India, Argentina, Thailand, and Brazil. In one way or another these countries control the import levels, so the local manager has a tendency whenever he can to stockpile what he thinks he's going to use for the next year or so."

Various customs and laws that affect employment can cause subsidiaries to adjust to business cycles by changes in inventory levels rather than production levels. Speaking to this point, one headquarters' official stated, "Inventories are higher abroad than here because there's a tendency in many foreign countries to retain people much longer during a downturn than in the United States, which has a higher mobility of labor. If we see a downturn in our sales in the United States, we will lay off people rather quickly. In Europe we find that it is very difficult to do because the custom is for people to join a company and make a career out of being with that company."

Performance schedules provided by local suppliers to the subsidiaries are often unrealistic. One financial manager said, "Take our locations in

Latin America, such as Argentina, Brazil, and Mexico. When they're not importing from the States, they're sourcing a lot locally; and they have the problem that local suppliers' schedules are nowhere nearly as dependable as suppliers' schedules are in the States. Consequently, just to avoid any risk of having to shut down for lack of a part, managers in these locations use a consciously longer lead time for orders."

The use of scientific, quantitative methods in an attempt to achieve optimal solutions for the problems of inventory management is widespread in the United States. To extend these principles abroad, headquarters' personnel of the multinational enterprise may write an inventory-control manual describing procedures to be followed. But the much greater uncertainty and rapidly changing conditions overseas make it difficult to apply domestically oriented quantitative techniques. Furthermore, those who take these methods beyond the seas encounter limitations of personnel and communications. "Generally speaking," observed a headquarters' official, "inventory management is not as sophisticated in the factories outside the United States, partly because communications and methods of control are better and more precise here." An official of another firm told of his efforts to introduce overseas "a fairly sophisticated procedure" for controlling inventories, based on the principle that a subsidiary cannot keep every product in stock at all times. He observed somewhat ruefully that "it is very difficult for managers to accept this," and "I am afraid that these procedures are not considered too seriously in the field."

Controlling the level of inventories typically involves managers responsible for a number of different business functions—finance, purchasing, production, marketing, and accounting. As a result, in the United States there often is organizational confusion about inventory management. Abroad, organizational relationships usually are defined less clearly than in the domestic operation, and at times subsidiaries report to three entities, whose responsibilities are in terms of product, function, and geography.[3] Thus, the responsibility of inventory management is often even more clouded than in the United States.

Small multinational enterprises rely heavily on local managers for inventory decisions, although headquarters' personnel in some Small firms recognize the dangers of this approach. Said one, "Too often at new locations, they would not know what they wanted. You could go into somebody's bonded warehouse in Geneva or Rotterdam and see that they were stocking obsolete items. I try to get over there once a year and see what's in there, and then try to distribute it to some place else if it's not salable quickly. It's rather difficult for the local management unless you ask them to admit they have some nonsalable goods sitting around in inventory.

And, of course, to me the longer that you let it sit there, the less likely you have the possibility of getting a return on it. It gets old and pretty soon you have 100 percent write-off. It's gone; it's scrap."

The inventory-control problem is accentuated in the Medium enterprises by the growing amount of intrasystem shipments and the attempt to effect a tight central control. In discussing this problem an official of a Medium firm noted that the coordination of production, shipments, and mainte-nance of inventories "is especially difficult to fit into any overall company-wide policy." The availability of inventories from subsidiaries rather than from the United States must be considered constantly, and so must the company's policy of allocating certain products in limited supply on a worldwide basis. The divisional controller receives copies of all purchase orders issued by foreign subsidiaries in order to review these continually for reasonability.

The Large enterprise, faced with its complex production–marketing–storage arrangements, relies more heavily than the others on financial-statement rules. But there is such diversity in the system that any one rule applied worldwide can result in strange events. A refinery manager for a major oil company told of an experience he had. An order from headquarters forced the refinery to reduce inventory to be used for refinery repairs to a specified limit by the end of the year. As no local market existed for the excess parts, they were discarded to a junk pile. When a major repair to the refinery took place the following year, the maintenance supervisors had to scour the junk piles in order to obtain sufficient parts to make the needed repairs.

This last episode highlights a nagging issue between managers in the United States and abroad. In a system with great uncertainty, poorly de-fined responsibilities, and wide variations in conditions from place to place, there is a strong tendency on the part of headquarters to identify low inventories with effective management. One company, for example, at-tempted to educate its overseas managers on the contribution to profits that could be made by curtailing inventories. The company distributed sta-tistics on the costs of keeping a dollar's worth of inventory on hand. "We find that in a weak-currency market such as Brazil, we have gotten our in-ventories down to a three-month level; and we are using it to show the rest of the managers what can be done."

In contrast, the subsidiaries desire a relatively large inventory and at times search for loopholes in the enterprise's procedures that can be ex-ploited to achieve it. In one case, when evaluating the effectiveness of local management, headquarters decided not to take into account the inter-est a subsidiary paid on loans from headquarters to support inventory.

This decision was reached because the borrowing had stemmed from the parent company's insistence upon the remittance of funds. Consequently, some subsidiaries built up their inventories with borrowed funds, thereby facilitating sales, but the interest incurred did not detract from their profit performance. Explained a headquarters' treasurer of this enterprise: "We feel that in some cases, such as South Africa, they may be taking advantage of the system by increasing inventories to give them a better chance for sales. This increases their profit, but probably not enough to offset the increased interest expense that we pay; but in terms of what is reported as their profit performance, they're better off."

Pattern and Trend

In the area of managing current assets, there are two major opposing tugs on the multinational enterprise. One, pulling from the direction of the foreign country, takes the form of local customs, governmental pressures, and institutional availability, all of which cause the overseas management to emulate the practices of its competitors. The other tug arises from headquarters which seeks to educate local personnel in the ways that U.S. companies handle their current assets.

As might be expected, which tug is the winner depends upon the particular circumstances. In general, however, the foreign influence is consistently present while that of headquarters is more uneven, sometimes strong and sometimes waning in importance. So by and large, foreign subsidiaries have relatively lower cash, but relatively higher levels of accounts receivable and inventories than U.S. firms. And the level of current assets needed to support an annual dollar of sales on the average does not appear to differ systematically from that of indigenous firms in the host countries. In the United Kingdom, for example, the ratio of current assets to sales was found to be approximately the same for U.S. subsidiaries as it was for a matched set of U.K. firms, in a variety of industries.[4] Although a similar study in France produced a less uniform pattern, as shown in Table 6–4, it was not substantially out of line with the general observations. In two industries (petroleum and chemicals) the ratios in U.S. subsidiaries were more like those of French industries than those of U.S. industries. In two other industries (automobiles and electrical machinery) it was the other way around: the ratios in U.S. subsidiaries were almost identical with those in the United States. In the other industry shown (nonelectrical machinery) the ratios in the United States, in France, and in the subsidiaries were nearly the same.

TABLE 6–4

Current Assets of French Subsidiaries of U.S. Multinational Enterprises Compared with French Industry and with Domestic Operations of U.S. Industry, 1966, Expressed as a Percentage of Annual Sales

	French Industry	U.S. Subsidiaries in France	Domestic Operations of U.S. Industry
Petroleum	20	18	54
Chemicals	42	39	48
Automobiles	32	45	43
Electrical machinery	61	44	45
Nonelectrical machinery	54	55	52

Source: Jean Marie Bonnet, "Comparison of the American Subsidiary with Its Parent and Its Local Competitor," unpublished MBA Research Report, Harvard University Graduate School of Business Administration, 1969. The financial information on French companies (including U.S. subsidiaries) in this report is unpublished data from Institut National de le Statistique et des Etudes Economiques. The information for U.S. corporations in this report is from "The Ratios of Manufacturing," *Dun's Review* (November 1967): 78, 81, with the medians of appropriate industry groups used.

Over the years, as the U.S. multinational enterprise becomes more aware of the benefits to earnings that could be achieved by tightening the reins of control in its own hands and learns how to use these reins more effectively, the influence of headquarters' policy is likely to become more apparent in the way foreign subsidiaries manage their current assets. As an illustration, we have noted that the availability of overdrafts has an important effect on the manner in which foreign subsidiaries handle their cash and investments. Following this policy, the overseas units of one Large multinational enterprise not only use overdrafts to the hilt but also are likely to apply any excess cash to reduce their overdraft position rather than to seek new short-term investment outlets. "We don't have to find any place to invest short-term," observed the firm's financial officer. "Security companies would like us to and they keep thinking we've got some cash but we don't. If we have any extra cash, we just repay part of our overdraft."

Contrast this policy with that of a Medium firm that gives more attention to central planning and does not place a similar automatic reliance on overdraft privileges. Instead, it favors a strategy that cuts costs by taking advantage of interest-rate differentials, and therefore, it may even frown upon the use of overdrafts, despite their convenience, if less expensive sources are available elsewhere in the corporate system. Thus, in response to the question of whether the subsidiaries employed overdrafts, an official responded firmly that with few exceptions the answer was "no." He then added, "We could get lots of overdraft facilities, but we look at the interest rate they charge, and we can obtain funds cheaper in the United States."

The outcome of a policy that makes less use of overdrafts but moves funds more efficiently would probably be that cash balances overseas would continue to be low; but the total of cash and marketable securities might increase as management broadens its investment horizons abroad and money markets develop throughout the world, for then holdings of foreign short-term marketable securities by U.S. multinational enterprises are likely to rise, resulting in increased system earnings through raising the return on short-term investments.

In the case of inventories, the delays created by distance and transportation, the overstocking that arises from government rulings, and the difficulty of applying technical U.S. procedures to different foreign sources all suggest that in many instances considerable fat exists in foreign inventories. Out of the $32 billion of inventories that foreign affiliates of U.S. foreign direct investors held at the end of 1970, as much as $15 billion of this amount might represent inventories in excess of those needed for a similar volume of operations in the United States. And even if this estimate is on the high side, here is an area that seems susceptible to better control and will probably attract increasing attention from headquarters. The net result would be to free considerable funds for further investment abroad or return to the United States.

The question of accounts receivable is different. The need to meet local competition may make it difficult for headquarters to bring about major changes of policy that would lead to cutting down the magnitude of receivables. Here, the shortening of terms is likely to come more gradually, therefore, and in tandem with a general tendency for greater harmonization to occur in trade terms throughout the world as the ties of international business become closer.

SEVEN / Protecting against Exchange Risks

Since the beginning, multinational enterprises have been preoccupied with the risks that go with doing business in many currencies. Note the emphasis on the word "risks." The problem has always been seen as asymmetrical: the fear of loss from those risks has greatly exceeded the hope of gain.

Stated in another way, the fear of loss from devaluations or revaluations abroad has always been more important as a governor of action than the hope of gain from devaluations and revaluations. A devaluation of a foreign currency relative to the dollar usually results in a reported loss; when Brazilian cruzeiros, for example, suddenly fall in value, cruzeiros held by subsidiaries in Brazil will buy fewer dollars, and the result is a loss in dollars on the books of the U.S. enterprise. A revaluation of a foreign currency relative to the dollar usually results in a reported gain, but not always, for debt denominated in a revalued currency increases in dollar value. Accounting principles have traditionally called for recognizing a loss when it occurs but not reporting certain types of gains unless offset by a loss. Also, governments are less likely to frown upon a firm's protecting against a loss than a firm's trying deliberately to profit from movements in exchange rates. All this contributes to the asymmetry of the exchange-rate problems as viewed by U.S.-controlled enterprises.

True, a lull in anxiety over foreign devaluations began in 1971 when the dollar itself was devalued in terms of other major currencies, such as the German mark, Swiss franc, French franc, British pound, and Japanese yen. Although a few U.S. enterprises had more liabilities than assets in these revalued currencies and thus recorded a loss (for a given amount of marks, more dollars would be required than before), most U.S. enterprises found themselves richer in dollar terms, for their assets in the revalued currencies exceeded their liabilities in the revalued currencies.

This development, however, did not alter the long-term asymmetrical nature of the exchange-risk problem. Many less-developed nations continued to have weak currencies relative to the dollar—that is, their reserves of dollars and gold were small enough to suggest the danger of devaluation. And even some of the major currencies were obviously not going to retain forever their existing high rate of exchange with the dollar.

Financial managers in U.S.-controlled systems kept right on being preoccupied with the perils hanging over their profit statements.

Their ever-present concern leads to protective measures—various sorts of "insurance" against losses. Most enterprises have regular programs of protection in countries with weak currencies. In addition to these normal arrangements, almost all multinational enterprises take some action when any sudden increase occurs in the level of currency risk in countries where they operate. The nature of these programs and these actions is the subject of this chapter.

It is possible to be overprotective, and financial managers sometimes magnify the exchange risk out of proportion of the real danger to the enterprise. No executive likes to have a loss on his record, especially a loss that with more prescience he might have avoided. Companies also do not enjoy reporting losses to their stockholders. Even though the consequences of such losses are not usually crucial, the prospect of their appearance in financial statements is real enough. The tendency to purchase more protection than would be optimal for the firm is no secret among financial officers. At a private meeting in 1971 of twenty financial managers from twenty different multinational enterprises, most heads nodded in agreement to the statement by one outspoken participant: "If the truth were known, everyone in this room should be fired for buying too much protection."

The choice of protective measures usually is related to the degree of exposure to risk. A multinational enterprise can calculate the exposure of its foreign operations to exchange risk in more than one way, as discussed in Chapter 2. In a loose sense, all the current assets held abroad by U.S. foreign direct investors (about $62 billion in 1970) and all the revenues collected by U.S. foreign direct investors in foreign currencies (well over $100 billion annually) are exposed to exchange risk.[1] But typically, a manager thinks of exposure in terms of the balance sheet, and defines exposure as (1) those *assets* that are subject to a reduction in value in the event of a devaluation, *minus* (2) those *liabilities* that are subject to a reduction in value in the event of a devaluation. An example of such an asset is the aforementioned cruzeiros held in Brazil; a devaluation will cause them to be worth less in dollars. But the exposure is lessened if some of the cruzeiros have been borrowed from a Brazilian bank, for the devaluation will lessen the dollar value of the loan to be repaid.

One method of offsetting effects of devaluation is to increase the prices of goods sold in local currencies so that the dollar value of the profits will not decline after devaluation. A free-market exchange rate that reflects the possibility of devaluation can be used as a guide to pricing. The general manager of one firm's Southeast Asia region gave an example: "We are apprehensive of the peso in the Philippines. It is soft and we know it, so we convert pesos at a different rate than the official rate. We sell a machine for $100 and calculate an equivalent number of pesos, which at present is 425 pesos although the official rate is 390 pesos; so the customer must pay 9 percent higher than the pesos calculated by using official exchange rates. Also, in the event of a formal devaluation, we would increase the price. We have to stay with the dollar."

But such an emphasis on pricing as a protective measure is exceptional; relatively few firms report that they routinely raise local prices in anticipation of devaluation. Instead, the focus of attention is on the balance sheet, where one of the normally accepted accounting practices is used to determine the amount of assets at risk.[2]

Current Assets

The makeup of a firm's current assets is always changing, and the amount of each type of asset can be somewhat raised or lowered at the discretion of financial managers. The idea is to minimize the subsidiary's holdings of those current assets that, in accordance with accepted accounting procedures, would be written down in the event of devaluation. These can be cash, accounts receivable in local currency, and certain inventories. Actually most of the emphasis is on cash or near-cash (marketable securities).

CASH AND MARKETABLE SECURITIES

Some enterprises follow a general policy of minimizing current assets in their subsidiaries by holding in the parent firm all such assets that are not needed in the day-to-day operations of the subsidiaries.

This is not usually the most profitable way to run a multinational enterprise. In order to gain insights into the potential costs of such a strategy, we used the simulation model to compare the effects of a financial policy in which the amount of cash and marketable securities held by the parent over the four years of the model was maximized with the results of a policy maximizing consolidated profits after taxes. The results are in Table 7–1.

To be sure, the model, when asked to maximize liquidity in the parent, accomplished that purpose, for the average amount of liquidity held by the parent was $450 million over a four-year period compared with only $13 million under the profit-maximizing policy. But maximizing liquidity in the parent reduces consolidated profits after taxes by 12 percent. Surprisingly, maximizing liquidity in the parent results in an exchange loss of $10 million, compared with an exchange profit of $53 million under the policy of maximizing profits. The reason for this outcome is that when effort is concentrated on remitting cash to the parent, other protective measures are overlooked. One such measure is to accumulate dollar assets in the form of intrasystem accounts in the subsidiary located in the country in which the devaluation is expected. These dollar assets allow additional borrowing in local currency and the funds thus generated can be used for local working capital, with the remainder converted to dollars and loaned to another unit in the system.

TABLE 7–1

Effect of Alternative Financial Policies on Selected Performance Indicators. Multinational Enterprise Model, Totals for Four Years (In Millions of Dollars)

	Alternative Financial Policies	
Performance Indicators	Maximize Consolidated Profits After Taxes	Maximize Cash and Marketable Securities Held by Parent
Consolidated profits after taxes	471	416
Average amount of cash and marketable securities held by parent	13	450
Exchange gain (loss)	53	(10)

Although a policy of centralizing all excess liquidity in the parent is not likely to be optimum in the real world either, such a policy is sometimes used, though exchange-risk protection is not the only motive. Following is an excerpt from a parent's memorandum to all of its foreign subsidiaries:

The general policy of the [name of company] is to transmit full profits after foreign taxes of all subsidiaries to the parent company in the United States as soon as practicable after these profits have been earned, except where, due to circumstances, it would be advantageous to retain a subsidiary's earnings abroad. There are several advantages to the policy of having full profit remittance after taxes to the United States parent. One of these is that it tends to minimize losses due to the depreciation of foreign-exchange rates, exchange restrictions, and other risks to which profits earned overseas are subject. Another advantage is the desirability of accumulating all surplus funds provided by operations in one place rather than in many. This permits more effective coordination of the investment of these surplus funds and removes the possibility of local operating management diverting their energies from their prime responsibility of manufacturing and merchandising. It follows that when a subsidiary needs additional funds for normal operations or for additional capital investment, the U.S. parent must stand ready to make such an investment.

Other enterprises follow a policy of moving cash only from those subsidiaries in countries with weak currencies. In these cases the cash is moved to the parent or to subsidiaries operating in countries with strong currencies. A number of intrasystem financial links are used: dividends,[3] debts, interest, royalties, management fees, and intercompany accounts. In fact, however, reducing the level of cash and marketable securities held in subsidiaries immediately prior to an expected devaluation does not play such a major role in protecting against devaluation as one might imagine, for most enterprises believe that the level of such assets *normally* held abroad is relatively low. That is, the Small enterprise keeps low balances abroad because it uses any excess funds for the inventory, accounts receivable, and fixed assets needed for expansion; the Large enterprise keeps low balances abroad as part of its normal procedure to control its far-flung network of subsidiaries. Medium enterprises are more likely than the Small or Large ones to be exceptions to this pattern, for they often invest short-term funds abroad to obtain a higher interest rate. Thus the Medium firm is more likely than the other firms to move cash in anticipation of changes in currency values.

LOCAL ACCOUNTS RECEIVABLE

A large volume of accounts receivable on the balance sheet heightens exposure and could be a source of concern. As one financial manager stated, "Our biggest problem overseas is financing accounts receivable. This is a problem that we face in the United States, obviously; but overseas we have the added problem of protecting receivables against currency risk."

A multinational enterprise can indeed reduce its exposure to currency devaluations by reducing the amount of local receivables and shifting the cash to stronger currency havens within the system. But in practice this is seldom done. Reducing the length of credit terms would reduce sales, which in turn would reflect on the performance of the marketing executive. And offering special discounts to speed collection either on sales already made or on new sales is likely to be more costly than viable alternatives.[4]

However, borrowing against receivables is somewhat more popular; this is especially so in those countries in which the cost of discounting receivables is about the same as that of borrowing. The Medium firm is more likely than the others to take such action with the explicit motive of protecting against a devaluation. Said an official of one Medium firm, "Receivables are another problem in a weak currency area. If it takes you, say, ninety days to convert receivables to cash, your currency can degenerate in value as much as 10 percent in that length of time. So we have followed the procedure of discounting accounts receivable and doing everything possible to speed up collections. Of course, the people that owe you have the opposite incentive, so it is a constant battle."

The Small enterprise is likely to shrug off the problem because of its lack of knowledge and lack of detailed supervision of its foreign operations. The Large enterprise is prone to pay little attention to changing the terms on accounts receivable, for it seeks automatic protection in rules that call for local borrowing to offset specified assets on the balance sheets of its subsidiaries.

INTERCOMPANY ACCOUNTS

Intercompany accounts provide a ready vehicle to reduce exchange loss when a devaluation is expected,[5] for as the treasurer of a subsidiary in a Large enterprise observed: "To safeguard against devaluation, we reduce exposure by promptly settling our foreign debts—which are all intercompany. Beyond this speeding up of intercompany settlements, we go on as usual." This treasurer was simply following a prudent policy of reducing his supply of a local currency before that currency dropped in value.

Another example: In 1968 when the French franc was under attack, the European treasurer of a Medium enterprise ordered the French subsidiary to pay immediately all invoices of other subsidiaries and any other debts not denominated in French francs. In addition, he ordered all other subsidiaries not to pay any funds owed to the French subsidiary until further notice. These two actions, of course, reduced the French subsidiary's supply of French francs prior to the expected devaluation. In such cases these funds are not replenished until after the devaluation occurs or until the franc weathers the attack.

Some enterprises refine this policy, and while signalling subsidiaries to pay their dollar debts, allow intercompany debts to remain outstanding between subsidiaries if the subsidiary in the country with the stronger currency owes the subsidiary in the country with the weaker currency even if both currencies are expected to devalue in relation to the dollar. For example, when a computer manufacturer became apprehensive about pound sterling, "Our fear was that if sterling was devalued, the Australian dollar would go down at least part of the way. So we asked both our U.K. subsidiary and our Australian subsidiary to pay down their U.S. balances but to leave outstanding a debt owed by Australia to the United Kingdom. If both the Australian dollar and sterling are devalued by the same amount, Australia doesn't lose anything; but if the pound is devalued more, they'll gain."

INVENTORIES

Assets held as inventories do not invoke the same degree of apprehension regarding foreign-exchange losses as cash, marketable securities, and receivables. The major reason is that the value of inventories, particularly those that have world-market prices, can be raised to offset currency devaluations. That is, in some methods of determining exposure, inventories imported from hard-currency areas are revalued upward in terms of the devalued currency so as to keep a constant value in hard currency in the expectation that the prices to consumers can be raised accordingly. Therefore, according to one corporate official, "Our imported inventories are not subject to exchange devaluation."

Indeed, a small number of enterprises, predominantly of Medium size and capable of relative flexible adjustments to changing conditions, go a step further and actually carry proportionately larger inventories abroad in order to serve as a hedge against inflation and the risk of devaluation. Two factors, however, tend to reduce deliberate stockpiling as a hedge against devaluation. First, it is relatively expensive, some 20 to 25 percent annually, for financing, storage, and obsolescence. Furthermore, inventory management seldom is the responsibility of the financial executive.[6] As in the case of local accounts receivable, this again illustrates the point that enterprises are not organized to use all possible tools in an optimal way.

Local Liabilities

If local sources of funds, such as loans or accounts payable, are used instead of dollars, then upon devaluation of the local currency, fewer dollars will be needed to repay the sources. As for accounts payable, a subsidiary can obtain "unexposed" funds by deferring payments of local accounts, but in fact this device is seldom used. If a trade discount is missed because of deferred payments, the effective annual cost is likely to be much higher than the cost of borrowing.[7]

Many overseas subsidiaries, when they need funds, routinely borrow locally in order to reduce exposure. Consider the case of a Large enterprise that has been overseas for a long time and once did its selling through agents, who were financed directly by the parent. In the postwar period the enterprise established manufacturing plants throughout the world. Its sales being mainly to retail customers on long-term credit, the enterprise found that its subsidiaries were carrying large amounts of receivables in areas where the currencies were not strong; funds to support such receivables were provided by the parent. As a result, substantial devaluation losses appeared in the consolidated financial statement. So the enterprise shifted the financial burden to the subsidiaries, adopting a policy of having the subsidiaries borrow locally to obtain funds to finance long-term receivables to the extent possible. Said an executive of the firm: "Now admittedly we still have some exchange losses, but they have become smaller, and although our interest expense has climbed, we have benefited. We like to have borrowing in every country in which we hold receivables and these receivables are nearly all installment receivables. So if we have a receivable in cruzeiros or Indian rupees, we want to have some borrowing in the same currency."

Another firm has records to show that in the twenty-two years ending in 1969 it saved $7 million by borrowing locally in local currency when it needed funds—rather than borrowing dollars in the United States, sending them abroad, and taking an exchange loss every time the local currency was devalued. For the last seven years of that period, however, the firm found that because of high local interest costs it had a loss of $362,000 by following this policy of borrowing locally rather than providing dollars and taking an exchange loss when the local currency was devalued, hardly evidence that local borrowing always pays.

A serious problem arises when a currency suddenly weakens. This is the moment when the firm most wants protection but also the moment when protection is least likely to be available. The most common response to the sudden weakening of a currency is to borrow locally and increase remittances to the parent. But such activities are likely to be limited by both tightness in the local money market and government restrictions on the outflow of funds. The international treasurer of one Large enterprise said that at such a time "we try to get all the money out of the country that we can but this is the problem: it's very difficult to borrow money when a devaluation is expected. Just like now, Peru is a bit shaky. We're trying to remit all the money that we can. We'd like to borrow more but the government has placed restrictions on borrowing."

There is no lack of data to indicate that the foreign units of U.S.-controlled enterprises do more short-term borrowing (relative to current assets) than their domestic counterparts do. The measure used for this analysis is the "current ratio," that is, the ratio of current assets to current liabilities.* Table 7–2 shows a time series of estimated ratios for foreign and domestic operations of 26 multinational enterprises—all those among our 187 enterprises for which sufficient information was available. All the ratios are greater than 1, indicating that current assets exceeded current liabilities; but the foreign ratios are consistently lower than the domestic ones, giving some statistical support to the clear lesson of our interviews and observations—to wit, that the exchange-risk factor leads to heavy

TABLE 7–2

Ratio of Current Assets to Current Liabilities, Foreign Operations Compared with Domestic Operations of Sample of U.S.-Controlled Multinational Enterprises, Selected Years, 1939–1966 [a]

	End of Fiscal Year							
	1939	1945	1950	1955	1960	1964	1965	1966
Foreign	1.9 [b]	2.1	2.0	1.9	1.9	1.6	1.5	1.5
Domestic	2.8	3.4	3.1	2.6	2.9	2.7	2.5	2.4

Sources: Published annual reports and 10-K statements to Securities and Exchange Commission.

[a] Sample consists of twenty-six enterprises, which accounted for about 20 percent of the total assets of U.S. firms that have direct foreign investments. The years chosen are at approximately five-year intervals except for the last three. For some firms in some years there were gaps in the data, and we supplied estimates based on ratios of year-to-year changes for consistent sets of companies for these before computing the averages of the whole group.

[b] Note that these figures are ratios. Hence, foreign current assets were almost twice as much as foreign current liabilities in 1939; but the domestic ratio was even larger, current assets being almost three times current liabilities.

short-term borrowing abroad in nondollar currencies. The same sort of evidence on current ratios is found in the three multinational enterprises—Small, Medium, Large—that provided us with extensive data. Current ratios for these firms in foreign countries and in the United States are given in Table 7–3. In some countries, of course, only short-term borrowing is available, so this also is a factor contributing to a lower current ratio.

* The parent's investment in the foreign operations has been omitted, so the current assets and current liabilities of the foreign operations are denominated primarily in local currency.

TABLE 7–3

*Ratio of Current Assets to Current Liabilities, Three Sizes
of Multinational Enterprises, Year End, 1963–1965*

Location of Operations	Small Multinational Enterprise			Medium Multinational Enterprise			Large Multinational Enterprise		
	1963	1964	1965	1963	1964	1965	1963	1964	1965
Canada	—	—	—	2.4	3.1	2.6	0.9	0.8	3.3
France	—	—	—	1.1	1.3	0.9	n.a.[a]	1.0	1.0
Germany	2.2	2.2	2.0	1.3	2.0	1.8	1.2	1.1	1.4
Spain	5.4	1.7	2.3	—	—	—	1.2	1.7	2.3
United Kingdom	—	—	—	1.8	2.6	3.2	1.1	1.1	1.6
Australia	1.2	1.3	2.0	4.5	4.5	2.1	n.a.	1.3	1.4
South Africa	—	—	—	1.7	1.6	1.9	4.3	5.9	2.9
Mexico	1.7	1.4	1.6	—	—	—	1.2	3.5	3.4
Colombia	n.a.	1.3	1.1	1.3	1.5	1.8	1.7	1.2	3.3
Argentina	1.4	1.4	n.a.	—	—	—	1.0	1.0	1.7
Brazil	3.2	1.8	1.3	2.4	1.1	0.8	2.6	5.0	3.5
TOTAL-FOREIGN	1.6	1.5	1.7	2.0	2.3	2.4	1.3	1.5	1.8
United States	3.0	3.1	2.3	3.0	3.6	3.2	2.3	2.3	1.9

Source: Unpublished records of three unidentified enterprises.

[a] n.a. = not available to authors.

Forward Exchange Market

At any point in time, a unit of a multinational enterprise system has a schedule of payments to be made in a nonlocal currency, typically dollars, at specified dates in the future. Such payments might be for dividends, goods purchased, funds borrowed, or interest. In many instances when the unit is located in a country with a weak currency, the enterprise will use local currency to purchase the dollars for delivery on the dates when the dollar payments are due. A premium must of course be paid for this service. The exchange rate is agreed to at the time the contract is made, and the dollars are paid for when they are delivered. If a devaluation does not occur, there typically is a loss on the transaction, representing the premium paid for a hedge against devaluation. (The difference between the price paid for the dollars at the time of delivery and the spot-rate for dollars at the time of delivery is the premium paid for the forward purchase of dollars.) But if a devaluation does occur, there is a gain on the transaction—not necessarily a gain in absolute terms when also considering the payments due, but a gain in comparison with what would have happened if there had been no hedge. The purchaser in effect has brought an insurance policy against the possibility that a devaluation will occur before the dollars are needed.*

A closely related form of protecting against exchange risk is a "foreign-currency swap," which typically is used in countries without a large market in forward exchange. In a foreign-currency swap an enterprise buys a given amount of local currency (usually at the spot rate in the foreign-exchange market) and simultaneously contracts to sell this amount of local currency at an agreed price at a specified future date. In a credit swap, the enterprise grants an interest-free loan in a hard currency to a bank outside a host country; a branch of the bank in the host country in turn lends local currency to a subsidiary in the host country at an agreed interest rate. At the end of a given time period, both loans are repaid in the currency in which they were denominated, so neither party is subject to exchange risk.

Such hedging or swapping to provide funds for known dollar payments in the future protects against "conversion" losses. Remember that these are losses due to settling a debt at an exchange rate different from that existing at the time the liability was recorded on the unit's books. Typically a tax payment is not due on such forward exchange transactions, for the unit buys only enough forward exchange to cover required payments; thus any profit the unit makes by purchasing in the forward market is offset by the conversion loss on the dollar payment due. However, "translation" losses, that is, losses due to restating the subsidiary's worth in terms of the parent's currency, are not tax deductible. Therefore, to offset these so-called losses on the parent's books, a firm would have to purchase enough dollars in the forward market to pay the taxes due on any profit from the transaction and at the same time cover the translation losses.[8]

Many multinational enterprises make little use of the forward market, mainly because of the costs. Typical of the remarks from such firms are: "We've thought about operating in the forward exchange market a couple of times, but the benefit is hardly worth the cost and we haven't bothered with it." "I've looked at our reports and I don't recall ever seeing anything that said we saved a significant amount by hedging. Our hedging costs run a little bit higher than what our devaluation losses would have been."

---

* Some authors distinguish between forward exchange coverage and hedging, in that the forward exchange cover is self-liquidating against an anticipated transfer of funds, whereas hedging involves a reversal of the original forward transaction on or before the due date. We use the two terms interchangeably.

The conclusion that hedging costs are approximately equal to devaluation losses, as economic theory would suggest if one assumes a perfect market, was supported by our calculation of the cost of a series of hypothetical transactions in the forward market. We used actual spot and forward quotations obtained from a bank and actual dividend remittances of one multinational enterprise during a three-year span in seven countries. Measured against $9.1 million remitted by subsidiaries in this multinational system, the amount of money lost by buying dollars forward (rather than accepting the reduced value of the proceeds at the spot rate after the close of the next three-month period) was $64,000, or only seven-tenths of one percent.

In like manner, some firms, comparing the cost of using dollars and hedging with the cost of local borrowing, have concluded that the differential interest cost between dollars and local currency tends to equal the premium paid for buying dollars in the forward market,[9] as economic theory would predict. Said an international treasurer: "Now we check the cost of local borrowing as opposed to the combination of putting the dollars in and hedging; and we find that the cost of the hedge is related to the difference in interest rates. So, we have settled on borrowing in the foreign currency as the easiest and most satisfactory way to provide the protection."

In some cases, after being "called on the carpet" for having foreign-exchange losses, some managers have tended to purchase forward exchange regardless of what the risk of devaluation is. But such widespread purchase of forward exchange by a company is not the usual practice. On the other hand, once there is a sudden increase in the level of the currency risk, the potential loss looms greater and the outcome of long-term experience offers less comfort. In these circumstances most companies tend to "run scared," as an official of a large farm equipment manufacturer put it, and then efforts to hedge the local currency by purchasing foreign-exchange contracts for future delivery become a very common course of action. Typical is the official who explained that the use of forward exchange was not "a strict policy followed in all cases" and that "as a rule, we do not need a forward position, but would take a chance on our anticipated transfers." But in discussing his reaction to an impending devaluation, he presented the standard case in which the forward market is used as a supplementary device without much consideration at that stage to cost factors. "If we figure there will be a devaluation in a currency, and if we have any earnings and the exchange controls permit, then we try to take out every dime as quickly as we can. In addition, we try to get assets in another form so that they are not denominated in a local depreciable currency.

Then, we try to cover dividends by buying forward exchange although we may be refused permission. We also cover payments for imports."

Again, though, just when the forward market is most needed, it is not likely to be available. The forward market in the country of the subsidiary may be closely regulated or nonexistent. True, in New York such major currencies as sterling, Canadian dollars, German marks, Swiss francs, and Dutch guilders can usually be purchased forward. But when a change in the value of even these currencies is impending, the foreign government must subsidize the market for any large forward transaction. The government, through its intermediary bank handling the transaction, usually will want to know the identity of the purchaser and the purpose of the transaction. In the cases of other European and most non-European currencies, a thinness in the forward market is commonplace, frequently because of foreign official regulations.[10] Moreover, the ability of the firms to do much in these circumstances is hampered by the fact that other companies are likely to be adopting similar tactics, thus increasing the demand for forward exchange at the crucial time of need.

Policies Used by Firms of Different Size

The attitude of a multinational enterprise to exchange risk varies sharply in accordance with the size of the enterprise and its experience.

The Small enterprise often feels less pressure than the larger ones to embark upon an organized program to protect against exchange risk, for many such firms do not consolidate their foreign operations and so foreign-exchange losses do not appear directly in the parent's annual reports (see fn. p. 39). Furthermore, the Small firm typically lacks knowledge in this highly complex area. As for the forward markets, the Small enterprise is less likely to use it than are the larger, more experienced firms. Such lack of use is generally by default rather than the result of an explicit plan.

As the enterprise grows and its management becomes more sensitive to multinational problems, its mounting current assets abroad raise the specter of currency losses. Concern with exchange risk looms prominently in its financial strategies and often appears as a motivating factor in formulating policy. From this time on, coping with the uncertainties of changing currency relationships becomes a way of life for its financial managers.

The international treasurer of a Medium enterprise, discussing his company's protection procedures, pointed out that "it is only logical to do it in headquarters where you can look at the whole thing and work out something that makes sense." He then described a situation in which he borrowed funds in Switzerland by an overdraft, then converted these funds into kroner for use in Sweden. Although the kroner was a sound currency, he concluded that "the Swiss franc was the stronger of the two—so I hedged it [purchased Swiss francs forward] in a transaction because I had an overdraft situation that I had to cover." This readiness to hedge is often found in Medium enterprises, which commonly use the forward market more than either of the other two sizes of firms.[11]

The rule-of-thumb philosophy of the Large enterprise is illustrated by a firm in which financial executives in headquarters and regional offices controlled exposure by setting tight limits on subsidiary cash, receivables, and inventories. They relied heavily on local borrowing to serve as an offset to these current assets in case of devaluation. The rule of thumb was that exposure, which they defined as current assets minus current liabilities, should be equal to 5 percent of total assets. The home office and regional executives did all the hedging, and the question of exchange risk was never discussed with subsidiary financial managers. As a critical control figure, the higher executives relied on the "exchange exposure" item that appeared on the monthly operating reports issued by the subsidiaries.

In a Large enterprise, a machine manufacturer that uses a different set of rules, the treasurer ticked off these points: "Here are measures we do in those areas where the threat of devaluation is greatest. We have sufficient local currency liabilities to match the local currency assets subject to exchange losses. On the intercompany accounts we instruct our subsidiaries to buy forward exchange where it seems prudent to do so; for instance, we're still hedging the pound."

In another Large firm, headquarters establishes exposure limits for the different countries and, if these are exceeded, it adopts measures to bring them into line. "We set ourselves objectives by countries; for example, in Mexico our exposure is not going to go over $2.5 million. We would do whatever is necessary to keep it there." Some Large enterprises issue administrative bulletins listing a number of checkpoints in protecting against exchange risks, as shown in the following list of checkpoints from a company manual:

Checkpoints for Managers of Subsidiaries of a Large U.S. Multinational Equipment Manufacturer in Protecting against Exchange Risk *

1. In order to pass the risk of exchange losses to customers, contracts involving the importation of equipment are required to have exchange clauses

---

* *Source:* Copied *verbatim* from company manual (name of company withheld to protect anonymity).

that protect [name of company] beyond the time of actual receipt of funds until their remission to the supplying factory. If a situation develops when a customer cannot pay in convertible currency, an exchange clause is no protection and all terms must be approved by headquarters; in these circumstances, typical protective terms are for the customer to provide a confirmed letter of credit in the currency of the supply works or to pay for all imported materials with a convertible currency that can be legally remitted to the supplying factory or headquarters.

2. All intercompany obligations must be paid when due, if necessary with funds borrowed for this purpose after obtaining headquarters' approval.

3. A "close-up" must be maintained on collections so as to keep receivables to a minimum and to avoid accumulations of cash "beyond the minimum necessary for day-to-day operation."

4. Obligations for future payment of foreign currencies may be protected against devaluation of local currency by buying forward exchange although ordinarily this course is not favored because the costs are likely to exceed the rate at which funds may be borrowed to make immediate remittance; it may be necessary if local borrowing is not available.

5. Actions that may be taken in exceptional circumstances with headquarters' approval are paying intercompany obligations in advance with borrowed funds and buying real estate.

6. Advance deposits required by governments in connection with import licenses must be made by the customer; if, in unusual circumstances [name of company] makes the deposits, the costs must be absorbed by the customer.

7. It may be possible for both the customer and [name of company] to hedge on exchange loss by advance payments.

8. Remittances should not be delayed in anticipation of improved exchange rates nor should any borrowings be made to obtain an exchange profit; borrowings may only be made to protect specific future obligations that are not otherwise protected.

Overall, though, the biggest firms are likely to accept exchange losses more readily than are the Medium enterprises, partly because the Large firm's widespread network of subsidiaries spreads the risk. Thus the Large enterprise is likely to be much more selective in its use of forward exchange, often employing it only to hedge foreign-currency payments expected to be made by the subsidiary in the near future. Other factors reinforce this relaxed attitude of the Large firm toward exchange losses. Their local managements are likely to be local nationals, who sometimes interpret hedging against the local currency as a lack of confidence in the country's economy. Furthermore, the Large firm's policy of maintaining an aura of "good corporate citizenship" hampers it from taking any action that could be construed as lack of faith in the local economy. Very large purchases of forward exchange would be required for full protection, and these could not be kept a secret within the local financial community.

Sources of Information

Obviously, the extent to which a manager can minimize the reported exchange loss due to an actual devaluation depends upon his ability to anticipate the event. As time runs out before the devaluation occurs, adoption of special measures becomes increasingly difficult. As one international treasurer ruefully observed, "As soon as I saw the article in *Business International,* I ran in and called our bank in New York and then asked them what it could possibly mean; but I found out that it was too late to do anything."

Very few firms make their analysis by recourse to basic data, such as those contained in publications of the International Monetary Fund; instead they rely on opinions of others expressed in newsletters and newspapers or given by banks, subsidiaries, and even other companies.

Even though most companies make use of an extensive array of such sources, the personnel of Small firms are much less specialized and their ability to anticipate future developments is comparatively inadequate. The international financial vice president of a Small firm, when discussing his company's measures to cope with a possible change in sterling that was attracting attention at that time, remarked, "Let's take the English pound as an example. One of our men is going to a conference in New York to improve our understanding of what protection we might be able to buy in the event that we thought the pound was to be devalued. The man who is working on treasury-type functions will gain knowledge and perhaps make recommendations—should we transfer funds, and if so, how should we do it—from England to here."

Banks are the most universally used source of information concerning exchange risk—mainly U.S. banks, but also foreign banks. Since these institutions, however, help make the market in forward exchange, they tend to recommend to their customers the automatic covering of exchange risks so that their customers can concentrate on the normal problems of their business without worrying about the added problem of fluctuations in exchange rates.[12]

Naturally, subsidiary managers are used by headquarters as a source of information. But the reliability of this source is reduced by the reluctance of subsidiary managers, especially local nationals, to admit the true weakness of the local currency. For example, a French treasurer of a French subsidiary of a Large firm stated that he would never put anything in writing that suggested that the franc was weak, although he might discuss it by telephone. In another case, a French treasurer of a French subsidiary was ordered to hedge against possible devaluation of the franc, but he was reluctant to do so because he thought such action would be disloyal to France.

The diversity of practice in relying on sources of information is revealed in the following contrasting answers to the same questions by financial officials in the headquarters of Large enterprises.

Question: Do you ever cooperate with other multinational enterprises on obtaining information about expected changes in currency rates?

Answer 1: No. The only time that we have any contact with other companies in the foreign field is when we have a credit problem about a specific customer.

Answer 2: Yes. We talk to our competitors about currency risks.

Question: To what extent do you rely upon the banks for information about exchange risk?

Answer 1: They don't know a damn thing. Half of them, you know, don't travel. So how do they know? All they know is what they read; it's like those newsletters. Maybe some guy writes a good newsletter, but about six others read that newsletter and write their own.

Answer 2: We rely mostly on banks. Banks are experts on most foreign currencies and they have large foreign trading departments. We speak to three or four banks and get different opinions from people whom we consider financial experts with respect to the stability of any particular currency.

Question: Are your own subsidiaries an important source of information?

Answer 1: We're a bit skeptical of their information. We've found that the person in a country doesn't quite see it the same as the fellow outside the country.

Answer 2: Our sources are basically the "subs." We expect our people in these countries to get to know the bankers, know the government officials, keep their ears open, and try to anticipate what's going on.

In the final analysis there seems to be no source of information that is clearly superior to the others. The successful manager most likely will use a variety of sources and eventually make his own decision.

An Example of a Protection Program

Even though Large multinational enterprises purchase less forward exchange—relative to the amount of their exposed assets—than do Medium firms, the Large enterprises are especially likely to evolve relatively elaborate programs to protect against devaluation losses. This is because the economies conferred by large scale operations permit a variety of specialists to be maintained at headquarters, regional offices, and in subsidiaries. An illustration is found in the actual program of Eta enterprise, our code name for a U.S. motor car manufacturer.

At the time of Eta's annual budget meeting, the overseas finance managers gather at the home office with headquarters' management to establish for the ensuing year the financial policy that will be presented to top management for approval. One of the aims of this policy is to give the overseas locations rather specific guidelines on the extent of forward protection that will be purchased. If the financial manager of a subsidiary thereafter desires a change, he must seek the approval of headquarters. A staff specialist in headquarters put it this way: "We might say to a subsidiary, 'Your currency looks a little bit weak, so for the forthcoming year we agree that you're going to cover forward against merchandise payments in dollars.' This gives them a general set of ground rules against which to work. If circumstances change to make these rules invalid, subsidiary management then comes back to us and we agree on any changes in the program."

To assess the status of foreign currencies, Eta's headquarters has specialists in the economic, political, and financing sections who are in constant touch with foreign personnel and representatives of U.S. financial institutions. In the typical manner of Large firms, this enterprise relies on an extensive array of resources for information to support its protection program. The assistant treasurer classified them as follows: "First come the company's own economists and economic analysts located in headquarters. It is the responsibility of this group to study economic conditions around the world, evaluate their results for top management, and to make periodic long-range predictions of future rates in different countries. Included in their information sources is all available published information in magazines and newspapers, banks with international operations, and the management of other American companies operating in host countries. The second resource is personnel located in regional offices. They have a responsibility and sources of information similar to the headquarters' personnel, except that they are limited to the countries for which their regional office is responsible. Third, there are local people in the subsidiaries. The financial manager of each subsidiary is expected to keep informed regarding conditions in the host country and to transmit his findings to the regional offices and headquarters."

In addition to the review at the annual budget meeting, currency conditions are evaluated frequently at headquarters. Each month a special subcommittee of the parent's finance committee meets to check problems of overseas financing, including the constantly underlying question of exchange risk. Among the matters discussed is a quarterly report prepared by the headquarters' staff. The report has a section entitled, "Worldwide Exposure to Exchange Risk by Currency." This section has two regular parts and sometimes a third. The first of the regular parts shows exposure approximately as defined by the financial-asset method, except that inventories purchased in countries with a "weak" currency are now included in the exposure. The second part is presented in the same form but shows exposure modified to include all inventory. These parts therefore contain exposure data—past, current, and projected—by countries classified into those with strong, average, and weak currencies. The third part, if there is one, highlights the data on a specific currency which is in the limelight at the moment.

The European treasurer's office has gone even further in protecting against exchange risk. An economist makes probability estimates of the likelihood of devaluation of each European currency for the next three, six, and twelve months. Then the treasurer's staff, armed with these probability estimates and a gauge of the cost of cover, uses the chart shown in Table 7–4, which is for a three-month hedge. For example, let us assume that the current cost of a three-month hedge is 2 percent on an annual basis. In the "cost of cover" column of the chart, the 2 percent row is located and cover is purchased if there is greater than a 24.5 percent probability of a devaluation of 2 percent within the next three months. Or cover is purchased if there is greater than a 9.8 percent probability of a devaluation of 5 percent within the next three months. And so on across the row corresponding to the expected devaluation percentage. Actually the probability estimates are not quite this fine. More likely, if the cost of cover is an annual 2 percent, the European manager will use approximate relationships as a guide. He will figure, say, that he will break even if there seems to be one chance out of ten for a 5 percent devaluation within three months, but will make money on the average if there is greater than one chance out of ten. Similar charts are available for periods of one, six, nine, and twelve months, though forward exchange typically is purchased for a period of one to three months. Decisions to hedge are cleared with headquarters' personnel, although at the time of our interview the European treasurer was attempting to obtain more authority in such matters.

In spite of all these relatively "sophisticated" measures, the headquarters' managers of Eta implied that overall the firm had a net loss on their actual purchases of forward exchange compared with the alternative of never purchasing forward exchange. And the European treasurer stated that the only time that the European region had had a net gain on purchasing forward exchange was immediately after the 1967 sterling devaluation.

TABLE 7–4

Form Used by U.S. Multinational Enterprise Eta to Aid in Making Decision to Purchase Forward Exchange (Three-Month Period of Cover)

Cost of Cover at Annual Rate, Percentage	Probability of Devaluation That Will Make Cost of Cover Equal to Expected Exchange Loss						
	2%	5%	8%	10%	12%	15%	20%
0.5	6.2	2.5	1.6	1.2	1.0	0.8	0.6
0.6	7.5	3.0	1.9	1.5	1.2	1.0	0.7
0.7	8.7	3.5	2.2	1.7	1.4	1.2	0.9
0.8	9.9	4.0	2.5	2.0	1.7	1.3	1.0
0.9	11.1	4.5	2.8	2.2	1.9	1.5	1.1
1.0	12.4	5.0	3.1	2.5	2.1	1.7	1.2
1.2	14.8	5.9	3.7	3.0	2.5	2.0	1.5
1.4	17.3	6.9	4.3	3.5	2.9	2.3	1.7
1.6	19.7	7.9	4.9	3.9	3.3	2.6	2.0
1.8	22.1	8.8	5.5	4.4	3.7	2.9	2.2
2.0	24.5	9.8	6.1	4.9	4.1	3.3	2.5
2.2	26.9	10.8	6.7	5.4	4.5	3.6	2.7
2.4	29.3	11.7	7.3	5.9	4.9	3.9	2.9
2.6	31.7	12.7	7.9	6.3	5.3	4.2	3.2
2.8	34.0	13.6	8.5	6.8	5.7	4.5	3.4
3.0	36.4	14.6	9.1	7.3	6.1	4.9	3.6
3.2	38.8	15.5	9.7	7.8	6.5	5.2	3.9
3.4	41.1	16.4	10.3	8.2	6.9	5.5	4.1
3.6	43.4	17.4	10.9	8.7	7.2	5.8	4.3
3.8	45.8	18.3	11.4	9.2	7.6	6.1	4.6
4.0	48.1	19.2	12.0	9.6	8.0	6.4	4.8
4.2	50.4	20.2	12.6	10.1	8.4	6.7	5.0
4.4	52.7	21.1	13.2	10.5	8.8	7.0	5.3
4.6	55.0	22.0	13.7	11.0	9.2	7.3	5.5
4.8	57.3	22.9	14.3	11.5	9.5	7.6	5.7
5.0	59.5	23.8	14.9	11.9	9.9	7.9	6.0
5.2	61.8	24.7	15.4	12.4	10.3	8.2	6.2
5.4	64.0	25.6	16.0	12.8	10.7	8.5	6.4
5.6	66.3	26.5	16.6	13.3	11.0	8.8	6.6
5.8	68.5	27.4	17.1	13.7	11.4	9.1	6.9
6.0	70.8	28.3	17.7	14.2	11.8	9.4	7.1
6.2	73.0	29.2	18.2	14.6	12.2	9.7	7.3
6.4	75.2	30.1	18.8	15.0	12.5	10.0	7.5
6.6	77.4	31.0	19.3	15.5	12.9	10.3	7.7
6.8	79.6	31.8	19.9	15.9	13.3	10.6	8.0
7.0	81.8	32.7	20.4	16.4	13.6	10.9	8.2
7.2	84.0	33.6	21.0	16.8	14.0	11.2	8.4
7.4	86.1	34.5	21.5	17.2	14.4	11.5	8.6
7.6	88.3	35.3	22.1	17.7	14.7	11.8	8.8
7.8	90.4	36.2	22.6	18.1	15.1	12.1	9.0

A Taste of How Computers May Help

When the computer model of a multinational enterprise is programmed to maximize the system's consolidated profit after taxes, exchange losses are not necessarily minimized; but the computer automatically generates a policy to protect against devaluation. As part of this policy, the model employs a number of financial practices that real-life firms use prior to an expected devaluation, such as increasing dividends to the parent, paying intercompany accounts to countries with strong currencies and delaying intercompany accounts to countries with weak currencies, increasing royalties and management fees, increasing local loans owed in a country with a weak currency and shifting the funds to a stronger currency.

The model does not include all options available to real-life enterprises, such as changing the terms on local accounts receivable or accounts payable, changing the price of goods sold locally, changing the amount of inventories, deviating from planned expenditures on fixed assets, delaying payment of taxes to local government, or buying forward exchange.

In principle, this model's transactions—sometimes chains of transactions—are directed at increasing local liabilities denominated in a weak currency and reducing liabilities denominated in a strong currency. For instance, year 2 sees devaluations of 10 percent in country B and 21 percent in country C. The model's response consists in part of having subsidiaries B and C, prior to the devaluations, use their liquidity (in weak local currencies) to pay (in dollars) all current liabilities owed to the parent, A. Borrowing capacity in local currencies exists in both subsidiaries after these operations are completed, so the model considers all possible alternatives of converting this debt potential into devaluation profits; two of these alternatives are: (1) both subsidiaries borrow in their local currencies and pay dividends to the parent prior to devaluation, and (2) C borrows and lends the proceeds prior to devaluation to B for investment by the latter in short-term financial investments denominated in B's currency. The relative merits of each of these alternatives can be followed in Table 7–5.

Part I shows the balance sheets of both subsidiaries as they would have appeared after devaluation if local borrowing had been undertaken only to pay off liabilities to the parent.

Part II shows the balance sheets as they would have appeared if alternative (1) had been implemented. Under the borrowing rules in effect for the model, subsidiary B would have been allowed to borrow in local currency

TABLE 7-5

Effect of Alternative Financial Practices on Devaluation Losses. Multinational Enterprise Model for Year 2 (Post-Devaluation Balance Sheets in Millions of Local Currency Units of B and C and Exchange Loss Savings in Millions of Dollars)

PART I: LOCAL BORROWING UNDERTAKEN ONLY TO PAY OFF DEBT TO PARENT

	Subsidiary B		
Current assets	157	Current liabilities	60
Fixed assets	52	Long-term debt and equity	149
	209		209

	Subsidiary C		
Current assets	102	Current liabilities	12
Fixed assets	22	Long-term debt and equity	112
	124		124

PART II: NEW FUNDS BORROWED BY BOTH SUBSIDIARIES AND
REMITTED TO PARENT AS DIVIDENDS

	Subsidiary B		
Current assets	157	Original current liabilities	60
Fixed assets	52	New borrowing	56
	209		116
		Long-term debt and equity	93
			209
Exposure reduction:	56	Exchange loss saving:	$5

	Subsidiary C		
Current assets	102	Original current liabilities	12
Fixed assets	22	New borrowing	57
	124		69
		Long-term debt and equity	55
			124
Exposure reduction:	57	Exchange loss saving:	$10

B some LC*B*56 million and subsidiary *C* would have been able to borrow in local currency *C* some LCC57 million.* Remittance of these funds as dividends to the parent would have cut exposure by exactly those same

---

* According to the rules of the model, subsidiary *B*'s current assets after devaluation had to be at least equal to (1) 1.2 times current liabilities excluding local borrowing, plus (2) 1.52 times the local borrowing. In subsidiary *C* the current assets after devaluation had to be at least equal to (1) 1.15 times current liabilities excluding local borrowing, plus (2) 1.54 times the local borrowing.

TABLE 7–5 (*Cont'd*)

Effect of Alternative Financial Practices on Devaluation Losses. Multinational Enterprise Model for Year 2 (Post-Devaluation Balance Sheets in Millions of Local Currency Units of B and C and Exchange Loss Savings in Millions of Dollars)

PART III: SUBSIDIARY C BORROWS FUNDS AND LENDS TO SUBSIDIARY B

		Subsidiary B	
Original current assets	157	Original current liabilities	60
New short-term assets	266	New borrowing from C	292 [a]
Total current assets	423	Total current liabilities	353 [b]
Fixed assets	52	Long-term debt and equity	122
	475		475
Exposure increase:	266	Exchange loss increase:	$24
		Subsidiary C	
Original current assets	102	Original current liabilities	12
New lending to B	321 [a]	New borrowing	266
Total current assets	423	Total current liabilities	278
Fixed assets	22	Long-term debt and equity	167
	445		445
Exposure reduction:	266	Exchange loss saving:	$46

[a] C's loan to B is denominated in dollars. Hence the $266 becomes LCB 292 after B's 10 percent devaluation and LCC 321 after C's 21 percent devaluation.
[b] Does not total because of rounding.

amounts. This would have reduced the exchange loss by $5 million in *B* and $10 million in *C* for a total saving of $15 million for the system.

Part III shows the balance sheet implications of alternative (2), that of intersubsidiary lending. The key element in this alternative is that *C* could increase its local borrowing more by granting loans to *B* than by paying dividends to *A*. The explanation is that the short-term lending in dollars to *B* becomes a current asset for *C*, against which *C* is entitled to borrow additional local currency. Each new borrowing makes possible the conversion of local currency to dollars and a new dollar loan to *B*, generating potential for further borrowing. Thus a multiplier is at work, thanks to which *C*'s original current asset base of 102 million in local currency *C* supports additional local borrowing of LCC 266 million. This leads to a net gain by subsidiary *C* from the 21 percent devaluation of 56 million in local currency *C*—or $46 million. *C*'s lending to *B* in turn forces *B* to increase its asset base in order to satisfy its requirements of a minimum current ratio. To this end, B makes no dividend payments and instead acquires short-term local paper denominated in local currency, and thus has an increase in exposure. The new short-term paper acquired by B generates an exchange loss of 27 million in local currency B—or $24 million. But B's loss of $24 million is more than compensated for by C's gain of $46 million, leaving a gain of $22 million for the system as a whole. This outcome is superior to the $15 million that would have been saved by full local borrowing and dividend remissions to the parent—alternative (1)—and as a result the model naturally includes (2) in its policy for the year.

When the timing and size of the devaluations are known, as is the case with the model, the development of a suitable policy is straightforward, although it may be very complex as has been illustrated in the foregoing example taken from the model. The exchange-risk problem arises in the real world, however, from the uncertainty surrounding both timing and size of devaluations or revaluations. Thus the design of a strategy of reducing exposure—and loss—requires not only estimating the future course of exchange-rate developments but incorporating explicitly the uncertainty surrounding such forecasts. In this setting the policies developed by the model become *conditional* policies for a *given* sequence of exchange-rate developments, for example, devaluations of 10 and 21 percent at the end of year 2 in B's and C's currencies respectively. A procedure incorporating uncertainty in exchange-risk policy could be developed by laying out the different time paths that the exchange rates subject to risk might follow and then working out a single optimal policy given that uncertainty is faced. This would require a change in the model to include the capability of "scenario programming." [13]

EIGHT / Evaluating Performance

The managers of each multinational enterprise, surveying the world from their aeries in American skyscrapers, think of their overseas ventures as a system and in different degrees operate them as a system. But when the moment arrives to add up the score and judge the performance of the individual foreign units, the system in all its interrelationships is apt to get hidden under an account book. This is a serious defect, though an understandable one. Evaluation of performance is perhaps the most confused aspect of the multinational scene.

The Basic Measures of Performance

"Our foreign subsidiaries are judged on precisely the same basis as domestic." Financial officers of almost all multinational enterprises say something of this sort. However, often the changes made in the financial reports of various foreign subsidiaries to reflect the different circumstances under which they operate render the similarity more superficial than real; but let's begin by looking at those basic criteria. They are (1) the rate of return and (2) the subsidiary's performance relative to a budget.

THE RATE OF RETURN

Rate of return on what? In a sizable minority of enterprises, primarily those engaged in rapidly expanding fields and thus strongly oriented toward growth, the main performance standard is a specified return on sales. An official of one such enterprise explained, "We are interested in annual sales growth and the gross margin earned on those sales. These two figures taken together indicate our ability to continue to grow. Return on investment is not as significant a figure." Such firms, however, are an exception to the general pattern, for typically the spearhead of the performance evaluation of foreign operations is some form of return on investment.

Such measures relate income to assets. The income figure is usually net income before taxes. Sometimes it is gross operating income, sometimes net income after taxes. Two measures are most often used as the invest-

143

ment base. One is equity and the other is total assets *after* depreciation, with about the same number of enterprises employing each. A much smaller number of firms use total assets *before* depreciation.

The simulation model reveals the different results obtained when using two different indicators of the investment base. When each unit in the system is operated at arm's length from the others, the system's return is 25 percent on total equity and 19 percent on total assets after depreciation. When the entire system is operated as an integrated network to achieve maximum profit, the return on equity is increased to 31 percent; but, owing to the massive short-term borrowing that protects the system against devaluation losses, the return on total assets after depreciation drops to only 13 percent.[1]

Because of this problem of specifying the appropriate investment base and because of other problems encountered in attempting to use return on investment as the sole measure of performance, most multinational enterprises use some supplementary device to gauge their foreign subsidiaries' accomplishments. The most important is the budget, and in many instances this becomes the primary tool while the rate of return becomes a supporting measure.

THE BUDGET

Management reasons that if suitable objectives are defined in the budgetary process, then a subsidiary that meets budgeted levels is likely to have performed well. (To be sure, the budgets contain a lot of judgment as to what is a "suitable objective," so in this respect it is a circular measure —good performance is what you once thought it should be.) Moreover, by stressing the need to adhere to the budget, management can place pressure upon the subsidiary to maintain high standards.

Multinational enterprises almost universally follow the same budgetary procedures in their foreign and domestic operations. All subsidiaries are required to report at the same time substantially the same information with the same format. Typically, the budget culminates in two sets of documents. A capital budget lists individual projects with an indication of their profitability. An operating budget contains pro-forma income statements, balance sheets, and cash flow projections. The capital budget is prepared on a yearly basis and the operating budget on a monthly or quarterly basis for the forthcoming fiscal year. The budgets of a solid majority of firms also cover longer periods such as three to five years. Approval of the subsidiaries' budgets is done at the highest levels of the company, not uncommonly by the president and on occasion by the parent company's board of directors.

Although standard budgetary procedures throughout a multinational system are commonplace now, their introduction for foreign subsidiaries is relatively recent, somewhat more than half the firms we interviewed having instituted such practices since 1960.

The Adjustment of Financial Statements

The fact that rate-of-return and budgetary procedures are similar to those used domestically gives the illusion that evaluation of foreign subsidiaries is performed in the same way. Actually a number of changes are made—and a lot more ought to be made—in the financial statements of foreign subsidiaries in an attempt to give headquarters a clearer picture of the performance of the subsidiaries.

Some of the needed adjustments grow out of the difficulty of allocating income within the system. Profit earned by the multinational enterprise as a whole is not always easily attributable to one subsidiary or another, and regular accounting statements can be unenlightening.

Our model illustrates the difficulty of allocating profit to the "right" subsidiary, assuming that "right" exists as an ideal concept—often it's unavoidable to be arbitrary. Remember that the simulated system has a parent and two subsidiaries, B and C. The performance of each subsidiary varies with the degree of the other subsidiary's integration into the system. For example, the inclusion of B as part of a group of units that functions in an optimum pattern increases the enterprise's profits by 2 percent if C is operating at arm's length, but by 10 percent if C too is part of an optimum pattern for the system. On the other hand, the inclusion of C as part of a group of optimized units increases the enterprise's profits by 5 percent if B is operating at arm's length, but by 14 percent if B too is part of an optimum pattern. Now, when both B and C operate in an optimum pattern for the system, does one assume that B is contributing 2 percent or 10 percent to the system or that C is contributing 5 percent or 14 percent?

Another example from the model: Under full optimization the greatest contribution is made by C; its after-tax profits over four years are $180 million compared with only $60 million in B. This relationship, however, is brought about only because the parent has required the subsidiaries to engage in a series of financial relations that benefited the entire system rather than any one subsidiary. If management standardized those relationships and insisted upon arm's-length dealings between all units of the system, the positions would be reversed; B's profits would be $75 million, C's only $66 million, as shown in Table 8–1.

So there are serious complications in measuring and assigning the bene-fits of intercompany transactions, and it is not surprising that most multinational enterprises are reluctant to use other than a standard inter-company price in weighing performance. A minority of firms do take into account the earnings of the rest of the enterprise system which could be at-tributed to the operations of the affiliate being judged. They have to use considerable judgment in making such allocations, for it is difficult to de-termine the exact state of affairs that would exist if the subsidiary did not exist. For example, the transfer of goods through the corporate system is influenced by tax considerations and other complicating features of inter-national business. As one manager stated: "When it's an export item from the United States, it can go through three or four companies."

TABLE 8-1

Distribution of Profits as a Result of Different
Financial Policies. Multinational Enterprise Model,
Totals for Four Years (In Millions of Dollars)

	Consolidated Profits After Taxes	
Unit of System	Arm's Length Financial Policy	Optimal Financial Policy
Parent A	264	231
Subsidiary B	75	60
Subsidiary C	66	180
TOTAL SYSTEM	405	471

The need for adjustment to intercompany transactions pertains not only to goods but also to services. When headquarters, for instance, instructs an affiliate in an area with low interest rates to finance an affiliate in an area with high interest rates, how are the costs and benefits to be assigned when performance is evaluated? In an enterprise that borrows heavily, interest charge is an important cost, as one headquarters' official observed. "In this company, who pays the interest is a very big deal because it can affect the operating results of individual subsidiaries tremendously. It is one of the complicating factors in measuring subsidiary performance. Oftentimes, loans are taken out in particular geographical areas because of attractive terms and sent back to the home office or invested in other areas. The question is who pays the interest. If the foreign jurisdiction pays, even though the borrowed funds are not used there, they are in effect covering part of someone else's costs." When each subsidiary is judged as a separate profit center, granting intercompany credit can create a conflict between the interests of the subsidiary and those of the system. An official described it this way: "Sometimes we tell a subsidiary to give more merchandise credit or charge lower interest rates to another subsidiary than the managers of the selling subsidiary would prefer, and we have quite a battle with them when we suggest from the corporate point of view that it's the thing to do. They're being judged on a profit-center basis and they can give you ten dozen reasons why you can do it some other way. We certainly don't like to force it on them because they have the profit-center responsibility, but nevertheless we use intercompany credit as a financing device, and it does help out one or more subsidiaries that way."

So much for adjustments due to the circumstance that the subsidiaries being evaluated are not independent companies but cogs in a machine. Managers who judge performance also have something else to worry about and allow for—the uncontrollable variety of the world scene. Each subsidiary's performance is affected by the national conditions in which it labors.

Government restrictions on such items as remittances on capitalization may press heavily upon the operations of some foreign subsidiaries and rest only lightly on others. Barriers against transferring funds to the parent may hold down a subsidiary's rate of return by causing an excessive accumulation of cash that has to be placed in local money-market outlets where it earns relatively little income and is subject to devaluation risks. Required capitalization ratios may produce an undesired build-up in the investment base. Variations in interest rates from country to country do not exactly result in equally favorable opportunities for all subsidiaries, and so adjustments have to be made, whereas, in the words of one official, "In the United States, we don't adjust for interest expense."

Now enters again the familiar problem of accounting. Under the accounting principles of one country, a subsidiary may show a profit that could be substantially raised or lowered if expressed according to the requirements of another country. For example, the timing of the recognition of revenues is important whenever a subsidiary engages in installment sales. In the installment method of accounting, profits are reported when realized through collection or sale of the account. In the accrual method, the profit is counted in income at the time of sale and the applicable provision for income taxes also is charged against income at the time of the sale. When a large portion of an enterprise's business arises from installment sales, and when the subsidiaries do not all employ the same accounting method, vexing complications arise in trying to evaluate their performance.

Evaluation can also be affected by the attitudes, customs, and institutions of different lands. Foreign managers in some countries, as in Japan, are accustomed to viewing results in terms of sales growth and employment stability; thus they tend to be relatively indifferent to the significance of the rate-of-return measures relied upon more heavily in the United States. They tend to resist the use of such measures and to oppose efforts at changing established habits. One official mentioned other cultural factors thus: "You have to make some allowance for the fact that you get greater productivity out of people in the United States and in some foreign countries than you get in other foreign countries. Also, your foreign subsidiaries have to grant credit to their customers for a longer period of time than in the United States, so that causes a reduction in your return on assets. Reasonableness has to be the criterion of evaluating anybody. If you impose upon your foreign managers controls that are not reasonable within their cultural pattern, you're not going to be able to retain the management. So, we work within cultural patterns."

Conditions abroad not only differ, but often change fast. An official referred to the need for making "adjustments to the original budget based on things we feel are not within the control of the affiliate at all. In this way the manager's actual performance is determined only for items we feel are really under his control. Massive devaluations, for example, in the Latin American countries are adjusted."

The subsidiary's performance may be downgraded or upgraded depending upon the reasons why actual results deviate from the budget. An official made reference to factors that contribute to such deviations: "We generally have an analysis by country that shows the items that affect profits; these are market penetration, industry volume, all the different elements of cost, economies achieved, and pricing. We try to show item by item what's really affecting profit versus budget versus last year."

Small, Medium, and Large

Behind the facade of generalizations about how multinational enterprises evaluate performance are the variations in tactics flowing from the different size characteristics of firms.

THE SMALL ENTERPRISES

The distinctive feature of the evaluation measures of the Small multinational firm is informality. This theme runs through the comments of the financial officials of these firms. Typical is this assertion: "I will not burden our foreign subsidiaries with specific reporting unless I need it. Many of them are small and their managers complain about the fact that even monthly statements are unheard of in their countries. And I don't think that our headquarters' people have time to do a detailed review of the subsidiary's reports."

Thus it is not surprising to find that when Small firms do make rate-of-return calculations they invariably make them solely on the basis of local operations without any reference to benefits received or costs incurred elsewhere in the enterprise.

Headquarters' managements of Small firms, reluctant to impose extensive reporting systems on their overseas subsidiaries and to evaluate reports that do come in, tend to rely pretty heavily on personal visits. As an official curtly observed, "You can't do it from home; you've got to have a man on the scene." Budget procedures often are timed to coincide with a meeting of headquarters and subsidiary personnel, even if it delays budget review and approval. One headquarters' manager explained, "We like to discuss the proposed budget with the local manager. We have been able to arrange in some instances for them to come here. Sometimes we have delayed it until we have a chance to make a trip to one of the locations." In the meantime the local operations may be substantially left alone.

Moreover, as a headquarters official of still another Small firm stated, "Budgeting is another process that in the foreign area is nowhere as near as sophisticated as it is domestically. Our foreign subsidiaries don't have the size of staff that the domestic divisions have. Furthermore, some of these foreign businesses are growing very rapidly. Also, they have some different seasonal factors than you have in this country. You may find that this is a slack time in the United States and therefore a good time to prepare a budget. In some other country it could be abolutely the worst."

All such factors not only contribute to informality. In some Small firms they almost remove the budget as an effective instrument of evaluation. Headquarters simply does not believe itself capable of making independent judgments. "After all, we don't know what the problems are," said one official. "Therefore, our subsidiary president has got to make the judgments. All that headquarters can do is look at the consequences and ask questions." And the treasurer of a Small firm, explaining further the superficial attention given to subsidiary reports, commented, "After all, we're not a company that has been international for many years like the big corporations."

THE MEDIUM ENTERPRISES

Remember that when the sales of a firm's foreign affiliates climb above $100 million a year or thereabouts, supervision by headquarters is tightening, often stage by stage geographically. The Medium firms use rate of return as an indicator of performance and a formal budget as a supporting measure, but the fact that headquarters' management keeps a close eye on the overseas activities means that its budgetary policies usually are relatively relaxed. Besides, many Medium firms, lacking experience with a tightly controlled budget, have not yet developed the extensive adjustments and rules of thumb that are sometimes used by Large firms in comparing one subsidiary with another.

When a rate of return is used to judge the performance of a subsidiary, the Medium firm is more likely than either the Small or Large firm to consider the income and assets of the entire system on an integrated basis rather than on the basis of only the subsidiary's records as an independent entity. For example, one official stated that return on investment was calculated on a consolidated basis and explained: "We take what a subsidiary has made and add to it the intercompany profits and the intercompany royalties; the result is what we say is the true profit contributed to the corporation." An official of another firm, also emphasizing each subsidiary's contribution to the overall system, spoke as follows: "We don't have a set formula for return on investment. We are so integrated that much material flows from one plant site to another. The parent company manufactures a product and sells it to one of the international export companies at an intercompany transfer price. The international export company sells it to a sales subsidiary, and the sales subsidiary finally makes the sale to a customer. So you see, there are two companies backing up this guy who's doing the actual selling, and each is skimming off some profit. It's only been recently that we've been able to add all of these profits up and find out what the true profit on that sale is."

THE LARGE ENTERPRISES

On the surface the difference between the Medium and Large enterprises in measuring the performance of their subsidiaries is not so great; both appear to rely on rates of return and on budgets. Yet, underneath, the difference is substantial. Whereas the reviews and procedures of the Medium enterprise still have an aura of informality, those of the Large enterprise have become rigid. To control and evaluate its scattered and diverse foreign subsidiaries, the big company must rely upon some formal scheme to bring order to what otherwise would be chaos. The budgeting and review process, characterized by carefully organized meetings, has become a compulsive ritual in which all elements of the system participate in establishing the objectives of the subsidiaries and the rules that they will follow to achieve these objectives. In this sense, the budgetary procedure becomes the structure that guides the financial activities of the subsidiaries without the necessity of constant overview by headquarters.

These Large companies have had extensive experience in controlling their far-flung empires by means of the budget. Most of the firms instituted their budgetary systems prior to 1960. An official of one Large firm noted how the system had become a way of financial life for the managerial group: "Everybody lives by the system. Many of the general managers and top people in this company came through the finance route and are highly indoctrinated with the system. Therefore, we do not have a great deal of difficulty in getting people to just follow the system." It is not surprising that in response to the question of the criteria selected to judge the performance of the subsidiary, the official said laconically, "The budget is the key thing."

Since the performance evaluation of the Large firm is built around procedures, directives, and rule-of-thumb standards, there tends to be a relatively impersonal evaluation at headquarters. This condition exists in domestic subsidiaries, too, but it is aggravated in the international area where distance and communication provide serious obstacles to direct exchanges. The Large firm is more likely than the Small or Medium firm to calculate and compare rates of return of individual foreign subsidiaries, specific foreign countries where more than one subsidiary operates, and broader geographical areas such as Europe and Latin America. The few multinational enterprises that use either total remittances or dividends to the parent as a measure of subsidiary performance are likely to be Large ones, which typically have a number of mature subsidiaries returning funds to the United States in such magnitudes as to make an important contribution to the parent's ability to pay dividends. One big firm provides specific checkpoints along these lines: "Are royalties payable remitted on a current basis? Are dividend remittances aligned with established policies? Are intercompany accounts settled within thirty days?" An official of another Large firm noted, "We judge our foreign subsidiaries on the progress they are making in maintaining the proper flow of dividends to us." But even in these cases, remittances are only one of several budget items considered in measuring performance.

Yet the headquarters' managements are ordinarily aware of the big differences in circumstances that may detract from the significance of such comparisons. Therefore, as already discussed, headquarters at times makes adjustments to the subsidiary's operating results. For example, an executive of one Large firm said, "We have what we call 'formula assets' for our overseas locations. For example, the supply lines are much longer and the plants carry quite a bit more inventory than a domestic plant would. Foreign subsidiaries very often have excessive amounts of cash because of regulations preventing the sending of cash out of the country. So what we do is formularize cash, receivables, sometimes inventories; this puts them on a comparable basis with a plant in Kansas City."

The budgetary approach to judging performance provides management, especially those of Large enterprises, with a simple means of ascertaining the extent to which the subsidiaries meet prescribed yardsticks. Headquarters can develop a series of supporting guidelines against which any deviations from the budget can be checked. Through reports received routinely through channels, managers in headquarters compare the periodic changes in various revenue segments to ascertain if prescribed rates of improvement are being achieved, and in the various expense segments to determine if desired reductions are being achieved. To the extent that the changes from year to year follow the expected course, a favorable light is shed on the subsidiary's performance.

One big firm uses the following guidelines to help evaluate each of its foreign operating units: "Does the gross income of each division increase by at least a given percentage of the accepted plans? Is the latest estimate of the current requested plan in line with the accepted plans? Do gross profits by division show improvement or at least remain stable? Do depreciation costs and custom engineering show stable or declining percentages? Are any operating expense items increasing faster than the growth in revenue and, if so, are they explained?"

In this same vein, an official of another Large enterprise stressed the need to give attention to variations in the level of the budget from year to year. So long as there is progress in the absolute levels of growth, there can be some minimum assurance of some degree of progress. "I must admit that all of us at headquarters, including top management, look at comparisons with last year. We don't always fully trust the budgeting system because there are so many adjustments."

In spite of the apparent willingness on the part of some Large firms to make adjustments for "peculiar circumstances" encountered abroad and to judge on the basis of changes from year to year, in fact their managers are trapped by the extensiveness of the international empire. They are forced to return again and again to the use of tangible measures embodied in budgetary guidelines so that subsidiaries might better know what is expected of them and so that headquarters can readily evaluate the results.

The case of one Large firm is typical. Its managers in headquarters recognize that some subsidiaries have never been profitable, others are only recently operating in the black and their returns are still at a distance from the target, and still others which once hit the mark are now far from it. So the managers actually judge performance by the subsidiaries' ability to meet budgetary levels which are immediately geared to the realities of local conditions—with the rule of thumb forever lurking in the background: "We have a target of making an 8 percent return on the assets. We're not doing that at any place, but that's our target overseas. When we reach that target we'll want more, I suppose. And some countries are harder than others. In Puerto Rico we'll possibly in my lifetime never achieve an 8 percent return on assets. But other subsidiaries I think will. Great Britain reached that sometime in the past and I think it will reach it again. In France we're losing money; our goal right now is to get France profitable. Once it's in the black, the drive will be to push it on and on until we reach that 8 percent. We have accepted a plan and we look at that plan monthly and measure just where they are against the plan. And if they're below plan, they're not doing well. And if they're above plan, they are doing well."

Of course, rules of thumb are used for items other than profits. An official of one Large firm told us: "We are getting hold of some yardsticks as to how much new product sales we are entitled to for a dollar invested. We are putting our finger on all of our subsidiaries to help them know what they have to do if they want to grow so much in the next five years. There is a formula and it is predictable to arrive at that growth." And, to be sure, the subsidiaries are judged by whether their growth in sales corresponds to the rule of thumb.

The evaluation picture for Large enterprises can be put into focus as follows: Although the budget is a tool employed by practically all enterprises in the evaluation of overseas subsidiaries, it assumes special significance in the Large enterprises. In such firms, the budget is a major yardstick against which subsidiary operations may be gauged. In these relatively sophisticated systems the managements use a number of supporting measures whose current changes help throw light on the subsidiaries' performance. The impersonality of this relationship and the desire to judge the relative performance of units within the network leads to the use of worldwide and regional comparisons. But it is often necessary to work out a series of adjustments in an attempt to hold the subsidiaries responsible for those items over which they have control. Yet, at the end, the adjustments made by Large firms are relatively minor in scope.

The Omnipresent Conundrums *

In spite of the adjustments made to provide an adequate means for measuring results, two unsolved problems continue to haunt the multinational enterprise.

CONUNDRUM NO. 1: CHANGES IN CURRENCY VALUES

In measuring performance, headquarters must decide the extent to which the managers of its overseas subsidiaries are held responsible for foreign-exchange losses. Concerning a subsidiary which has experienced a devaluation or revaluation, management would reach different conclusions depending upon whether the outcomes are expressed in dollars or local currency. In our simulation model, for example, subsidiary C's average rate of return on total assets is 13 percent calculated on the basis of local currency and 10.5 percent when based on dollars. In the real world there is no clear-cut solution used by all firms. Slightly less than half judge the subsidiary in terms of local currency and about the same percentage judge the subsidiary in terms of dollars, with only a small minority using both standards.

Enterprises that judge subsidiary performance in terms of local currency do not believe that local managers have the primary burden for protecting against devaluation. Often this is an area in which headquarters issues pronouncements *ex cathedra* that determine the action taken by the subsidiary to reduce its exposure risk. To be sure, local management ordinarily is expected to make recommendations, but headquarters is regarded as better equipped to view the full range of currency problems, consult with specialists in the international field, study the protective actions that may be pursued, and select the best alternatives.

An official described as follows his company's policy of substantially freeing local management from the responsibility of protecting against large fluctuations in exchange rates: "The management of the subsidiary is not responsible for devaluation losses. The treasury office here [in headquarters] is very much concerned with what happens from a devaluation point of view, and in this sense we're quite centralized. We sit here trying to figure out at all times how to minimize the exchange loss that we have on whatever devaluation occurs. All sorts of analyses are made to figure out how we did. Did we gain, did we lose, did we do all the things that

* Conundrum: A problem to which only a conjectural solution is possible (Webster).

could have been done in hindsight to minimize or eliminate the exchange loss? But as far as the subsidiary performance is concerned, devaluation is excluded."

In short, many enterprises believe that the objective of a performance review is to gauge the operating efficiency of local management rather than its financial acumen, particularly with respect to avoiding exchange losses.

Still, judging a subsidiary only in terms of local currency ignores the fact that the subsidiary's operating results are affected, sometimes substantially, by the factors that cause devaluations and revaluations. As an extreme case, measuring the performance of a Brazilian subsidiary in the 1960's by using profits reported in cruzeiros not adjusted for purchasing power would have given a grossly overoptimistic picture.

Enterprises that hold their subsidiaries responsible for dollar performance point to the fact that a U.S. multinational company eventually must express the outcome of all its operations in dollars. Since the entire system is judged in terms of dollars, they think each element within it also must be judged on this basis. "When you make a consolidated statement," one official said, "you have to have a prominent currency, and if you're a U.S. company it has to be dollars." He then stressed top management's position: "They're interested just in dollars. They don't even want to know how many pesos are in a dollar, what's an Australian dollar worth compared to the U.S. dollar, or what's sterling worth. They don't give a damn. It's strictly dollars."

The same official mentioned the problems the firm has encountered in getting its subsidiary managers to think in terms of dollars. Along the same lines, an official of another company, which had recently switched to making valuations in terms of dollars, declared that reaction to a dollar review was especially acute when local management was in the hands of nationals rather than Americans. "Well, I think that we are getting them a little more oriented to dollar thinking. I know that a good many of them, particularly in some of the countries where we don't have American personnel, tend to think in local currencies. They try to ignore this idea of devaluations because they say, 'We are dealing in pesos, the currency of this particular country, and therefore should be judged in pesos, and not dollars, because even though there is a devaluation of, say 40 percent, the rise in the cost of living locally may be only 10 percent. Therefore we cannot adjust for this big devaluation.' "

Even if one agreed that in all circumstances dollars were a more appropriate measure of a subsidiary's profits than local currency, difficulties would still arise because of the one-year period often used to judge performance. Consider the case of a subsidiary with profits that rise rapidly each year in local currency, but much of the rise is due to rapid inflation. In a given year rapid inflation can substantially increase the dollar value of local earnings, whereas in the next year devaluation, a direct result of the inflation, can substantially *reduce* the dollar value of local earnings. Hence, in dollars, the subsidiary is reporting profits that oscillate from year to year rather than the relatively smooth profit picture that would occur if longer periods of time were used as performance intervals.

CONUNDRUM NO. 2: THE BENT MEASURING STICK

Although managers make adjustments to income streams and asset bases when evaluating foreign subsidiaries, most evaluations still take place with an implicit standard that the subsidiary is an independent company. The underlying assumption is that this entity is subject to review by using return on investment if only a few adjustments are made in the results. The truth is that this is an incorrect standard or "bent measuring stick," for its use neglects to consider the reasons for which the subsidiary was originally founded.

As mentioned at the outset of this book, foreign investments by U.S. multinational enterprises are typically defensive in nature, being part of a long-run strategy to preserve the enterprise's position in a world economy, or at least slow the decline of its position.

In manufacturing subsidiaries, a foreign investment typically takes place when the U.S. enterprise is in danger of losing a foreign market because of the cumulative effects of a number of items, such as freight, tariffs, and factor costs. These effects combine to make it necessary to have a local plant in order to serve the local market. The manager perceives that if his enterprise doesn't make the investment, a rival will do so and capture the market. Further, by manufacturing in a country, the enterprise will obtain more information about market conditions within the country. Alternatively, and increasingly in recent years, the market in question is not the country in which the plant is established: it is the United States or a third country. But the basic motivation of survival and growth in a world industry is still the same, for in these cases the manufacturer invests abroad to obtain low-cost foreign labor or materials in order to remain competitive with his rivals, many of whom at this stage of an industry's development are European and Japanese.

This defensive psychology also is at work in the natural-resource industries, where foreign investments consist mainly of acquiring new reserves and of developing more diverse sources to match those of competitors.

In sum, there is a common desire to reduce risks by diversifying and acquiring knowledge regarding new markets and new sources. At all times the matching of oligopolistic rivals and the keeping out of newcomers are underlying motives.

To be sure, multinational enterprises have formal capital budgeting systems, and the request to the board of directors for specific authorization to make the investment contains the results of elaborate calculations, varying in sophistication from a simple computation of average return on average investment to computer models that calculate a large number of possible outcomes based on different sets of assumptions.[2] Yet, since the investment decision is of a strategic nature, such formal documents are likely to be collections of assumptions and resulting estimates which operating management must provide to its board of directors but for which formal approval is a foregone conclusion.[3] (Anyone who has prepared such documents knows from experience the great variation in estimated profitability that results from a relatively minor change in one of several key variables, such as product price, product volume, or raw material costs.)

Such calculations often include tangible income to be received or costs to be incurred by other units in the enterprise's system. For example, when an automobile company constructs an assembly plant abroad, profits received by the parent because of the components shipped from the United States are included. So are royalties and management fees to be received by a parent.

Certain other tangible items that represent income or costs to the system are more difficult to value and so usually are omitted from the calculations. One example is a parent's guarantee of a loan made by a subsidiary —and, of course, there usually is a substantial difference between the cost of the guarantee to the parent and the worth of it to the subsidiary. Another example is the cost of holding a safety inventory in the United States to serve several foreign operations in addition to the U.S. operations. As in the case of the loan guarantee, the cost of this extra safety stock needed in the United States for the foreign plants is smaller than the cost of safety stock if each subsidiary held its own.

Then there are the intangible items. Their worth or cost is even more elusive, and to date they have universally been omitted from the formal calculations because of the difficulty of quantifying them. No major oil company, for example, wants to risk being left out of a potentially giant oil field, even though calculations of expected costs and returns might show a loss when discounted cash flow procedures are used. The risk of a rival's finding a huge low-cost oil field and thereby gaining a superior long-run competitive position is too big for an enterprise to take. And in manufacturing, the long-run risk to a firm is great if a rival expands more rapidly and thereby achieves greater economies of scale.

All these items—whether tangible or intangible—that were not entered formally into the original investment calculations are rarely taken into account by any multinational enterprise in evaluating the performance of its foreign subsidiaries.

Perhaps two or more years after final approval of the investment, the subsidiary's physical plant is completed and begins operations. The subsidiary then is incorporated into the regular control system of the enterprise. By this time the top executives in the parent firm, who made the decision to invest, are preoccupied with other strategic problems. Chances are, too, that many of the managers who were involved in the studies which preceded the investment decision have moved to other assignments or have largely forgotten the strategic nature of the investment decision, the intangibles involved, and the crudeness of the profitability estimates. Thus, with the passage of time, the estimates that were put in the request to the board of directors for funds have taken on weight.

Those are some of the reasons why a firm attempting to adjust all records so as to allocate income perfectly to the appropriate units within the system encounters acute complexities.

Even the simplest problem of all, that of allocating profit on the items that were included as part of the original profitability estimates, does not yield an easy solution. To be sure, when the original investment decision is being made, some managers try to determine the true economic consequences of the decision to the enterprise by estimating all relevant costs and income that the new subsidiary would have. However, firms rarely attempt to make precise determinations after the subsidiary commences operation, for such determinations are unwieldy, often involving a number of products and subsidiaries. Further, the operations of the subsidiary are likely to be considerably different from those originally planned and to be constantly changing in terms of products and markets.[4] Thus, for the purpose of measuring the performance of the subsidiary, a standardized price derived from the company's accounting system is used. An official of a manufacturing enterprise is speaking: "In considering a new foreign investment, we take into account all profit over the marginal cost of all components shipped from our Michigan factory to the foreign plant. But later, when we report the profit or loss of the subsidiary, we use a standard intercompany price that is based on average costs plus a profit."

The principle of using marginal cost for the investment decision and a standard price for measuring performance is not restricted to intercompany sales of components, but also applies to capital equipment and a variety of services. In one case, a multinational enterprise started a subsidiary in Brazil with used equipment that had little value in the United States, but the equipment had substantial value in Brazil and the Brazilian subsidiary was charged accordingly. Little managerial time was needed in starting the subsidiary because the manufacturing know-how was low in technology and easy to transfer and the marketing programs were transferred from the United States and modified by a locally hired sales manager. The cash investment was small because of local borrowing. After the subsidiary commenced operation it was expected to meet the enterprise's goal (used for all subsidiaries) of earning, after taxes, 10 percent on the subsidiary's equity; and in addition it was expected to pay a fee of 5 percent of sales for managerial and technical know-how.

Charges to the subsidiary for technology or services are often seen in a different light by the managers on opposite sides of the boundary. Sometimes these charges are related to the needs of the parent for funds, but even in cases in which an attempt is made to determine an "economic value" the results are cloudy. The actual costs to the parent of providing the services to the subsidiary usually are quite low, but the value to the subsidiary can be substantial. Yet when no free market exists for such services, the "true" value is indeterminate and sets awry any measures involving profits. An official said concerning this problem, "Our foreign operations pay technical service fees to the United States, and it is difficult to figure how much of these technical service fees are really earned and how much of them are just a means by which the parent obtains some return on its investment."

In the case of one chemical enterprise, all new products are introduced in the United States. Then only those products that have succeeded and are deemed likely to succeed in Europe are introduced in Europe. No attempt has been made to capture the cost of such screening in the United States by adjusting the technical fees charged by the parent to the European operations; yet records show, and it is widely believed in the firm, that European operations are more profitable than U.S. operations.

In brief, managers evaluating performance tend to forget the purpose of the original investment and the melange of numbers that went into the profitability calculations. Or, if they remember, they are likely to make adjustments which are so incomplete that it is self-delusion to believe that the true economic benefits of the subsidiary are measured. Presumably the true economic benefits of the subsidiary could be determined by comparing the entire enterprise system with and without the subsidiary in question, but such an exercise on a regular basis for a number of subsidiaries would be hopelessly complex. So the evaluation problem usually is solved by relying heavily on the meager hard data that are available—the profits reported by accountants.

The problem might not be so bad if the arbitrariness and limitations of profits as measured by accounting records were kept in mind, but they seldom are. Two examples will illustrate.

First, take the case of the Brazilian investment based on used equipment (mentioned on page 158). The executive committee of the parent firm, at one meeting, actually held a serious discussion of whether to sell the subsidiary, on the ground that it was unlikely to meet the corporate goal of 10 percent after taxes.

Second, consider the world oil industry. Oil companies make large investments in European refineries and marketing facilities as an outlet for crude oil from Africa and the Middle East. But the price structure is such that most profits are attributed to crude oil production; and therefore some subsidiaries engaged only in refining and marketing run continuous losses. Oil company executives, bank newsletters, and other responsible sources state that refining and marketing operations in Europe are not profitable. Within the enterprises there is a well-known feeling by managers that refining and marketing are not profitable but are just necessary "evils." Yet the companies continue to invest hundreds of millions of dollars in such operations for they are necessary to the profitability of the overall system. Of course, the oil industry is not the only one for which observers take at face value the statements that are published about the profitability of foreign subsidiaries.[5]

In sum, it is not realistic to consider a subsidiary as an independent operation when in fact it is an organic part of the worldwide corporate network. The profits reported by a subsidiary inevitably contain a high degree of arbitrariness, for the "true" value of a subsidiary to the system exists only as an ideal concept. Yet such conclusions are overlooked when it comes time to evaluate the performance of the subsidiary.

NINE / Maximizing Profits

Very few multinational enterprises try to integrate the financial links available to them into a grand design that embraces all elements of the system. For the big firms any such planning structure would be extraordinarily complex and would place heavy demands on both the prescience and skills of the managers; accordingly, policy is likely to be fashioned by using simplifying rules. For the Small firms, planning of this scope usually is beyond their financial ken. Moreover, the latitude of accounting conventions enables managers to make cost and revenue allocations that obscure the actual contribution of any unit to the profits of the system. On top of all this, when we study actual cases, the interrelationships among motivations, policies, and financial results are blurred by the inadequacy of information. Thus optimal action for a firm in the real world depends on the system, the environment, and the various constraints on management—and those constraints are formidable.

Accordingly, the computer model offers insights into optimality that a review of actual cases would not. In prior chapters we presented isolated actions taken by the model in optimizing its results; in this chapter we present a broader picture of the results.

Let us review the conditions in the world of the model. The production and sales plans are assumed to be beyond the control of the financial manager; hence, except for prices on sales between units of the system, all production and sales figures are exogenous inputs into the model. The results of a variety of financial policies may be studied at will. There are only a parent A and two subsidiaries, B and C; the future can be predicted with certainty; information and implementation are costless; the enterprise is not "risk averse" and so the value of earnings to the enterprise is not reduced by variations that occur in the earnings; and the enterprise has a linear preference function, that is, a dollar gained is valued the same as a dollar lost. The object of policy is to maximize profits after taxes for the consolidated enterprise over four time periods, each one of which simulates a year's activity. Achieving an optimal policy requires the utilization of all available financial linkages in a system that is in general equilibrium. Despite these simplifications, the issues that arise and the type of decisions that have to be reached prove to be useful simulations of real-world situations.

161

Like the financial executives of most multinational enterprises, the model increases profits by placing major emphasis on minimizing taxes, saving interest costs, and avoiding exchange risks. As would be expected, it places substantial profits in subsidiary C, which is located in a low-tax jurisdiction; and it allows C not to pay discretionary royalties or management fees. The model reduces interest costs by instructing C, which is located in a country with high interest costs, to borrow from subsidiary B and parent A when C needs funds. And it avoids exchange losses by having C borrow heavily in the local money markets just prior to country C's several devaluations and move funds to units in the system operating in areas with stronger currencies. By and large, these tendencies follow the patterns that managements in real life commonly pursue.

Where the model begins to strike off on an independent route is in its extensive use of intercompany financial links. In one period or another, it takes advantage of every link at its disposal to move funds within the system. A summary showing the extent to which these links are used is given in Appendix B. Management of an actual firm usually does not exploit such a wide gamut of opportunities.

Whether handling a vast array of financial links, as occurs in the model, or a small number, as more often takes place in fact, officials of a firm have to resolve conflicting issues. For this purpose the model measures the influences of the pertinent factors in its ambit and elects a course that makes the maximum contribution to profits. Rarely do managers in real life undertake a rigorous analysis of this type. Yet optimality requires such an approach in order to find the most appropriate one solution, for, as we illustrate below, the optimal solution is not obvious.

Transfer pricing is used by the simulation model primarily as a means of reducing the overall tax incidence. For this purpose, the relative impact of corporate taxation and duties is always considered. For example, since income taxes are lower in country C than in A and B, it is desirable from the system point of view for both A and B to price their products to C as low as possible, thereby recording profits in C rather than A and B so as to reduce the system's income tax payments. Furthermore, low prices on imports by subsidiary C minimize the payment of import duties to country C which are high. Thus, as both country C's income tax relative to A's and B's and country C's import duties indicate a low transfer price from both A and B to C, it is not surprising that the model adopts this solution in all years. It is not equally clear, however, whether C should raise its price to B in order to deflect more profits to itself, or lower this price in order to permit B to pay less in custom duties. By measuring the results that follow from each choice, the model chose to raise prices to B as much as possible because under the conditions of the model that method provides the greatest benefit to earnings.

Because transfer pricing is important in shifting profits to minimize taxes, it would appear desirable for parent *A* to raise prices to *B*, as *B* pays the highest rate of income taxes in the system. At the same time, one would expect *B* to pay extensive interest charges on all its intercompany debts as well as to collect the minimum allowable interest on its loans to other units in the system. But the results of the model indicate that the optimal policy does not coincide with the intuitively obvious solution. Indeed, parent *A*, when selling to *B*, actually reduces its sales price to the floor. And *B* pays only the minimum allowable interest charges on its borrowings from *A*.

At least part of the explanation of this set of policies lies in *B*'s role as a conduit. The parent shifts taxable income through *B* to *C*, because *C* is subject to the lowest tax rate in the system. By charging *B* a low price for goods and freeing it from the burden of paying interest charges, *A* provides additional income to *B*. In turn, *B* lowers its selling price to *C* and raises its buying price from *C*, thereby transmitting the extra profit to that unit. The shifting of profit from *A* to *B* enables *B* to serve in this conduit capacity because without the added income *B* would have had zero earnings and under constraints built into the model, a unit is barred from employing financial tools in such a way as to produce a deficit in its own operations; furthermore, with zero earnings, *B* would pay no income taxes and therefore would have no incentive to shift profits to *C*.

Subsidiary *C* borrows from its parent and affiliated subsidiary in year 1 and year 3 in order to keep down the system's borrowing costs, but in year 2 and year 4 it runs into a conflict between the two subgoals: minimizing interest charges and avoiding exchange losses. To minimize interest charges, *C* ought to continue to borrow from *A* and *B*. On the other hand, to strengthen its position with respect to devaluation, *C* ought to borrow locally and remit the funds elsewhere in the system. The model evaluates the costs of paying higher local interest rates against the benefits of reducing exchange exposure, and it elects the latter course.

Still another problem that requires solution arises from the implementation of credit policy. On the one hand, *C* might collect all accounts receivable from *B* as promptly as possible in order to invest them at the high rate available in its own area. On the other hand, it might defer collections in order to charge *B* interest, thereby creating a deductible cost in a high-tax jurisdiction and providing offsetting income in a low-tax country. In years 1, 2, and 4, the model finds that the desirable course is for *C* to permit receivables from *B* to remain uncollected up to the 180-day limit and to charge interest on the outstanding amount. But in year 3, *B* pays off all receivables due to *C* from year 2 as well as paying cash for all purchases from *C,* thereby not generating any intercompany accounts.

In the formulation of optimal strategy, an analytic chain is linked together to determine the successive effect of each financial transaction. For example, Figure 9–1 indicates that transfer pricing has a bearing on the corporate income taxes of both seller and buyer as well as on the import duty of the buyer. Thereafter, the liquidity of seller and buyer becomes a factor in the outcome because liquidity is closely tied to their borrowing capacities. Changes in the ability to borrow influence both interest costs and the foreign-exchange exposure of each of the units involved. These two aspects then feed back on the enterprise's profits before taxes and hence on taxes. Even in the simple equations on which the model is based, this and other analytic chains are sufficiently complex to result in enor-

FIGURE 9–1

The Transfer Pricing Chain

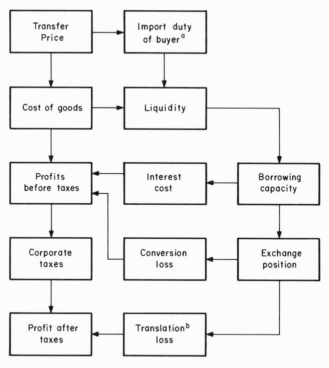

[a] Only item not affected for both buyer and seller.

[b] Under certain conditions a translation loss could affect profits before taxes, see note 8, chapter 7.

mous difficulties in obtaining an optimal solution without the assistance of a computer, and unexpected optimal solutions often emerge. So it is not surprising that in the real world the maze of interrelationships embodied in a firm's intricate web of subsidiaries forces managers to adopt various compromise solutions rather than strive for a system optimum using all possible financial links.

The model was used to determine the results of the financial policies typically used by our three size categories of multinational enterprises— the arm's-length policy simulating the Small multinational enterprise, the rule-maker simulating the Large multinational enterprise, and the optimal policy simulating the Medium multinational enterprise. Table 9–1 shows results of performance indicators for the three major types of financial policy.

TABLE 9–1

Performance Indicators of Three Basic Financial Policies.
Multinational Enterprise Model, Totals for Four Years
(In Millions of Dollars)

	Policy		
	Arm's-length	Rule-maker	Optimizer
Consolidated profits			
after taxes	405	436	471
Effect on profits:			
Exchange profit			
or loss	−18	3	53
Total income tax			
and import duty	−483	−477	−482
Interest earned minus			
interest paid	−33	−30	−40

As might be expected, the lowest consolidated profits after taxes are recorded when the units operate on an arm's-length basis, that is, none of the financial links connecting the units can be maneuvered to increase profits. On this basis, the profit figure is $405 million over the four-year period simulated by the model.

The use of the intrasystem financial links allowed under the rule-maker policy lifts the system profits to $436 million, or 8 percent higher than those achieved under the arm's-length policy. The increase in profits is achieved primarily by converting an exchange loss of $18 million to a gain of $3 million (a net gain of $21 million); reducing taxes and customs duties by $6 million despite the higher amount of profits earned; and saving

$3 million on interest charges. The saving of interest costs was small because of the greater borrowing required under the rule-maker policy in order to make the exchange gain.

Under an optimal policy, consolidated profits after taxes are $471 million, which is 16 percent higher than the arm's-length figure and 8 percent higher than the rule-maker. Once more the major reason for this enhancement is the system's ability to take advantage of currency relations, as an exchange profit of $53 million is now shown. Interest charges, at $40 million, actually are greater than under the other two policies because of the additional borrowing required in order to make the exchange gains. Also the tax total is higher than that of the rule-maker policy, and this is because of larger before-tax profits, which in turn require higher payments of income taxes. These higher income taxes result even though the shifting of taxable profits between tax jurisdictions actually produces an average tax rate (including duties) of 51 percent compared with 52 percent under the rule-maker policy and 54 percent under the arm's-length policy.

At least two aspects in which the model and the real world differ have an important impact on profits—the number of units in the system and the opportunity for exchange gains.

Compared with the parent and two subsidiaries in our multinational enterprise model, the giant multinational enterprise system in real life may contain over 100 units, in which several dozen are engaged in manufacturing. An increase in the number of subsidiaries means an increase in the number of national environments and a widening of the disparities in national interest rates and national tax systems. At the same time, the financial links over which funds may be shifted are multiplied.

Table 9–2 offers some clues to the significance of increasing the number of subsidiaries in the model. The numbers in the first and last columns are the same as those given in the preceding table—that is, all arm's-length and all optimal. But the two middle columns are different. In the all-arm's-length column, consolidated profits after taxes are $405 million. But if all of the financial links connecting parent A with subsidiary B can be maneuvered within limits to increase profits (while C continues to deal at arm's length with A and B), the profits of the system increase by about 2 percent, to $414 million. On the other hand, if full use can be made of the financial links between the parent and C while B operates at arm's length with A and $C,$ the profits of the system are increased to $427 million, or 5 percent greater than the arm's-length profit of $405 million. The greater improvement through optimizing the parent-C links rather than the parent-B links is due to the large difference in the exchange loss, from $17 million down to $6 million. When the financial links connecting both subsidiaries to the parent and to each other are used, the profits of the system spurt to $471 million, which represents a gain of 14 percent over the parent-*B* combination and 10 percent over the parent-*C* combination. Thus, the inclusion of two subsidiaries in the optimization network raises the system's profits by a larger percentage than adding one.

The reason why added subsidiaries offer new opportunities for profits is fairly obvious. More financial links exist for the shifting of funds and profits among units of the system without running up against some constraint in the model. Moreover, the existence of three units rather than two in the optimization network permits one unit to function as a financial pipeline through which funds and income may be shifted between two other units. In addition, there are more opportunities to shuttle funds back and forth

TABLE 9–2

The Effect on Financial Results of Number of Subsidiaries Included within System Optimization. Multinational Enterprise Model, Totals for Four Years
(In Millions of Dollars)

		Financial Policy		
	Arm's-length	Optimization of Parent-*B* Links (*C* is at arm's length)	Optimization of Parent-*C* Links (*B* is at arm's length)	Optimization of All Links (No units at arm's length)
Consolidated profits after taxes	405	414	427	471
Exchange profit or loss	−18	−17	−6	53

between units in order to take into account differences within the environment, such as different rates of interest.

To be sure, in real life a system probably reaches a point in its development when the incremental profits from one additional unit do not justify the costs of the extra managerial burden. To the extent that this negative effect occurs, however, it may well be very far out in the size range.

The second aspect in which the profit potential indicated by the model differs from that in the real world is gains from devaluations. Such gains are of less potential importance than the model itself suggests. First of all, changes in exchange-rate parities are probably smaller and less frequent in real life than in the model. Of the two subsidiaries in the model, one is assumed to be located in a developing country where heavy devaluations occur every second year. The second subsidiary operates in a developed area, and the 10 percent devaluation every fourth year is bigger than would be expected for areas of this sort. Moreover, in the model, funds are moved in and out of the developing country with much greater freedom than ordinarily would be possible. In addition, the model, operating with no doubts about future movements in exchange rates, is able to increase profits beyond what they would otherwise be every time a devaluation occurs. Finally, the model is uninhibited on political grounds in earning a profit on devaluations.

Thus offsetting influences must be taken into account in comparing the model with the real world. Because of the limited number of units in its system, the model is deprived of important potential benefits that could be garnered by effective use of added financial links. On the other hand, it enjoys special and significant advantages in the foreign-exchange area. Without attempting to assign exact weights to these two factors, we think it not unreasonable to assume that one comes near to balancing the other, and therefore neither enters into our conclusions about the profits that can be made by real multinational enterprises by improving their financial practices.

Our interest is in the actual increase of earnings that might be achieved by a firm in any given size class that learns effectively to use all the financial tools and links at its disposal. For this purpose, we estimate roughly that in 1968 the typical Small multinational enterprise earned $30 million in consolidated profits after taxes from its worldwide activities (including U.S. operations), the Medium enterprise $60 million, and the Large enterprise $400 million.[1] Then, putting the model to work, we can estimate how much a firm with an arm's-length policy or a rule-maker policy loses as a result of its nonoptimizing approach.

We have already seen (from the figures in Table 9–1) that when the model followed an optimizer policy it made 16 percent more profits than it did with an arm's-length policy and 8 percent more than it did with a rule-maker policy. Now, assuming that the firm with an arm's-length policy has worldwide profits of $30 million, as did the average Small multinational enterprise in 1968, we see that such a firm would have made $4.8 million more by pursuing an optimal policy (16 percent of $30 million). If one assumes that the rule maker has annual worldwide profits of $400 million, as did the average Large multinational enterprise in 1968, then such a firm would make $32 million more by pursuing an optimal policy (8 percent of $400 million). This is about as far as we can go at present in using the model to estimate potential gains to be made in the real world. For any single enterprise, however, the model could be modified to simulate the firm's financial system and an estimate of potential gains could be made by comparing profits using current practice with the profits that could be earned using an optimal policy derived from the model.

For all U.S. foreign direct investors—not just the 187 companies identified as multinational enterprises in this book—we estimate that the potential savings to be made by improving their financial policies are about one-quarter of their total *foreign* earnings; this would have been an improvement of some $3 billion in 1972 and presumably more in subsequent years.[2]

The gain to be derived from optimum financial policies depends to some extent, of course, on the characteristics of the industry in which a firm operates.

For example, a high ratio of current assets to total assets permits opportunities to maneuver current assets and create current liabilities so as to reduce exposure and even to make exchange gains. The number of subsidiaries per dollar of foreign sales and the proportion of intrasystem sales are rough indices of the degree to which intrasystem relations arising from the movement of goods may be used to shift funds and income. If this index is high, transfer pricing, interaffiliate receivables, and interaffiliate interest payments may be important tools. The proportion of wholly owned subsidiaries provides a gauge of management's freedom from conflicting interests when employing intrasystem financial links. The technology level reflects the usefulness of technical fees as a device for transfer of funds. High advertising expenditures suggest a relatively high degree of product differentiation, which in turn makes it easier for management to use transfer pricing. Also, a firm with high advertising expenditures is likely to be able to collect a high management fee from subsidiaries.

Illustrations of industries that appear to have above average opportunities to employ financial tools to increase profits are drugs, cosmetics and soap, farm machinery, office machinery, and electrical machinery. Except for the cosmetics and soap industry, which is in the low-technology category, each industry has an "average" or "above average" designation in every benchmark mentioned in the preceding paragraph.

The picture is somewhat different for fruits and vegetables, industrial chemicals, and transportation. In these cases, the opportunities to use financial tools to increase profits are average or below average. Enterprises engaged in the canning and distribution of fruits and vegetables have a relatively large number of subsidiaries per dollar of foreign sales, thereby providing opportunities for intrasystem shifting of funds. Offsetting this advantage, however, is their low technology level and only average designations in the other characteristics. True, the industrial-chemicals industry has a high technological content; but firms in this industry are handicapped by a high proportion of joint ventures, which limits their freedom to use intrasystem financial links, and a low ratio of current to total assets, which limits their facility to engage in foreign-exchange and interest arbitrage.

Petroleum refining, tires and tubes, and nonferrous metals are examples of industries where important barriers to optimization seem to exist. For one thing, the presence of joint ventures creates a hampering influence; and in petroleum refining and nonferrous metals the ratio of current to total assets tends to be particularly low. Though the intrasystem flows of goods are relatively high in these industries, many of the products are sufficiently standardized that variations in transfer prices cannot be very wide.

However, as individual enterprises vary widely in status within one industry, an analysis for an individual firm is needed to determine the level of potential savings.

Regardless of what industry a multinational enterprise finds itself in, optimization has its costs. At the outset, out-of-pocket charges arise from the additional personnel, time, communication interchange, and computer facilities required to do various things. These things include making an accurate description of the system, gathering the required information, formulating an appropriate policy, and monitoring the transactions with the various units involved. But most firms have planning staffs for their domestic operations, and many have staffs for their foreign operations as well, for even firms following an arm's-length policy are likely to have made some limited efforts at overseas planning. It is also commonplace in the United States to use computerized accounting systems that could provide the basis for the additional record-keeping and model-designing activities entailed in a full-blown optimization program for worldwide financial activities. Typical Medium and Large enterprises will have made steps in this direction through adoption of financial policies tied to some subgoal, such as tax minimization, or through formulation of rules to govern the relationships among their subsidiaries. In general, therefore, the added charges required to design and implement a profit-maximizing system will not prove prohibitive.[3]

But these tangible costs could be overshadowed by intangible ones caused by frictions generated through requiring subsidiaries to take action counter to their own interests although beneficial to the system. Complaints on this score by local managements are common.

Table 8–1, in the preceding chapter, showed the wide variations that occur in the reported earnings of the different units in the computer model

when different financial policies are used. For example, subsidiary *B*'s after-tax profits were $75 million when operating at arm's length but only
$60 million when operating as a cog in an optimal system. Furthermore,
B's earnings under an arm's-length policy are relatively stable, starting at
$15 million in year 1 and showing a slight increase in all subsequent
years. In contrast, under an optimal policy, *B*'s earnings plummet from
$15 million in year 1 down to zero in year 2.

If these conditions existed in the real world, it would not be surprising
for *B*'s management to object on two grounds—its earnings are lowered,
and they are changed from a consistent to an erratic pattern. As discussed
in Chapter 8, multinational firms have adopted different ways to deal with
this problem, such as judging local management on its ability to meet variables presumed to be controllable—that is, amount of sales, costs of manufacturing, and similar items. Despite these efforts at eliminating distor-
tions in results created by centralized planning, local executives are loath
to see a good performance eroded. Accordingly, the restraints imposed on
headquarters' management in its dealings with different units represent an
intangible cost of seeking an optimal policy.

In any given case the ultimate decision of management rests upon how
it evaluates the benefits and the costs. However, as the pressures of worldwide competition mount, the U.S. multinational enterprise will find it more
essential to explore all the financial tools at its command to achieve an optimal outcome. In taking this course, the firm sometimes may find it desirable to adopt policies that governments believe are hostile to their own
interests.

TEN / The Future

Like the Holy Grail, optimality is something to strive for. It represents an alluring prize to the multinational enterprise searching for greater profits. The potential gain of over $3 billion for all U.S. foreign direct investors is a rich stake. The extent to which firms can capture $3 billion or more depends on (1) the continuation of the environmental differences among countries and (2) the freedom that the firm has to use its financial links. The outlook for these two factors, therefore, is vital to the quest for optimality.

The Environmental Differences

Environmental factors of particular importance to the financial manager of the multinational enterprise are currency strength, interest rate, and the tax charge. Inequalities in these elements among countries allow the enterprise to increase its profits after taxes by moving funds throughout the system; thus, a look at the future of these inequalities is important in any projected vision of financial management in the multinational enterprise.

EXCHANGE RATES

International considerations are paramount in determining exchange rates. Since the creation of the International Monetary Fund in 1944, an official mechanism for working out agreements has been available. The original idea was to obtain adjustment of balance-of-payment positions through infrequent modifications in otherwise rigid exchange rates. The system provided for the United States to buy gold at the designated price of $35 an ounce and for other countries, in turn, to maintain the market values of their currencies within a narrow band of one percent on either side of par values established in relationship to the dollar.

For years the system worked well, but after a long period of U.S. balance-of-payments deficits and the resulting heavy speculation against the dollar, President Nixon effectively devalued the dollar on August 15, 1971, suspending the convertibility of dollars into gold. Subsequently the price of gold was set at $38 an ounce, but dollar convertibility into gold was not restored. To provide more flexibility for small adjustments in currency val-

173

ues, other countries agreed to hold their currencies within a band of 2¼ percent on either side of par values established in relationship to the dollar. In 1973 the dollar was again devalued.

The devaluation of the dollar, the setting of wider bands, and the floating of key foreign currencies shattered the relatively inflexible arrangements advocated by the International Monetary Fund. Nations nowadays are less inclined to suffer reduced economic growth, unemployment, and loss of currency reserves just in order to avoid a change in the value of their currency. Thus the wider bands and the floating of some currencies, plus this more flexible attitude on the part of governments, have increased for the multinational enterprise the perils of greater exchange losses or, depending on one's viewpoint, the opportunities for exchange gains.

INTEREST RATES

Interest rates are an important instrument of economic control. High rates discourage business firms from borrowing and thus are anti-inflationary. Low rates are conducive to borrowing and thus provide capital for business growth. Governments regulate rates directly through law and indirectly through their central banks, which control the reserves of commercial banks and thereby affect their ability to grant loans.

Though the domestic aspect of interest is paramount, the domestic and international aspects are to some extent interdependent. Interest rates have been regulated by governments to affect international flows of capital. For example, during the early 1960's the United Kingdom often raised rates to curb the outward flow of funds. Raising the rates also may have the effect of attracting short-term capital from abroad, and this too has sometimes motivated governments. On the other hand, in July 1971, to discourage the influx of speculative capital, West Germany did not allow financial institutions to pay interest on part of the funds brought into Germany by nonbanking corporations.[1] A month later, as the international currency crisis heightened, the French government prohibited banks from paying interest on foreign deposits of less than ninety days in order to stem the inflow of dollars. For the same reason, the Swiss government ruled that any funds deposited by a nonresident after a specified date would receive no interest.[2]

In order to stimulate exports, central banks have granted preferential rates to foreign bills of credit. For twenty-five years, Japan held its export financing rate below the discount rate and only abandoned this policy in August 1971 to ease the pressure for a rise in the value of the yen.[3]

The influence of interest rates on the movements of short-term capital was reflected in the 1970 annual report of the International Monetary

Fund. The Fund pointed to the desirability of better international coordination so that interest rates and other credit policies can be more uniform among nations, thereby minimizing speculative flows of short-term capital. As part of its program to equalize interest rates, the Fund also urged nations to make more use of tax policy for domestic purposes.[4]

Even though there has been external pressure for nations to harmonize their interest rates, this influence has been moderate. It is hardly likely to unbend national policies that have hardened to the use of interest-rate changes as a device for helping to manage domestic economic conditions as well as international capital flows. Thus it is unlikely that international agreements on interest-rate policy will smooth to any marked degree the rate dissimilarities that arise among countries because of domestic requirements.

TAXATION

Taxes not only give national governments a source of revenue but, like interest rates, are a means of economic control. The United Kingdom, for example, changed its laws in the 1960's to provide for a separate tax on income distributed as dividends by corporations, in order to encourage the retention of earnings and enlarge the amount of funds available for capital investment. In contrast, the West German law was changed to permit a low rate of taxation on corporate earnings that are paid as dividends. Because of the multiplicity of domestic interests at play, taxes, unlike exchange rates and interest rates, are considered almost solely the domain of the national government. Indeed, national governments value their prerogatives to manipulate the corporate tax structure to such an extent that taxes have seldom been equalized across a number of countries.

It is true, however, that in recent years forces have been moving in the direction of equalizing differences. A number of bilateral tax treaties between countries have been made. In the 1960's the European Economic Community reached agreement on a common value-added tax. In July 1970, the Organization for Economic Cooperation and Development agreed to undertake a study of the international aspect of taxation. A year later, the U.S. Secretary of the Treasury proposed that consideration be given to the feasibility of creating a continuing secretariat with its own staff of experts to work on development of international codes of conduct on tax policy.[5]

Pressure for more international coordination undoubtedly will persist. Multilateral agreements, primarily between developed countries, will be worked out to resolve tax questions. Initially the agreements will cover such items as value-added taxes, withholding taxes on foreign investment income, and discriminatory treatment of foreign investors. With respect to the last item, for example, the European Economic Community has put forth tentative plans for harmonization of efforts to attract new plants through investment incentives such as fast tax write-offs.[6]

Later, perhaps, multilateral agreements will be used to bring together the tax policies affecting multinational enterprises. But this development will be slow in coming, and national governments will jealously guard their own spheres of interest. This means the continuation of substantial tax differences among countries for the next decade or longer.

Freedom to Use Financial Links

Sometimes, when governments deliberately create differences in environments among countries, they do it to encourage enterprises to take actions that both increase the enterprise's profits and meet the goals of the government. An example is the raising of interest rates to attract short-term capital.

On the other hand, adversary conditions sometimes exist between multinational enterprises and nations, for the additional profits from multinationality are often earned either directly or indirectly at the expense of governments. If a firm moves money to avoid an exchange loss, currency relationships may be upset. Interest arbitrage by a firm may interfere with a nation's monetary policy. If an enterprise takes deliberate action to save taxes, some governments usually will have less revenues.

Thus, moves by the enterprise to operate as a worldwide system may run head on into countermoves by governments to keep steady the value of their currency, collect revenues, and control their interest rates. The severity of these countermoves in limiting the ability of the enterprise to transfer funds will be strongly influenced by how important those transfers are to the revenues and balance of payments of the affected countries.

IMPLICATIONS FOR GOVERNMENT REVENUES

It is hard to gauge the effects that a move toward optimality by multinational enterprises will have on the revenues of a government. In the world of the model, however, this information is readily available.

The redistribution of revenues to governments as a result of the adoption of an optimal financial policy instead of an arm's-length policy by the multinational system in the model is illustrated in Table 10–1. The substantial impact on income taxes and custom duties is clearly revealed. The optimal financial policy for the model reduces Country A's revenues from

TABLE 10-1

Distribution of Revenues to Governments Caused by Alternative Financial
Policies. Multinational Enterprise Model, Totals for
Four Years (In Millions of Dollars)

Financial Policy of Multinational Enterprise	Country A			Country B			Country C			A+B+C
	Income Tax	Import Duty [a]	Total	Income Tax	Import Duty	Total	Income Tax	Import Duty	Total	Totals
Arm's-length	265	0	265	118	16	134	36	49	85	483 [b]
Optimal	237	0	237	94	16	110	95	39	134	481

[a] Country A receives no import duty because the parent does not purchase from the subsidiaries.
[b] Does not total because of rounding.

the multinational system by 11 percent—from a four-year total of $265 million to $237 million—and country B's revenues by 18 percent. On the other hand, country C's revenues rise by 58 percent because its lower tax rate encourages the enterprise to record its profits in that country. Hence the total amount of income taxes and custom duties paid to all three governments is about the same with an optimal financial policy as with an arm's-length policy, although the system's consolidated profits after taxes are 16 percent higher. Should the enlarged earnings later be disbursed by subsidiary C as dividends to the parent, country A's income would rise, but such a payment could be deferred indefinitely.

Not only are the total revenues of each government in the model affected by the financial policy of the multinational system, but the pattern of change also undergoes considerable modification. For example, the jagged movement of country's C's revenues from year to year when the system follows an optimal policy is in sharp contrast to the very mild changes under an arm's-length policy, as shown in Figure 10–1. Similarly, country B's revenues experience a severe depression from $27 million in year 1 to $6 million in year 2 and go back up to $35 million in year 3 under the optimal policy, but revenues follow a smoothly ascending curve when arm's-length conditions prevail. On the other hand, the introduction of optimality does not materially change the shape of country A's revenue curve.

The results of the simulation model, of course, do not measure what would actually happen to any particular country's revenues. They are suggestive, however, of the degree of revenue variations that could be introduced as a multinational enterprise moves towards an optimal financial policy. The magnitude of potential changes points to the likelihood that governments will respond by increasing their reviews of the financial links available to the enterprises falling within their jurisdiction.

Also, the results of the model suggest that a nation wishing to increase its revenue from multinational enterprises could do so by having a lower rate of income tax than certain other nations. Indeed, this is in principle what some of the smaller nations have done in order to attract multinational enterprise affiliates engaged in financial, sales, or shipping activities. However, a large nation might find that an attempt to increase revenues by lowering the rate of income tax would fail, for more revenue might be lost from indigenous firms than gained from multinational enterprises.

IMPLICATIONS FOR BALANCE OF PAYMENTS

As described earlier, the multinational enterprise tends to speed funds out of a country in which it expects a devaluation and correspondingly to draw funds into those countries where there are prospects of revaluation or

FIGURE 10–1

Variations over Four Years in Governments' Revenues Caused by Alternative Financial Policies of Multinational Enterprise Model
(In Millions of Dollars)

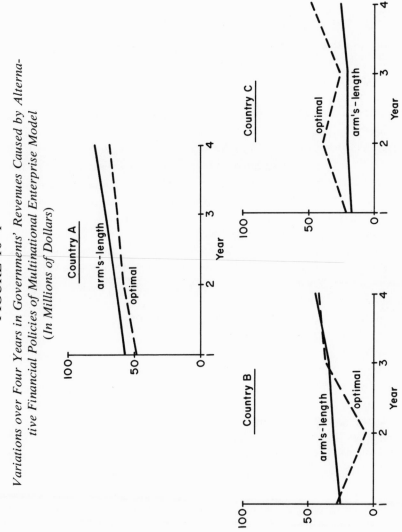

where interest rates are high and devaluation is not imminent. Because a firm that adheres to an optimal financial policy responds with particular vigor to this changing panorama of currency relationship, it characteristically engages in much larger shifts than one using an arm's-length policy. This condition is demonstrated in Figure 10–2 for the computer model.

When the multinational system uses an arm's-length policy, all three countries experience little variation in their balance of payments. In contrast, the optimal financial policy produces widely varying financial flows in all years. These movements are especially large in country C, whose currency experiences the most devaluations. Here, for three years, the span of oscillations is over forty times that experienced under the arm's length policy.*

Underscoring the differences between movements associated with revenue and movements associated with balance of payments is the fact that a country suffering a loss of revenue when the multinational system shifts to an optimal policy does not necessarily experience a shrinkage in its balance of payments. For example, when the system uses an optimal rather than an arm's-length policy, country B's four-year revenues are $110 million instead of $134 million (Table 10–1). In contrast, its balance of payments shows a deficit of $160 million under arm's-length policy but a positive $297 million when the enterprise uses an optimal policy. On the other hand, country C's revenues improve while its balance of payments worsens when the enterprise follows optimality as its goal.

Of course, the massive changes in balance of payments of the three countries in the model when the enterprise uses the optimal financial policy rather than an arm's-length policy may exaggerate the results that would occur in the real world if multinational enterprises generally undertook to use an optimal policy. Nevertheless, the model results are likenesses of reality, and there is evidence that the policies of multinational enterprises have the potential of bringing about major adjustments in balance-of-payments relationships.

The importance of the multinational enterprises' financial policies to the

---

* A word of caution: The balance-of-payments flows shown in Figure 10–2 do not imply that the results of foreign direct investment are either positive or negative for either the country of the investor or the host country. A number of relevant factors are omitted from the financial flows, such as the original investment, the purchase and sale of goods outside the multinational enterprise system, the efficiency of the country, and what the flows would have been if the investment had not been made. For an excellent discussion of the difficulties of using simple financial flows to determine the effects of foreign direct investment on the balance of payments, see Raymond Vernon, *U.S. Controls on Foreign Direct Investments—A Reevaluation,* New York: Financial Executives Research Foundation, 1969.

FIGURE 10–2

Variations over Four Years in Balance of Payments of Countries Caused
by Alternative Financial Policies of Multinational Enterprise Model
(In Millions of Dollars)

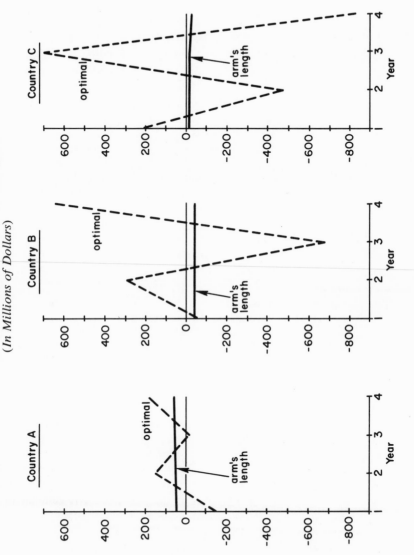

balance-of-payments issue may be seen in several ways. One is the size of the enterprises' holdings of liquid assets relative to the currency reserves of central banks. We estimate that at the end of 1971, the approximately 100 U.S. multinational enterprises in our Medium and Large groups— firms with centralized financial controls—had worldwide holdings of $25 billion in cash and marketable securities and $50 billion in *net* current assets (current assets minus current liabilities) including about $20 billion in foreign subsidiaries.[7] The $25 billion of cash and marketable securities held by these 100 firms overshadowed the central reserves of any nation in the world, as shown in Table 10–2. And the inclusion of non-U.S. multinational enterprises would increase this excess.

TABLE 10–2

Estimated Currency Reserves Held by the Eight Largest
Reserve Holders (Non-Communist), August 1971
(In Billions of Dollars)

	Gold	Foreign Exchange	Total [a]	No. of Months of Imports Covered by Reserves
Germany	4.1	11.4	16.9	6.1
United States	10.0	0.3	12.5	3.3
Japan	0.6	8.8	10.4	6.2
France	3.5	2.4	6.3	3.7
Italy	2.9	2.7	6.1	4.7
Canada	0.8	3.2	4.9	4.1
Switzerland	2.9	1.5	4.4	7.5
Britain	1.1	2.3	3.9	2.0

Source: The Economist (August 21, 1971): 54.
[a] Includes reserve positions in the International Monetary Fund and Special Drawing Rights.

Large-scale, short-term flights of capital ordinarily come about because of expected currency devaluations or revaluations rather than interest-rate arbitrage. When such movements occur, it is extremely difficult to ascertain with assurance the proportion attributable to so-called currency speculation and that attributable to the defensive efforts of multinational firms seeking protection for the purchasing power of their liquid assets. But if all the multinational enterprises simultaneously decided to move all their funds held as cash and marketable securities and not being used in their day-to-day operations into just one or two countries, there would be a huge increase in the reserves of the countries receiving the flows. For example, if all debts owed to U.S. parents by foreign affiliates were paid immediately, the central reserves of the United States would triple.[8] Conversely, such flows could deplete a considerable portion of the central reserves of some countries. These are extreme examples. For one less extreme, let us take the case of payments on intercompany accounts.

Within many multinational systems, as a matter of practice, debts are quickly paid to an affiliate in a country whose currency is expected to be revalued upward while that affiliate defers its payments to other units in the system. Conversely, payments are delayed to an affiliate in a country whose currency is expected to be devalued while that affiliate speeds up its payments to other units in the system. Because the central reserves of most countries are only several times their monthly volume of trade as indicated in Table 10–2, and because multinational enterprises account for a large segment of the foreign trade of many countries, these routine actions by enterprises on intercompany accounts can have serious effects on nations' central reserves. Take the case of Britain, and assume for the purpose of illustration that exports are about equal to imports, and further assume that multinational enterprises account for one-third of total imports and one-third of total exports. On those assumptions, a three-month change in credit terms of both imports and exports of multinational enterprises could wipe out all of Britain's reserves. While it is utterly unlikely that all multinational enterprises would act in concert, it is equally clear that their potential actions can have a material effect on a nation's currency reserves.

Although manipulations by multinational enterprises can be helpful as well as harmful to countries, the governments cannot stand the randomness of the outcome. They would prefer a less favorable but relatively stable balance of payments rather than a more favorable balance with large random swings. And this preference for steadiness also holds true, albeit to a lesser extent, for governmental revenues.

The Coming of the Shackles?

What are the prospects for relations between the multinational enterprise and the various governments with which it must deal? [9]

One possibility is for the multinational enterprise to be dismembered and each of its subsidiaries to become an independent unit that is treated equally with other local firms by the governments. Although antitrust proceedings might check growth in specific cases, there does not seem to be any serious prospect for a wholesale breakup of the multinational system. Quite the contrary: we foresee continued growth of multinational enterprises, in part due to the growth of many of the existing enterprises and in part due to the entry of many other firms into international operations.[10]

A second possibility is for the U.S. government to negotiate arrangements with the various local governments concerning the behavior of multinational enterprises. To be sure, at times when faced with very adverse conditions, such as nationalization, managers of multinational enterprises have requested governmental support. However, the growing strength of these firms, the uncertainty of U.S. measures, and the need for more prompt action than might be feasible through such arrangements are all negative scores against the wholesale representation of U.S. multinational enterprises by the U.S. government.

A third possibility is to settle any issues between governments and multinational firms through some form of international arbitration. But this route seems distant. Experience suggests that tax and interest-rate considerations are so important to domestic economic conditions that national governments will be wary about surrendering their authority in these areas.

A fourth outcome might be the creation of a world body to which the multinational enterprise with its roots in many different jurisdictions would have legal allegiance. This notion has a symmetrical appeal because it balances global government against global enterprise, and indeed this possibility has been discussed by several authors.[11] This could be done either through a new organization or one of the existing international bodies. However, such an approach remains for the present a chimera in the face of the enormous difficulties presently encountered in persuading governments to cede economic independence to international agencies or regional organizations. Over the near term the most likely development is the negotiation of multilateral treaties for controlling a few financial items.

Thus, we are left with the conclusion that for many years multinational enterprises will continue to deal directly with nations on most financial matters. Which way are those dealings likely to go?

First, let us consider the financial tools of multinational enterprises that mainly affect governmental revenues rather than balance of payments. Intercompany transfer pricing is the major device in this category, others being royalties, management fees, and interest payments. National governments are aware of the usefulness of these devices to the multinational enterprise in effecting shifts of income and have tended to increase their surveillance in this area. For example, in early 1971, Germany negotiated with the oil companies in order to reach a "fair" income-tax payment rather than use the posted prices to determine such a tax.[12] In another instance, a multinational enterprise had to reach agreement with both the U.S. and Taiwan governments regarding the technical fees its Taiwan subsidiary would pay the U.S. parent.[13] Nevertheless, there are enough counteracting influences to suggest that governments will not embark upon a wholesale policy of restraint.

For one thing, it is often extremely difficult, as discussed earlier, to establish a true arm's-length price for the types of goods moving between members of a multinational system. And in the case of royalties and management fees the problem may be insuperable. To formulate a basis for determining values, each firm has personnel working on the problem. On the opposite side, each government usually has a relatively small group of duty and tax collectors to police this broad area of uncertain pricing, covering a multitude of goods and services provided by a number of firms. So the advantage rests with the many managers seeking the most expedient means of shifting funds rather than with the comparatively small number of supervisory government officials.

Moreover, a country's possible loss of tax revenues because of transfer-pricing policies is likely to be a minor consideration compared with the benefits that the multinational enterprise can bring to the local economy in the form of employment, local purchase of goods, high-technology industry, research facilities, and exports. Governments have given ample evidence that in order to attract desired investments they are willing to grant tax holidays, provide special tax rates, and even agree with an enterprise that it can use transfer pricing to allocate a lion's share of taxable profits to other governmental jurisdictions with low taxes. In lieu of these direct tax favors, the governments may find it preferable to make arrangements, either explicitly or implicitly, with multinational enterprises to allow their management to exercise judgment in transfer pricing without much hindrance. Through this means, the discriminatory tax treatment would be obscured, thereby limiting dissent from local interests and avoiding the dissipation of regulatory control.

Moreover, the experience of the simulation model suggests that transfer prices are relatively easy to use, for an optimal solution calls for profits to be shifted in the same direction over a number of time periods. In the model, for example, profits are moved from parent *A* to subsidiary *B* in all four years. Thus, a given transfer-pricing policy may be optimal for long intervals; in the real world this is desirable because it avoids frequent renegotiations with governments.

Even though some governments will attempt to dampen the swings in their revenues that would result from optimal financial policies on the part of the enterprises, we do not believe that the effort will be effective worldwide, especially since the changes in a country's total income due to firms' financial policies probably would not be sufficiently great to interfere with the government's ability to control economic activity through traditional monetary and fiscal measures. In these circumstances, a national government probably would move cautiously in pushing controls over a financial link that is helpful to a company but of no great consequence to the government's revenues.

Thus we foresee continued opportunity for multinational enterprises to make extensive use of revenue-shifting tools, especially transfer pricing.

But, for those tools having a major effect on the balance of payments, the story is different. For we have seen that large movements of short-term capital by multinational enterprises can have profound effects on the central bank reserves of individual countries. And though all multinational enterprises are unlikely to act in concert, the fact that they have the potential for upsetting a nation's currency value will cause governments to put more restraints on short-term capital movements.

There are signs that the wind is blowing in this direction. During the international currency crisis of August 1971, for example, the Japanese government prohibited advance payments to Japanese exporters and developed plans to limit foreign borrowing by its corporations.[14] In order to curb disruptive capital flows, the International Monetary Fund has suggested that members consider standby tools that may be quickly activated such as regulations on bank reserves and on foreign borrowing and lending by major companies. At the same time the Fund has opposed comprehensive exchange controls.[15] But none of the proposals to date have been sufficient to protect the nations' currency reserves.

It will be recalled that the multinational enterprise achieves mobility in the movement of funds through its financial links concerned with credit. These are ordinarily available because a debtor-creditor relationship between units of a system arises out of a variety of business circumstances such as the sale of goods, provision of services, or grant of loans. The parent has considerable latitude in determining when the transfer of cash will take place to pay the debt—by permitting the original terms to remain unchanged or by accelerating or deferring the payment date.

Sooner or later government action will severely limit the multinational enterprise's use of credit tools in shuttling funds throughout its system; thus the enterprises will be shackled in their ability to protect against currency changes.[16] As a result, multinational enterprises may come to accept losses and gains from devaluations and revaluations as a routine element in operating internationally. As long as all multinational enterprises are faced with the same rules, no one enterprise will suffer unduly. In fact, such rules will remove a major tension between firms and national governments and thereby make multinational enterprises more welcome than they might otherwise be.

Furthermore, the managers of the enterprise can then concentrate on using their other competitive weapons, such as marketing and technology, which were the basic reasons for their foreign investments in the first place.

As managers improve their ability to use intercompany financial links and as governments become more aware of their use, we see a new sphere for bargaining between the multinational enterprise and the state. The enterprise will be seeking greater permissiveness to shift profits and move funds, and the state will be agreeing, provided certain conditions are met —such as the firm's importing more capital, exporting goods, and not moving such large amounts of funds that the currency value will be jeopardized. Accordingly, important requirements for the multinational executive of the future will be his ability to take the system point of view in planning intercompany financial links and his skill in negotiating with government officials in order to obtain the freedom to use these links in implementing his ideas.

APPENDIX A / Methods Used in Determining Financial Practices Employed by U.S. Multinational Enterprises

Interview Analysis

One or more corporate executives were interviewed at each firm. Usually the corporate executives permitted the discussions held with them to be recorded on tapes. Sometimes, though, an executive was reluctant to have an actual transcription made because he felt that it inhibited his freedom to talk. In these cases the analyst summarized the results during breaks in the interviews and at the close of the interviews. Depending on the time available, not all questions were asked of all firms.

The information on financial behavior of multinational enterprises collected in the interviews was analyzed both qualitatively and quantitatively. The qualitative analysis consisted of a study of each interview to gain an understanding of the financial behavior of the responding firm and the underlying elements at work.

In the quantitative analysis, the interviews were studied to identify a series of typical financial practices, such as:

Parent uses rule of thumb in determining the ratio of debt to equity for new affiliates.

Parent usually accompanies its initial investment in an affiliate with a loan.

Parent usually grants credit on accounts receivables as a means of financing a new affiliate.

An analyst further evaluated the interviews to determine whether each surveyed company followed the particular practice. These judgments were based on the analyst's best estimate of what practices the firm actually followed and at times these differed from an initial generalization made by an executive as to these practices. For example, if an executive stated that

189

the parent did not accompany a new investment with a loan, the interviewer then would ask about specific cases. If it was found through interviewing this executive or other executives or through an examination of company records that the parent usually had accompanied initial investments with a loan, then the analyst concluded that it was their usual practice to do so. The analyst then coded a sheet and the results were punched on computer cards. We were interested in determining what influenced financial practices, and in that sense, the observations on financial behavior were the dependent variables in the statistical analyses. There were a total of 500 practices formulated, of which 191 were regarded as major behavioral observations.

The Explanatory Variables

At the start of our research, no theory other than that of the profit-maximizing entrepreneur of classical economics existed to explain the financial behavior of multinational enterprises. Therefore, at the very beginning of the project before the explanatory variables were defined, several exploratory interviews were held to enable us to formulate hypotheses. Based on these interviews, the following explanatory or independent variables were selected:

1. Sales of the foreign operations of the multinational enterprise ("foreign sales")
2. Number of years since the first manufacturing facility was established abroad
3. Number of countries in which the enterprise manufactures
4. Average sales in each foreign country in which the enterprise manufactures
5. Foreign sales as percentage of total sales
6. Total sales of enterprise
7. Percentage of subsidiaries wholly owned
8. Technology level of the firm

Of these independent variables, the first five provide some gauge of the foreign involvement in terms of either size or experience. It was found that the total sales of foreign operations was the only variable to be correlated significantly with each of the other four variables; furthermore, this variable was correlated significantly with total sales of the enterprise.

On the other hand, the remaining two variables—percentage of subsidiaries wholly owned and technology level (percentage of total sales spent on research and development)—were not correlated significantly with any of the other variables nor with each other (Table A–1). Accordingly, the reduction of the first five variables by use of factor analysis was explored. Since it was found that those factor scores that represented foreign involvement had statistically significant correlations with the size of foreign sales, for ease of interpretation we chose the natural variable (foreign sales) rather than an artificial variable (a factor score obtained from a factor analysis). Also, as mentioned above, the size of a firm's foreign sales was correlated significantly with the size of a firm's total sales; thus, the one variable—size of foreign sales—could be used as a proxy for the first six variables on the list above.

Crosstabs: Classical Approach

On the basis of the foregoing analysis there remained foreign sales, percentage of subsidiaries wholly owned, and technology level as the major unrelated variables to explain the differences in financial practices. An analysis using a cross-tabulation table with a chi-square significance test was performed for each of these three explanatory variables with each dependent variable.

For these chi-square significance tests, the three explanatory variables were split into several ranges; for example, based on our perception of the proper dividing line, enterprises were divided by their foreign sales into (1) less than $100 million; (2) $100 million to $500 million; and (3) more than $500 million. Experiments were conducted to determine the effects of shifting these size boundaries, but the resulting analyses showed that the results were insensitive to moves of the boundaries of plus or minus 25 percent. These analyses revealed that financial practice was more often correlated with foreign sales than with either of the other two explanatory variables. For this reason and because our qualitative study of the interviews had revealed its overriding importance, the size of a firm's foreign sales was adopted as the explanatory variable on which attention was focused in the study.

Crosstabs: Bayesian Approach

One can think of three universes of firms, with each universe containing firms with a different range of foreign sales: the first with foreign sales less than $100 million, the second with foreign sales of $100 million to $500 million, and the third with foreign sales greater than $500 million.

A series of crosstabs employing probabilistic (a Bayesian approach) analyses was used to determine on the basis of sample evidence the proba-

TABLE A–1

Correlation of Selected Variables for Thirty-nine U.S.-controlled Multinational Enterprises

Variable Number [a]	Description	(1) Foreign Sales	(2) No. of Years Since First Manufacturing Facility Established Abroad	(3) No. of Countries in Which Firm Manufactures	(4) Average Sales in Each Country in Which Firm Manufactures	(5) Foreign Sales as a Percentage of Total Sales	(6) Total Sales	(7) Percentage of Subsidiaries Wholly Owned	(8) Technology Level of Firm
1	Foreign sales	+1.00							
2	No. of years since first manufacturing facility established abroad	+0.44 [b]	+1.00						
3	No. of countries in which firm manufactures	+0.48 [b]	+0.30	+1.00					
4	Average sales in each country in which firm manufactures	+0.92 [b]	+0.37	+0.11	+1.00				
5	Foreign sales as a percentage of total sales	+0.52 [b]	+0.27	+0.48 [b]	+0.38	+1.00			
6	Total sales	+0.86 [b]	+0.35	+0.30	+0.84 [b]	+0.03	+1.00		
7	Percentage of subsidiaries wholly owned	+0.28	+0.16	+0.20	+0.23	+0.36	+0.13	+1.00	
8	Technology level of firm	−0.12	−0.34	−0.20	−0.05	−0.27	−0.00	−0.21	+1.00

[a] Variable numbers 1 through 7 are logarithmic functions. [b] Significant at 0.01 level.

bility that one universe of firms with a given range of foreign sales had financial practices that were different from the other two universes combined. While these analyses were made for 191 questions, for illustrative purposes, only some examples are presented here (see the left-hand part of Table A–2 and Table A–3). These two tables present some of the data underlying the material presented in Chapters 4 and 5 in the text. Thus, the third question on Table A–2, which contains information pertaining to Chapter 4, shows a probability of 0.99 that parents in a universe of Small multinational enterprises are less likely than parents in a universe of Medium and Large enterprises to use a rule of thumb in determining the ratio of debt to equity for new (foreign) affiliates; this finding is reported on page 57 of the text. (In some cases the findings are discussed in a series of pages, but only the initial page is listed in Tables A–2 and A–3.) Whereas about half (15 out of 29) of all firms reporting on this practice use a rule of thumb, none of the five Small firms do so. Although the probabilities shown in these exhibits are for the difference between one universe of firms compared with the other two universes of firms combined, analyses showed that the probabilities also were high that the universe in question was different from either one of the other two universes.

The Logistic Multiple Regression Tests

The other analyses shown in Table A–2 and Table A–3 use a logistic regression model, as explained in Table A–4. For an independent and dependent variable, the logistic regression model fits an *s*-shaped, or logistic, curve to the data; the curve takes the form shown below.

The dependent variable expresses the probability that a firm uses or does not use a stated financial practice and hence cannot be greater than one or less than zero.

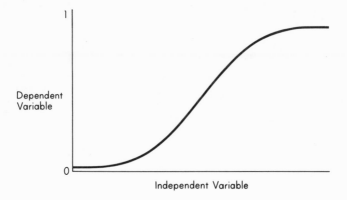

TABLE A-2

Statistical Analysis of Interview Results: Chapter Four

Page Number in Text	Financial Practice		Number of Answers	Bayesian Crosstabs by Size of Firm — Small	Medium	Large	Probability[a]	Regression Coefficients for Logistic Regression Model[b] — Size	(Size)²	Peak or Valley[c]	Technology	Ownership
50	Parent usually accompanies initial investment with loan	Yes	22	not significant				not significant				
		No	10									
53	Parent usually grants credit on accounts receivables as a means of financing new affiliate	Yes	21	not significant				not significant				
		No	0									
57	Parent uses rule of thumb in determining ratio of debt to equity for new affiliate	Yes	15	0	8	7	0.99 *	+8.4			+0.76[d]	+0.01
		No	14	5 *	4	5		(0.71)			(1.5)	(0.04)
60	Parent lends to foreign affiliates that need working capital but cannot borrow funds locally because of restrictive monetary policy	Yes	19	3	10 #	6	0.97 #	not significant				
		No	12	5	2	5						
61	Standard practice to charge interest on intercompany receivables	Yes	9	3 #	2	4	0.94 #	−20.0[d]	+1.8[d]	350	+1.3	−3.0
		No	14	1	8 *	5	0.92 *	(1.6)	(1.6)		(0.2)	(0.9)
63	Parent takes interest rate differentials into account in financing foreign affiliates	Yes	25	5	13 #	7	0.99 #	not significant				
		No	8	3	0	5						
66	Affiliates typically borrow locally from banks	Yes	33	not significant				not significant				
		No	0									
69	Foreign affiliates borrow money from institutions other than banks	Yes	16	1	6	9 #	0.94 #	+1.6[d]			−0.23	−1.31
		No	12	4 *	5	3	0.96 *	(2.0)			(0.4)	(0.5)
70	Enterprise obtained funds from the Eurobond market	Yes	21	1	9	11 #	0.99 #	+1.7[d]			−0.20	+1.4
		No	18	8 *	8	2	0.99 *	(2.3)			(0.4)	(0.6)

[a] Probability that the universe of firms of the size category whose number in the sample is marked with an * or # would in fact have a lower or higher percentage of "yes" responses than the universes of the other two size categories combined. See Robert Schlaifer, *Analysis of Decisions under Uncertainty* (New York: McGraw-Hill, 1969), section 15.1. A cutoff value of a 0.92 probability was used.

[b] "Not significant" means that no coefficient is significant at a probability level of 90 to 93 percent depending on the degrees of freedom (a cutoff value of 1.5 for t was used for convenience). t values are in parentheses below the coefficients. See Table A-4 for description of logistic regression model.

[c] Calculated from regression coefficients before they were rounded for insertion in this table.

[d] ...

TABLE A-3

Statistical Analysis of Interview Results: Chapter Five

Page Number in Text	Financial Practice	Number of Answers	Bayesian Crosstabs by Size of Firm				Regression Coefficients for Logistic Regression Model[b]				
			Small	Medium	Large	Probability[a]	Size	(Size)²	Peak or Valley[c]	Technology	Ownership
75	Withdrawal of funds a major financial issue in recent years	Yes 25 / No 13	5 / 4	8 / 8	12# / 1	0.99#	not significant				
77	Amount and form of funds determined primarily by parent	Yes 27 / No 4	6 / 0	13 / 1	8 / 3*	0.95*	−2.0[d] (1.8)			+0.32 (0.5)	−0.55 (0.1)
77	Needs of system play more dominant role in determining amount of funds withdrawn from an affiliate than do needs of the affiliate in question	Yes 7 / No 24	0 / 6	6# / 8	1 / 10	0.99#	+170.0[d] (1.5)	−16.0[d] (1.5)	210	−1.5[d] (1.9)	+0.85 (0.3)
77	Has dividend policy rather than "ad hoc" decisions	Yes 23 / No 10	2 / 4*	10 / 6	11# / 0	0.99# / 0.93*	not significant				
79	Uses rule of thumb for percentage of foreign earnings to be paid in dividends	Yes 14 / No 16	1 / 5*	5 / 8	8# / 3	0.98# / 0.94*	+0.12[d] (1.6)			+0.93[d] (1.5)	+10.0[d] (1.8)
85	Parent expects to wait for substantial period before receiving dividends from new affiliate	Yes 29 / No 0	not significant				not significant				
86	Desires to maintain uniform dividend policy for a subsidiary to prevent host country from stopping remittances	Yes 13 / No 25	1 / 8*	4 / 12	7# / 5	0.99# / 0.93*	not significant				
86	Ability of subsidiary to borrow locally has significant influence on dividends	Yes 7 / No 30	2 / 7	1 / 15*	4 / 8	0.95*	+1.3[d] (1.7)			+0.92[d] (1.5)	−5.0[d] (1.9)
91	Parent adjusts transfer prices to move funds to and from foreign affiliates	Yes 14 / No 23	not significant				not significant				

See notes for Table A-2.

TABLE A-4

Description of Logistic Multiple Regression Model [a]

$$log_e \frac{p}{1-p} = \beta_0 + \beta_1 X_1 + \beta_2 X_2 + \beta_3 X_3 + \beta_4 X_4$$

where:

$p =$ "true" but uncertain long-run fraction of multinational enterprises that engage in a specified financial action with specified values of X_1, X_2, X_3, X_4 as defined below.

$X_1 =$ logarithm (to base 10) of foreign sales in thousands of dollars of total enterprise in 1965.

$X_2 = (X_1)^2$. Note: The square of the logarithm of foreign sales (X_1) was entered as a separate variable in cases in which a parabolic relationship was hypothesized.

$X_3 =$ technology level of firm, as determined by the ratio of R&D expenditures to total sales ($1 =$ low, $2 =$ medium, $3 =$ high). Based on unpublished data prepared by John Stopford for use in *Growth and Organizational Change in the Multinational Firm* (unpublished doctoral thesis, Harvard University Graduate School of Business Administration, June 1968).

$X_4 =$ logarithm (to base 10) of the percentage of firm's foreign subsidiaries with common stock owned 90 percent or more by parent company either directly or indirectly.

Example:

An example of one equation is:

$$log_e \frac{p}{1-p} = 56 - 20X_1 + 1.8X_2 + 1.3X_3 - 3.0X_4$$
$$\phantom{log_e \frac{p}{1-p} = 56} (1.6) \quad (1.6) \quad (0.2) \quad (0.9)$$

$n = 23$

where

$p =$ "true" but uncertain long-run fraction of multinational enterprises that have a standard practice of charging interest on intercompany receivables.

t values for the coefficients are in parentheses.

---

[a] Professor Arthur Schleifer, Jr., provided advice on the use of the model. For further details of this method of analysis, see his "Bayesian Multiple Regression Computer Programs," MEPD-13 (preliminary), Harvard Business School, May 14, 1968.

In our use of logistic regression models, all three independent variables are entered into one equation; thus, the effect of each variable on the dependent variable is determined by a logistic curve when the effects of the other two independent variables are held constant at any specified levels. For example, with respect to the third practice in Table A–2, the coefficient for the size of foreign sales is positive, but with a *t* value less than one (with a *t* value of one, there is about an 83 percent probability that the independent variable has an effect on the dependent variable). The coefficient for the technology level is positive with a *t* value of 1.5; this means that there is a little more than 90 percent probability that high-technology firms are more likely than low-technology firms to use a rule of thumb in determining the ratio of debt to equity for a new affiliate when the effects of the other two explanatory variables—size of foreign sales and ownership—are held constant. The coefficient on the ownership variable —the percentage of foreign affiliates wholly owned—is negligible in this case.

The logistic regression model was used for another type of analysis. When the Medium firm was hypothesized to be more likely (or less likely) than the other two size categories of firms to use a specified financial practice, the size of foreign sales was also entered as a squared term in order to test for the hypothesized peaked relationship, as shown below.

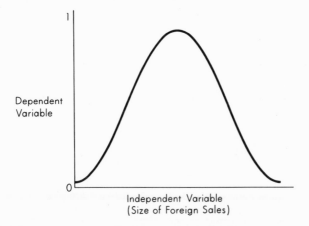

For example, the results of the Bayesian crosstabs tests shown on the left-hand part of Table A–2 for the fifth practice in that table demonstrate that Medium enterprises are less likely than other enterprises to charge interest on intercompany accounts ($p = 0.92$). When the effects of technology and ownership are held constant in the logistic regression model, the coefficient of the "size of foreign sales" is negative and that of the square

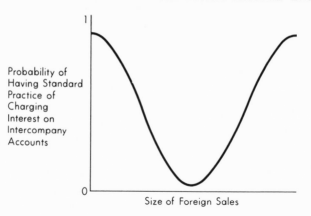

of "size of foreign sales" is positive; that is, as the size of foreign sales increases, the curve starts off with a negative slope and gradually changes to a positive one.

The position of the peak (or valley in this case) indicates the value of foreign sales most likely to be connected with a stated financial practice. To solve for the size of the firm at the peak (or valley) in the curve, the first derivative of the equation with respect to the *foreign sales* variable is set equal to zero and solved for the foreign sales variable. For example, take the equation in Table A–4 (fifth practice in Table A–2):

$$log_e \frac{p}{1-p} = 56 - 20X_1 + 1.8(X_1)^2 + 1.3X_2 - 3.0X_3$$

$$\frac{d(log_e \frac{p}{1-p})}{dX_1} = -20 + 3.6(X_1)$$

Set this first derivative as equal to zero and the solution is:

$$X_1 = 5.56$$

As X_1 is expressed in base 10 logarithms, the antilog must be used in order to have the result expressed in millions of dollars; the antilog of 5.56 = \$350 million. Therefore, a U.S. multinational enterprise with *foreign sales* of \$350 million is less likely to have a standard practice of charging interest on intercompany receivables than multinational enterprises with foreign sales either lower or higher than \$350 million. This figure is of interest not because of the exact amount, but rather because it falls within the range of \$100 million to \$500 million that we specified for Medium firms; thus, it confirms the findings of the Bayesian crosstabs test shown on the left half of Table A–2. Both of the peaks reported in Tables A–2 and A–3 are between \$100 million and \$500 million, and, in fact, the majority of peaks obtained from all of our logistic regression models fall within this range.

For this practice (the fifth practice in Table A–2), the *t* values of the other two independent variables are less than one; thus, the probability is less than 0.83 for either variable that its effect on the dependent variable exists.

Size seems to have an effect on fewer financial practices when the results of the regression analyses are compared with the results of the crosstabs test. For example, refer to the 18 financial practices described in Tables A–2 and A–3. The probability is greater than 92 percent (*t* value of about 1.5 or higher, depending on degrees of freedom) in only seven of these financial practices that the size of foreign sales of an enterprise has an effect on the enterprise's financial practice. In contrast, for 13 of these financial practices, the Bayesian crosstabs analyses show that the probability is greater than 92 percent that the financial practice of one universe of enterprises with a specified range of foreign sales is different from that of the other two universes combined.

One of the reasons that size seems to have an effect on fewer practices for the regression analyses compared with the Bayesian crosstabs test for the three universes is that more variables are tested with the regression model with the same number of observations; thus the degrees of freedom are less so that the distribution is spread. This greater spread of distribution makes it more difficult to achieve significant results. However, regardless of statistical significance, the signs of the regression coefficients on the "size" variable in the logistic regression analyses usually support the results of the Bayesian crosstabs model. In the case of technology and ownership patterns, the regression analyses show these regressions have less of an influence on financial practices than does size of foreign sales, thus confirming the results of our contingency table tests. Overall, however, we made little use of the logistic regression analyses in drawing conclusions for our text; however, these analyses were used in drawing the tentative conclusions on page 45 concerning the probable effects of technology level and ownership patterns.

Even though the logistic multiple regression analyses had only a nominal effect on the main findings presented in the text, we present the results of these analyses for another reason. The use of a logistic multiple regression equation with a dependent variable having only two values, zero and one, is relatively new and has not been widely used; in fact, prior to our use of it on this project, we had not encountered it in the field of business administration. Thus, we present information about it and some results in the hope that it will aid other researchers.

APPENDIX B / Simulation Model of a Multinational Enterprise

The simulation model is a dynamic linear program designed to produce a full set of financial statements for one parent A and two subsidiaries B and C. Various analytic tools were also developed and some of the more important ones are discussed briefly in this appendix.

Each unit of the model operates in a different country, with an environment that reflects its economic character. The relevant aspects of these financial environments are summarized in Table B–1.

TABLE B–1

*The Financial Environment in which the Units of the
Multinational Enterprise Model Operate*

A. THE SYSTEM AS SUPPLIER

System Unit	Public
Company A	60-day receivables, no interest charge; dividends at 11.75% per annum on equity; short-term securities purchased at 5%.
Subsidiary B	60-day receivables, no interest charge; short-term securities purchased at 6%.
Subsidiary C	60-day receivables, no interest charge; short-term securities purchased at 8%.

B. THE SYSTEM AS CLIENT

Public	A		B	C
Supplier credit	60-day payables, no interest charge		60-day payables, no interest charge	60-day payables, no interest charge
Money market	first 100% of equity	6%	7%	9%
	next 40%	7%		
	the rest	8%		
Capital market	first 100%	7%	8%	—
	next 40%	8%		
	the rest	9%		

TABLE B–1 (*Cont'd*)

	A	B	C
	C. THE GOVERNMENT		
Corporate taxes [a]	50%	60%	30%
Import duties	—	10%	50%
Collection lag	25% of corporate taxes	25% of corporate taxes	25% of corporate taxes

[a] No carryover of losses.

TABLE B–2

The Inflationary and Monetary Environment of Countries
B and C in the Multinational Enterprise Model,
Four Years

	Country B (Host Country of Subsidiary B)			Country C (Host Country of Subsidiary C)	
Year	Price Increase Percentage	Devaluation Percentage	Year	Price Increase Percentage	Devaluation Percentage
1	5	—	1	10	—
2	6	10	2	10	21
3	7	—	3	10	—
4	8	—	4	10	21

Prices increase moderately in country B which experiences a devaluation at the close of year 2. Prices rise much more rapidly in country C which has two major devaluations—one at the close of year 2 and the other at the close of year 4. These conditions are summarized in Table B–2.

Certain constraints were imposed on the system to make certain that each unit had sufficient cash and inventories to sustain operations and that it maintained sufficient liquidity to ensure its financial well-being. These constraints are summarized in Table B–3.

The basis of the financial activity of the system stems from the production and sales undertaken by the parent and each subsidiary in each year as summarized in Table B–4. Except for prices on sales between units of the system, all production and sales figures are exogenous inputs into the model, because the production and sales plans are assumed to be beyond the jurisdiction of financial policy.

TABLE B–3

Operating and Financial Constraints Affecting the Multinational Enterprise Model System

	A	B	C	Consolidated
Operating constraints				
Cash	min. 10 day sales	min. 10 day sales	min. 10 day sales	
Inventories	15% of sales at public prices	15% of sales at public prices	15% of sales at public prices	
Financial constraints				
Long-term debt/equity	0.5 : 1	total: 1 : 1 public: 0.5 : 1	1 : 1	
Current assets/current liabilities [a]	2 : 1	1.2 : 1	1.15 : 1	
Current assets/fixed assets				Year 1. 1.5 : 1 2. 2.5 : 1 3. 3.0 : 1 4. 3.5 : 1

[a] In devaluation years local borrowing counted predevaluation.

TABLE B–4

Production and Sales of the Units in the Multinational Enterprise Model, Four Years

	Year	1	2	3	4
1. *Production*					
Company A	Dollars	319.6	351.5	386.7	425.4
Company B	Local currency	51.7	60.0	69.8	82.5
	Dollars	51.7	60.0	64.3	75.7
Company C	Local currency	46.7	56.2	67.8	81.7
	Dollars	46.7	56.2	56.5	68.0
2. *Sales*					
a. Sales to public:					
Company A	Dollars	400.0	440.0	484.0	532.4
Company B	Local currency	126.0	146.9	172.8	205.4
	Dollars	126.0	146.9	157.1	186.7
Company C	Local currency	88.0	106.5	128.8	162.1
	Dollars	88.0	106.5	106.5	133.3

TABLE B–4 (*Cont'd*)

Year		1	2	3	4
b. Intercompany sales:					
Company *A*					
to company *B*	Dollars	16.0	17.6	19.4	21.3
to company *C*	Dollars	10.0	11.0	12.1	13.3
Company *B*					
to company *C*	Dollars	10.5	12.2	13.1	15.6
Company *C*					
to company *B*	Dollars	17.6	21.3	21.3	21.3

Note: All intercompany sales and resulting production costs are shown at arm's-length prices.

The model is constructed to optimize an objective function; the one that we primarily used is the sum of consolidated profits after taxes for four years simultaneously. In addition, tests were run to determine the effects of using the following alternative objective functions: minimize taxes paid; minimize interest costs; minimize foreign-exchange exposure; maximize cash and securities at the parent; and maximize shareholder wealth.

Results were obtained from computations that simulated the behavior of financial management under three basic financial policies that reflect the developmental stages of the multinational enterprise, as discussed in Chapter 3. Under an arm's-length policy, each unit in the system operates on an arm's-length basis (Table B–5). Under a policy of centralized control, the parent uses the financial links of the system as fully as possible to optimize the objective function selected. The financial links that are available within the system and which could be used under a centralized policy are

TABLE B–5

Settings on Intercompany Links, Arm's-Length Financial Policy, Multinational Enterprise Model

Item	Setting
Intercompany receivables	60 days, 8% interest
Royalties (*B* and *C* to *A*)	3% of sales, payable at year end
Management fees (*B* and *C* to *A*)	3% of assets, payable at year end
Dividends (*B* and *C* to *A*)	11.75% of equity, payable at year end
Short loans	None allowed
Long loans	None allowed

summarized in Table B–6. For example, parent *A* is given the leeway to vary the prices of the products that it sells to either subsidiary *B* or *C* within a range of plus or minus 20 percent, and subsidiaries *B* and *C* have the same leeway on prices of goods sold to each other. (Pages 12–31 of Duerr [1] indicate that many disputes between U.S. companies and the U.S.

TABLE B–6

Intercompany Financial Links Available to the Multinational Enterprise Model under a Centralized Financial Policy

		Receivers	
Suppliers	*A*	*B*	*C*
A			
Products		±20%	±20%
License and know-how		yes	yes
Management		yes	yes
Credit:			
Receivables		0–180 days @ 0–8%	0–180 days @ 0–8%
Short loans		0–max @ 4–9%	0–max @ 4–9%
Long loans		0–max @ 4–10%	0–max @ 4–10%
Royalties and fees		0–50% no interest	0–50% no interest
B			
Products			±20%
Royalty	3–5% of sales		
Management fee	0–3% of assets [a,b]		
Dividends	0–retained earnings		
Credit:			
Receivables			0–180 days @ 0–8%
Short loans			0–max @ 7%
C			
Products		±20%	
Royalty	3–5% of sales		
Management fee	0–3% of assets [a,b]		
Dividends	0–retained earnings		
Credit:			
Receivables		0–180 days @ 0–8%	
Short loans		0–max @ 7%	

[a] Excluding intersubsidiary loans.
[b] Holds on values after devaluation.

government on transfer pricing have involved a range greater than ±20 percent.) *B* pays *A* royalties that amount to 3, 4, or 5 percent of sales; the exact percentage is at the discretion of management. All intercompany sales are on terms that may vary between 0 and 180 days and at an annual rate of interest on the amount outstanding ranging from 0 to 8 percent. Table B–6 contains still other financial links not discussed here.

The third financial policy provides for some central guidance but incorporates selected rules: those used in the "rule maker" policy discussed in Chapter 9 are summarized in the following list:

Setting on Intercompany Links,
Representative-Rules Financial Policy,
Multinational Enterprise Model

A. The same freedom existed to adjust the following items as in the centralized financial policy (Table B–6):
   1. Transfer pricing
   2. Granting of credit on receivables in year of devaluation
   3. Short-term loans
B. The following items were set at a specified value as used for the arm's-length policy (Table B–5):
   1. Interest on receivables
   2. Interest on short-term loans, same as on receivables
   3. Long-term loans
   4. Royalties
   5. Credit on royalties
   6. Management fees
   7. Credit on management fees
   8. Dividends by *B* and *C*, except set at 50 percent of profits after taxes rather than 11.75 percent of equity as in arm's-length policy

In the real world, financial policies may be marked by shades of differences rather than by firmly defined lines. Accordingly, simulations also were formulated and studied for five intermediate financial policies, such as excluding the use of transfer pricing from full centralization.

The Use of Discretion

Figure B–1 provides a summary of the discretionary use of financial policy tools by the model to obtain the highest consolidated after-tax profits under a centralized financial policy. The table is constructed so that ac-

FIGURE B–1

Summary of the Discretionary Use of Financial Policy Tools,
Multinational Enterprise Model

From \ To / Period	A 1	A 2	A 3	A 4	B 1	B 2	B 3	B 4	C 1	C 2	C 3	C 4
A Transfer pricing, sales by A — Up												
Down					▨	▨	▨	▨	▨	▨	▨	▨
Receivables on sales of goods									▨		▨	
Interest rebate on receivables									▨		▨	
Short-term loans									▨		▨	
Interest rebate on short-term loans									▨		▨	
Long-term loans					▨		▨		▨		▨	
Interest rebate on long-term loans					▨		▨		▨		▨	
Rebate on royalties					▨		▨					
Royalties and management fees receivable									▨		▨	
B Transfer pricing, sales by B — Up												
Down									▨	▨	▨	▨
Receivables on sales of goods									▨		▨	
Interest rebate on receivables									▨		▨	
Short-term loans									▨		▨	
Management fees		▨										
Dividends												
C Transfer pricing, sales by C — Up					▨	▨	▨	▨				
Down												
Receivables on sales of goods					▨		▨					
Interest rebate on receivables												
Short-term loans					▨		▨					
Management fees												
Dividends		▨	▨									

▢ Discretionary nonuse   ▨ Discretionary use

tive behavior is read across rows whereas passive behavior is read down columns, that is, the treatment accorded by parent *A* to subsidiaries *B* and *C* can be seen by looking across the rows corresponding to parent *A* and inspecting the columns corresponding to *B* and *C*. On the other hand, to determine the treatment accorded parent *A* by subsidiaries *B* and *C*, it is appropriate to read down the column corresponding to subsidiary *A* (that is, *A*'s passive behavior). The table is further divided into four sub-columns for each unit in the system corresponding to the four years for which the model produces a policy. This allows a judgment to be formed on the stability of the optimal policy emerging.

Examining the active behavior of the parent, as an example, we read A's rows and find:

A transfers prices downwards to B and C in all years

A grants credit on accounts receivable only to C and only in years 1 and 3

A rebates (i.e., does not charge) interest on C's receivables when they are outstanding

A makes short-term loans only to C and only in years 1 and 3

A rebates (i.e., charges minimum allowable) interest on C's short-term debt when it exists

A maintains long-term loans to B and C in all years and rebates interest (i.e., charges minimum allowable) thereon

A rebates (i.e., charges minimum allowable) royalties to B in all years except year 2 and to C always

A extends credit through royalties and fees receivable only to C and only in years 1 and 3

Examining in turn the passive behavior of A, we read down A's column to ascertain the treatment it received from B and C. We find:

B pays A management fees only in year 2

B pays no dividends in any year

C pays no management fees in any year

C pays dividends in years 2 and 3

Financial Statements

Income statements, balance sheets, and cash flow statements were produced. In order to facilitate internal analysis, the income statements show the breakdown of the destination of sales as well as the use of transfer pricing and other discretionary financial tools. At the same time, the format of the statements respects to the extent possible the conventions of public reporting.

The translation rules used are based on the assumption that devaluation occurs after the close of business on December 31. As a result, for purposes of consolidation, income statements are translated at the historical rate in force during the period. For the translation of the balance sheets, the following modified AICPA rules are used: (1) translated at current (i.e., end of period, post devaluation) rates—all current assets and liabilities and long-term loans; (2) translated at historical rates—fixed assets.

On the local-currency balance sheet, the following items are considered to be denominated in foreign currency: intercompany receivables, intercompany short and long loans, and royalties and management fees outstanding. Conversion losses appear in subsidiary income statements when devaluation requires the payment of a dollar loan to the parent in a larger number of local-currency units than were required at the time the debt was incurred. Translation gains or losses appear in the consolidated statement as a result of the different rates at which the various items in the financial statements are translated.

Financial statements were turned out for each unit in the system for each year covered under the various financial policies and objective functions that were studied. These statements follow conventional forms. For this reason as well as the very large number of statements involved, the statements have not been reproduced in this book.

The Matrix Tables

For analytic purposes, it was found helpful to recast the conventional statement into a matrix form. Use of this form allows a double-entry table to be set up in which payer and payee, debtor and creditor, or source and use can be identified on the same page. As a result, the various interrelationships among the accounts of the model system could be inspected at one time.

Table B–7 shows a matrix income statement for the flow of funds under a centralized financial policy that maximizes consolidated profits after taxes. In general, the flow is from the source of the funds, represented by the units of the system and the public along the horizontal line at the top of the chart to the users, represented by the units of the system and the public along the vertical line at the left of the chart. Thus, in year 3, parent A moves funds by means of a loan of $120.5 million to subsidiary C which then reverses the flow by repaying the loan in year 4.

The Marginal Contribution of Policy Tools

The computer program provided the marginal contribution of relaxing the constraints on the system under different policy conditions; these marginal contributions are measures of the marginal contribution to four-year consolidated profits after taxes of the system of changes in different restrictions, internal and external, on the system's behavior.

TABLE B–7

The Flow of Funds in the Multinational Enterprise Model Using All Available Financial Links to Maximize Consolidated Profits After Taxes (In Millions of Dollars)

Uses	A First Year	A Second Year	A Third Year	A Fourth Year	B First Year	B Second Year	B Third Year	B Fourth Year	C First Year	C Second Year	C Third Year	C Fourth Year
A												
Sales					15.3	14.1	15.5	17.0	5.5	12.8	4.9	15.
Royalties and fees					4.0	8.8	5.0	6.0	1.7	5.5	2.0	6.
Interest					2.4	2.0	1.7	1.4	5.1	1.7	6.2	1.
Dividends					—	—	—	—	—	3.8	55.3	—
Securities					—	—	—	—	—	—	—	—
Short loans					—	—	—	—	—	78.6	—	120.
Long loans					—	10.1	8.4	7.1	—	8.5	7.1	6.
B												
Sales									5.7	14.0	5.4	17.
Interest									7.2	—	23.7	—
Securities									—	—	—	—
Short loans									—	406.6	—	705.
Long loans	60.4	—	—	—					—	—	—	—
C												
Sales					13.0	23.4	38.3	11.0				
Interest					0.8	22.2	—	26.9				
Securities					—	—	—	—				
Short loans	78.6	—	120.5	—	103.3	—	641.8	—				
Long loans	51.2	—	—	—	—	—	—	—				
SUBTOTAL	190.1	—	120.5	—	138.8	80.6	710.7	69.4	25.2	531.5	104.6	873.
Public												
Cost of production	288.0	308.7	338.8	371.7	45.8	51.6	54.8	64.8	44.9	52.9	52.6	63.
Freight	—	—	—	—	3.4	3.9	4.1	4.3	2.1	2.3	2.5	2.
Interest	20.9	15.3	19.7	12.7	4.2	2.4	22.5	—	—	23.9	—	28.
Overhead	5.0	5.3	5.6	5.9	2.1	2.3	2.4	2.7	1.1	1.3	1.2	1.
Taxes:												
Corporation	46.3	54.7	61.7	67.2	22.0	7.0	23.4	36.6	10.4	25.1	18.3	31.
Import	—	—	—	—	3.4	3.9	4.1	4.3	8.1	9.3	10.1	11.
Dividends	46.4	54.5	58.7	77.6	—	—	—	—	—	—	—	—
Fixed assets	44.9	49.0	54.7	61.1	9.7	11.6	12.4	15.1	4.4	5.5	5.2	6.
Securities	—	—	—	—	—	369.8	—	410.2	230.0	—	532.1	—
Short loans	—	69.5	—	59.1	—	59.8	—	321.2	25.1	—	219.5	—
Long loans	—	21.1	19.2	49.2	22.5	—	5.0	—	—	—	—	—
Subtotal	451.5	578.1	558.4	704.5	113.1	510.3	128.7	859.2	326.1	120.3	841.5	147.
Difference in Cash Holdings	0.7	1.2	1.3	1.4	1.2	1.0	0.3	0.9	1.5	0.7	0.6	0.
TOTAL	642.3	579.3	680.2	705.9	253.1	591.9	839.7	929.5	352.8	652.5	946.7	1020.

TABLE B–7 (*Cont'd*)

The Flow of Funds in the Multinational Enterprise Model Using All Available Financial Links to Maximize Consolidated Profits After Taxes (In Millions of Dollars)

				Sources							
Subtotal				Public				Total			
First Year	Second Year	Third Year	Fourth Year	First Year	Second Year	Third Year	Fourth Year	First Year	Second Year	Third Year	Fourth Year
20.8	26.9	20.4	32.4	393.3	433.4	476.6	524.5	414.1	460.3	497.0	556.9
5.7	14.3	7.0	12.7	—	—	—	—	5.7	14.3	7.0	12.7
7.5	3.7	7.9	2.6	—	—	—	—	7.5	3.7	7.9	2.6
—	3.8	55.3	—	—	—	—	—	—	3.8	55.3	—
—	—	—	—	47.5	—	—	—	47.5	—	—	—
—	78.6	—	120.5	25.5	—	97.5	—	25.5	78.6	97.5	120.5
—	18.6	15.5	13.2	141.9	—	—	—	141.9	18.6	15.5	13.2
5.7	14.0	5.3	17.7	123.0	143.4	153.2	181.8	128.7	157.4	158.6	199.5
7.2	—	23.7	—	—	22.5	—	24.6	7.2	22.5	23.7	24.6
—	—	—	—	5.5	—	336.1	—	5.5	—	336.1	—
—	406.6	—	705.6	51.3	—	321.2	—	51.3	406.6	321.2	705.6
60.4	—	—	—	—	5.5	—	—	60.4	5.5	—	—
13.0	23.4	38.3	11.0	86.9	103.9	103.4	129.5	99.9	126.8	141.7	140.5
0.8	22.2	—	26.9	19.0	—	42.6	—	19.8	22.2	42.6	26.9
—	—	—	—	—	238.0	—	532.1	—	238.0	—	532.1
181.9	—	762.3	—	—	265.6	—	321.2	181.9	265.6	762.3	321.2
51.2	—	—	—	—	—	—	—	51.2	—	—	—
354.1	612.1	935.7	942.6	893.9	1211.8	1530.6	1713.7	1248.2	1823.8	2466.3	2656.3

First Year	Second Year	Third Year	Fourth Year
378.7	413.2	446.2	500.1
5.5	6.2	6.6	7.2
25.1	39.6	42.2	41.6
8.2	8.9	9.2	10.0
78.7	86.8	103.4	135.6
11.5	13.2	14.2	15.9
46.4	54.5	58.7	77.6
59.0	66.1	72.3	83.1
230.0	369.8	532.1	410.2
25.1	129.3	219.5	380.3
22.5	21.1	24.2	49.2
890.7	1208.7	1528.6	1710.8
3.4	3.9	2.2	2.9
1248.2	1823.8	2466.5	2656.3

For example, the transfer price from A to C in year 1 has a marginal price of $0.648, that is, if the invoiced value of A's sales to C in year 1 decreases by another dollar, the four-year consolidated profits after taxes will rise by 64.8¢. This figure is explained in the main so as to give a flavor of the interaction between various constraints in the model. Through an additional reduction of the invoiced value of its sales to C, A reduces its income by $1 and its tax payment by $0.50, leaving a reduction in consolidated profits after taxes of $0.50. C reduces its import costs by $1 and its import duty payment by $0.50; therefore, C's income increases by $1.50 and its tax payment by $0.45. This leaves an increased contribution to profits after taxes in C of $1.05 for a net balance between C and A of $+$0.55. In addition, C is able to purchase new short-term financial assets equal to its additional income of $1.05 plus a quarter of its new tax payment of $0.11. A yield of 8 percent on the additional short-term assets of $1.16 sums to $0.0928 before taxes and $0.065 after taxes. The sum of $0.55 and $0.065 is $0.615; the remaining $0.033 to obtain the marginal price of $0.648 requires tracing through all the stages of the adjustment of the system to A's one dollar reduction in transfer price.

Example of Equations

The simulation model is a dynamic linear program designed to produce three accounting statements—income statement, balance sheet, and cash flow—for one parent and two subsidiaries. Thus, the model consists essentially of three sets of equations (linear constraints) each defining one type of accounting statement. In what follows, the parameters for year 1 will be used, other periods differing in minimal respects only.

Since an example equation will be shown only for year 1, the year to which the activity refers will not be explicitly stated if it is year 1, otherwise a 0, 2, 3, or 4 will be used. When there is an originator and a destinee of a transaction, the respective activity will be subscripted, listing first the originator of the transaction and then the destinee. The use of A, B, and C refer to the units of the enterprise; P refers to the public (rest of the world). Thus, for example, $0T_{AB}$ means year 0 transfer pricing base for A's sales to B.

On the income statement, profits after taxes and retained earnings are defined through the use of four subsets of equations linked sequentially. The first of these defines adjusted operating profit, the second net profits, the third exchange gain/loss, and the fourth profits after taxes and retained earnings. An equation for adjusted operating profit is the example selected for this appendix. Adjusted operating profit is equal to operating profit plus (minus) the effect of transfer pricing because the difference between sales and cost of goods sold, both at arm's-length prices, is an exogenous input into the model, since the production and sales plans are assumed to be outside the decision space of the chief financial officer.

Where:

$T^{\pm}$ = invoice value at arm's-length prices on which transfer pricing is applied

$A \atop BNOP \atop C$ = net operating profit not adjusted for transfer pricing

$A \atop IBNOP \atop C$ = net operating profit adjusted for transfer pricing

IS = value of sales at arm's-length prices

Then:

1. $-0.2T^{+}_{AB} + 0.2T^{-}_{AB} - 0.2T^{+}_{AC} + 0.2T^{-}_{AC} + IANOP = ANOP$

2. $+0.22T^{+}_{AB} - 0.22T^{-}_{AB} - 0.2T^{+}_{BC} + 0.2T^{-}_{BC} + 0.22T^{+}_{CB} - 0.22T^{-}_{CB}$
   $+ IBNOP = BNOP$

3. $+0.3T^{+}_{AC} - 0.3T^{-}_{AC} + 0.3T^{+}_{BC} - 0.3T^{-}_{BC} - 0.2T^{+}_{CB} + 0.2T^{-}_{CB} + ICNOP = CNOP$

4. $T^{+}_{AB} + T^{-}_{AB} \leq IS_{AB}$

5. $T^{+}_{AC} + T^{-}_{AC} \leq IS_{AC}$

6. $T^{+}_{BC} + T^{-}_{BC} \leq IS_{BC}$

7. $T^{+}_{CB} + T^{-}_{CB} \leq IS_{CB}$

More extensive sets of equations are available in a statistical working paper available from the authors.

NOTES

ONE

1. International Business Machines Corporation, *Annual Report for the Year Ended December 31, 1964,* p. 19.

2. See Robert B. Stobaugh and Associates, "U.S. Multinational Enterprises and the U.S. Economy," in *The Multinational Corporation,* pt. 1, Bureau of International Commerce, U.S. Department of Commerce (Washington, D.C.: 1972), esp. p. 28; for a brief summary, see Robert B. Stobaugh, "How Investment Abroad Creates Jobs at Home," *Harvard Business Review,* 50 (September–October 1972): 121. A detailed account of the growth and motivation of U.S. foreign direct investment is given in Raymond Vernon, *Sovereignty at Bay: The Multinational Spread of U.S. Enterprises* (New York: Basic Books, 1971), Chapters 2 and 3. For studies explicitly showing the importance of market size in influencing U.S. foreign direct investment, see Robert B. Stobaugh, "The Product Life Cycle, U.S. Exports, and International Investment," unpublished D.B.A. thesis, Harvard Business School, June 1968, Chapter 4; and A. E. Scaperlanda and L. J. Mauer, "The Determinants of U.S. Investment in the EEC," *American Economic Review,* 59 (September 1969): 558–68.

3. See U.S. Department of Commerce, Office of Business Economics, *U.S. Direct Investments Abroad, 1966, Part 1: Balance of Payments Data* (Washington: Superintendent of Documents, 1970), pp. 20, 109.

4. For example, two offices in the Department of Commerce, the Office of Business Economics and the Office of Foreign Direct Investment, differ substantially in their estimates of overseas investment. In part, the differences may be caused by variations in samples, but another part is caused by factors unknown to the Department (Office of Business Economics, U.S. Department of Commerce, *U.S. Direct Investments Abroad, 1966, Part 1: Balance of Payments Data* [Washington: Superintendent of Documents, 1971], p. 34). Compounding the problem, accounting reports for overseas operations tend to be less accurate than for domestic operations because of such factors as the looseness of foreign accounting for reserves and greater ease in varying depreciation allowances. Also, as we indicate in numerous subsequent illustrations, the balance sheets and income statements of individual subsidiaries within a multinational enterprise, rather than reflecting arm's-length negotiations on intercompany transactions, are the outcome of much more arbitrary allocations of costs and profits, made in order to achieve a particular set of goals. Finally, book value understates the market value of foreign affiliates by a substantial, but unknown, amount.

5. *U.S. Direct Investments Abroad,* pp. 49, 77.

6. For data from 1897 to 1929, see E. R. Barlow and Ira T. Wender, *Foreign Investment and Taxation* (Englewood Cliffs: Prentice-Hall, 1955), pp. 11, 14.

7. A thorough discussion of the role of the product life cycle in affecting U.S. foreign direct investment is given in Vernon, *Sovereignty at Bay,* Chapter 3.

8. Unless otherwise noted, the statistics in this section are from U.S. Treasury Department, Internal Revenue Service, *Statistics of Income . . . 1964–1966,* Supplemental Report, *Foreign Income and Taxes Reported on Corporation Income Tax Return* (Washington: Superintendent of Documents, 1973). The number of U.S. foreign

direct investors seems not to have grown dramatically. According to the census of U.S. foreign direct investors, some 3,400 persons (firms or individuals) filed reports in 1966 compared with 2,800 in 1957. In contrast, the number of foreign affiliates grew from about 10,000 in 1957 to 23,000 in 1966. See *U.S. Direct Investments Abroad,* pp. 2, 177; and Office of Business Economics, U.S. Department of Commerce, *U.S. Business Investments in Foreign Countries* (Washington: Superintendent of Documents, 1960), p. 6.

9. The estimate that there were 1,500 U.S. branches abroad in 1962 rests upon the fact that the ratio of branches to subsidiaries for all U.S. foreign direct investment was 15 percent in 1966; see *U.S. Direct Investments Abroad,* p. 183.

10. For a more detailed description of the selection of the 187 firms, their characteristics relative to other U.S. firms, and their relative importance at home and abroad, refer to Vernon, *Sovereignty at Bay,* Chapter 1. For a list of firms, see J. W. Vaupel and J. P. Curhan, *The Making of Multinational Enterprise* (Boston: Harvard Business School, 1969), pp. 6–8.

11. In 1967, the 187 enterprises had 7,927 foreign subsidiaries and 3,646 of these were engaged in manufacturing; see J. W. Vaupel and J. P. Curhan, Chapter 3. The estimate that the 187 enterprises had perhaps 1,000 branches rests upon the fact that the ratio of branches to subsidiaries for all U.S. foreign direct investment was 15 percent in 1966; see *U.S. Direct Investments Abroad,* p. 183.

12. J. W. Vaupel, "Characteristics and Motivations of the U.S. Corporations that Manufacture Abroad," unpublished working paper, Harvard Business School Multinational Enterprise Project, 1971, p. 38

TWO

1. Michael T. Wells, "Devaluation and Inflation and Their Effect on Foreign Operations," in Kenneth B. Berg *et al.* (eds.), *Readings in International Accounting* (Boston: Houghton Mifflin, 1969), p. 271; and Martin O. Binger, "Translation of Financial Statements Expressed in Foreign Currencies," *Readings in International Accounting,* p. 276.

2. Even though a draft of the proposed new rule was withdrawn from circulation pending further study, some accounting firms allowed enterprises to adopt the new rule. See *Wall Street Journal* (December 15, 1971): 2, and American Institute of Certified Public Accountants, *Accounting Research Association Newsletter* (January 28, 1971). As a sidelight, in 1972 the American Institute of Certified Public Accountants was preparing to replace the Accounting Principles Board with a new organization to determine policy. See *Wall Street Journal* (May 2, 1972): 42, and (May 23, 1972): 20. The U.S. tax rules with respect to conversion and translation losses differ from the financial treatment thereof and are quite complex in themselves (see generally Donald R. Ravenscroft, "Taxation of Income Arising From Changes in Value of Foreign Currency," *Harvard Law Review,* 82 [1969]: 772–97; Herbert J. Korbel, *Foreign Earnings and Profits and Recordkeeping* [Washington, D.C.: Tax Management, Inc., 1967]; and Treasury Regulation § 1 964–1, d and e).

3. For more details on this complex subject the reader should refer to the original sources. For example, there are exceptions to this general rule, for under certain circumstances inventory can be stated at the acquisition rate. Furthermore, long-term debt and fixed assets can be stated at the new rate when the debt was issued in connection with the acquisition of long-term assets shortly before a substantial change in the exchange rate. For further details, see American Institute of Certified Public Accountants, *Inventory of Generally Accepted Accounting Principles for Business Enterprises,* Accounting Research Study No. 7 (1965), pp. 330–34.

4. National Association for Accountants, *Management Accounting Problems in Foreign Operations,* N.A.A. Research Report 36, 1960, pp. 16–24.

5. C. Willard Elliott, "The Lower of Cost or Market Test for Foreign Inventories," *Readings in International Accounting,* pp. 292–99.

6. Profits from subsidiaries of U.S. multinational enterprises have continued to rise in the face of numerous devaluations of foreign currencies, and to our knowledge no study has been made showing what profits would have been if no devaluations had taken place. For a hypothetical example of deviations between accounting profits and economic profits see Robert B. Stobaugh, "How to Analyze Foreign Investment Climates," *Harvard Business Review,* 47 (September–October 1969): 100–108. For a mathematical formulation of the difference between accounting and economic values, see Donald Heckerman, "The Exchange Risks of Foreign Operations," *Journal of Business,* 45 (January 1972): 42–48. Members of the accounting profession are beginning to suggest that the difference between accounting and economic values be recognized; see Donald R. Mandich, "Devaluation, Revaluation— Re-Evaluation?" *Management Accounting,* 52 (August 1970): 27–29; and Donald J. Hayes, "Translating Foreign Currencies," *Harvard Business Review,* 50 (January–February 1972): 6–19.

7. *Business International* (April 30, 1971): 143.

8. U.S. tax law limits the foreign tax credit so that a firm pays the higher of the U.S. or foreign tax rate (this is the "effective" foreign rate determined in accordance with U.S. tax accounting principles) on its taxable income from foreign sources; this limit may now be calculated by either the per-country or overall method. In the former case, the rate is applied separately on the taxable income from sources within each country, while in the latter case the rate is applied separately to the taxable income from all foreign countries. The per-country limit used above could penalize a multinational corporation with subsidiaries in the countries some of which had higher and others lower tax rates than those in the United States; the overall method, on the other hand, could penalize a firm where a subsidiary's losses in one country reduced total foreign income, and thus the available foreign tax credit, without lowering the amount of foreign taxes actually paid. From 1954 to 1961 only the per-country option was available, but starting in 1961 the law gave taxpayers a one-time choice between the two methods. The prompt response of firms to this relaxation is indicated by the fact that in the initial year of its availability more than one-third of the foreign taxable income was shown on taxpayer returns using the overall limitation. See U.S. Treasury Department, U.S. Internal Revenue Service, *Foreign Tax Credit Claimed on Corporation Income Tax Returns with Accounting Periods Ended July 1961–June 1962,* "Supplemental Report, Statistics of Income, 1961" (Washington, D.C., Superintendent of Documents, 1967).

9. For a good introduction to this very complex field, refer to Boris I. Bittker and James S. Eustice, *Federal Income Taxation of Corporations and Shareholders* (Boston: Warren, Gorham & Lamont, Inc., 1971, with 1972 supplement, no. 1), Chapter 17. Except for a number of special situations, such as cases involving subpart F or Western Hemisphere Trading Corporations, U.S. tax treatment of foreign losses is symmetrical with the tax treatment of profits. For more details, see William C. Gifford, Jr., "United States Tax Treatment of Foreign Losses" (forthcoming). Such losses are not large in relation to profits; during the year 1962, for example, of the total of 10,539 U.S.-controlled foreign corporations, 2,803 reported net losses totaling $334,912,000 (IRS, *Foreign Income and Taxes Reported on Corporation Income Tax Returns*).

10. These data are from *Foreign Tax Credit Claimed on Corporation Income Tax Returns.*

11. Under Section 963 of the Revenue Act of 1962. For an analysis of the tax

principles governing the election by a domestic corporation to receive a minimum distribution from one or more controlled foreign corporations and the resulting Section 963 exclusion of subpart F, see William C. Gifford, Jr., *Controlled Foreign Corporations—Section 963* (Washington, D.C.: Tax Management, Inc., 1970). The fact that this publication has more than 200 pages suggests some of the complexity involved. Similar publications are available for other sections of this Revenue Act of 1962. Although U.S. firms have proceeded to work within the Revenue Act of 1962, it is so complex that certain rulings by the Internal Revenue Service are believed to be incorrect. For example, see William C. Gifford, Jr., " 'Excess' Distribution under Section 963: Computation of the Foreign Tax Credit," *Tax Law Review,* 26 (1971): 371–78.

12. For more detail on financial accounting, see Kenneth B. Berg, Gerhard G. Mueller, and Lauren M. Walker, *Readings in International Accounting* (Boston: Houghton Mifflin, 1969). Tax accounting also presents a problem, for regardless of an enterprise's policy on consolidating financial reports, the profits of a foreign subsidiary for U.S. tax purposes must be computed in accordance with U.S. tax accounting principles.

13. John M. Stopford and Louis T. Wells, Jr., *Managing the Multinational Enterprise: Organization of the Firm and Ownership of the Subsidiaries* (New York: Basic Books, 1972), Chapter 7. For a study of instability in joint ventures, see Lawrence E. Franko, *Joint Venture Survival in Multinational Corporations* (New York: Praeger, 1971).

14. Chamber of Commerce Istanbul, "Turkiyede Ozel Sermaye Yatirimlari ve Ekonomiye Yarali Olmasi Icin Dusunlen Tedbirler" ("Foreign Private Capital Investments in Turkey and Measures Being Considered to Make Them Useful for the Economy"), Istanbul (1967), p. 48. [In Turkish.]

15. Max W. Thornburg, *Turkey: An Economic Appraisal* (New York: Twentieth Century Fund, 1949), p. 21.

16. Richard D. Robinson, *The First Turkish Republic* (Cambridge, Massachusetts: Harvard University Press, 1963), p. 105.

17. Most of this section on Turkey was drawn from Hasan Bilgin, "Socio-Economic Constraints Operating in Turkey and the Projection of Their Effect upon the Financial Statements of American Subsidiaries," unpublished working paper, Columbia Business School, 1970.

THREE

1. Other studies have noted different types of organizational phases of businesses. For example, the Business Policy area at Harvard Business School has referred to stages of corporate development and Stopford and Wells have defined the stages of multinational organization. See Malcolm S. Salter, "Stages of Corporate Development," Harvard Business School case BP–902; and John M. Stopford and Louis T. Wells, Jr., *Managing the Multinational Enterprise: Organization of the Firm and Ownership of the Subsidiaries* (New York: Basic Books, 1972), Chapter 2.

2. This was a frequently cited reason as to why companies did not have a separate international financial executive. The NICB study, covering nearly 300 industrial firms with international operations, found that only 17 percent of those companies with total sales of less than $100 million and with less than one-quarter of their sales abroad had a separate international financial executive. See National Industrial Conference Board, *Managing the International Financial Function* (New York, 1970), pp. 2–3.

3. Our data do not allow an estimate to be made solely for manufacturing opera-

tions. Estimate was made on the basis of data from Office of Foreign Direct Investment, U.S. Department of Commerce, "Foreign Affiliate Financial Survey 1966–1969," (July 1971); U.S. Treasury Department, Internal Revenue Service, *Statistics of Income . . . 1962,* Supplemental Report *Foreign Income and Taxes Reported on Corporation Income Tax Returns* (Washington, D.C.: 1969); and unpublished U.S. government data made available to us in the form of carefully controlled aggregate statistics so as to maintain confidentiality.

4. See preceding note.

5. *Managing the International Financial Function,* p. 92.

6. See note 3.

7. See note 3.

8. See William H. Gruber, Dileep Mehta, and Raymond Vernon, "The R&D Factor in International Trade and International Investment of United States Industries," *Journal of Political Economy,* 75 (February 1967): 20–37; and Raymond Vernon, "Organization as a Scale Factor in the Growth of Firms," in Jesse W. Markham and Gustav F. Papanek (eds.), *Industrial Organization and Economic Development: In Honor of E. S. Mason* (Boston: Houghton Mifflin, 1970), p. 47.

FOUR

1. The six-month interest-free period applies to intercompany accounts arising in the ordinary course of business out of sales, leases, or the rendition of services. Section 482 applies to sales of goods and services between members of a multinational service system. For a study of the experience of more than 500 U.S. companies with Section 482, see Michael G. Duerr, *Tax Allocations and International Business* (New York: The Conference Board, Inc., 1972). This study reports that about two-thirds of U.S. firms with significant commercial relations with related parties abroad indicated that the Internal Revenue Service had allocated income from one of their subsidiaries to the U.S. parent (*ibid.,* p. 7). However, the Revenue Act of 1971, which allows U.S. exporters to choose between one of several methods in setting transfer prices on inter-company sales to a Domestic International Sales Corporation (DISC), reduces the scope for conflict between enterprises and the IRS (see "Domestic International Sales Corporation," TB 71–16 [December 21, 1971], issued by Ernst & Ernst, 140 Broadway, New York, N.Y.).

2. For examples of restrictions by various countries, see *Financing Foreign Operations* (New York: *Business International,* various dates).

3. This executive did not know the source of the four-to-one ratio, but because of the *Talbot Mills* decision—on a domestic case—many observers think that the Supreme Court has made it clear that a four-to-one ratio of intercompany debt-to-equity is not "obviously inadequate." See 326 U.S. 521 (1946). For a discussion of this issue, see Richard B. Stone, "Debt-Equity Distinctions in the Tax Treatment of the Corporation and Its Shareholders," *Tulane Law Review,* 42 (1968): 251–88; and William M. Goldstein, "Corporate Indebtedness to Shareholders: 'Thin Capitalization' and Related Problems," *Tax Law Review,* 16 (May–June 1960): 1–79. The Tax Reform Act of 1969 added Section 385 to the Internal Revenue Code, authorizing the Treasury to issue detailed guidelines with respect to the acceptable level of shareholder indebtedness. No such regulations have yet been issued. It is well known, however, that the Internal Revenue Service does accept a four-to-one debt-to-equity ratio in its advance rulings to offshore financing subsidiaries formed for the purpose of raising capital abroad. Total debt, not just intercompany debt, is used in calculating this ratio.

4. E. T. Penrose, "Foreign Investment and the Growth of the Firm," *Economic Journal,* 66 (June 1956): 220–35.

5. See note 6, Chapter 1.

6. See note 4, above.

7. See source and note a in Table 7–2.

8. Raytheon Annual Report, 1969; "Italian Failure Casts Shadow on All Firms," *Business International* (1968): 201.

9. See Stopford and Wells, cited in note 13, Chapter 2.

10. David K. Dodd, "An International Capital Market?" *Financial Analysts Journal* (November–December 1967): 159; *The Economist* (December 25, 1971): 86.

11. Fritz Machlup, *Euro-Dollar Creation: A Mystery Story* (Princeton: Princeton University, International Finance Section, Department of Economics, 1970), Reprint no. 16 in *International Finance* (reprinted from *Banca Nasionale del Lavoro Quarterly Review,* no. 94 [September 1970]).

12. *Wall Street Journal* (March 16, 1972): 12.

13. Estimated by authors from unpublished U.S. Government data made available to us in the form of carefully controlled aggregate statistics so as to maintain confidentiality.

FIVE

1. This distinction is made by Michael Z. Brooke and H. Lee Remmers, *The Strategy of Multinational Enterprise: Organization and Finance* (New York: American Elsevier Publishing Company, 1970), Chapter 6.

2. For further support of this conclusion, see Irene W. Meister, *Managing the International Financial Function,* National Industrial Conference Board, Business Policy Study No. 133 (New York: 1970), Chapter 4.

3. Calculated from data in the Office of Business Economics, U.S. Department of Commerce, *U.S. Direct Investments Abroad 1966, Part 1: Balance of Payments Data* (Washington, D.C.: Department of Documents, 1970), pp. 63, 85, 114, 137, 177. This finding is consistent with David B. Zenoff, "The Determinants of Dividend Remittance Practices of Wholly-Owned European and Canadian Subsidiaries of American Multinational Corporations," unpublished D.B.A. thesis, Harvard University Graduate School of Business Administration (1966), Chapter 4, and with George F. Kopits, "Dividend Remittance Behavior within the International Firm: A Theoretical and Empirical Analysis," unpublished Doctoral dissertation, Georgetown University (June 1971). Kopits found that for foreign subsidiaries of U.S. foreign direct investors, other things being equal, a subsidiary's dividends would be greater, the more it earns and the slower it grows.

4. Dividend policy was found to be the most important problem between multinational enterprises and their foreign joint venture partners. See John Stopford and Louis T. Wells Jr., *Managing the Multinational Enterprise: Organization of the Firm and Ownership of the Subsidiaries* (New York: Basic Books, 1972), Chapter 7. The problems involved in dealing with minority stockholders are exemplified by the case of Sinclair Venezuelan Oil Company, a company operating in Venezuela and owned 97 percent by Sinclair Oil Corporation. The Venezuelan unit paid dividends of $108 million over a nine-year period although its earnings were only $38 million for the same period. A court, as a result of a suit by a minority stockholder, ruled that Sinclair had breached its duty to the subsidiary by requiring it to pay excessive dividends; a higher court later reversed this ruling. See *Del. Ch. 261 A.2d 911* and *Wall Street Journal* (June 23, 1971): 11.

5. For all U.S. foreign direct investors in 1969, for example, management fees (and service charges) were $729 million and royalties (and license fees and rentals)

were $641 million. Royalties were 60 percent of the total fees in the manufacturing and trade industries and only 14 percent in petroleum and other industries. David T. Devlin and George R. Kruer, "The International Investment Position of the United States: Developments in 1961," *Survey of Current Business* (October 1970): 21–37.

6. Consistent with this attitude, transfer pricing appears to be used more in Latin America than in other areas as a method of withdrawing funds from subsidiaries. Whereas income receipts from sales affiliates averaged 8 percent of net earnings for all foreign operations of U.S. foreign direct investors engaged primarily in manufacturing, the comparable figure for Latin America was 14 percent. See *U.S. Direct Investments Abroad, 1966, Part 1: Balance of Payments Data*, p. 69.

7. Estimated by authors from data in Marie T. Bradshaw, "U.S. Exports to Foreign Affiliates of U.S. Firms," *Survey of Current Business* (May 1969): 34–57; and R. David Belli, "Sales of Foreign Affiliates of U.S. Firms, 1961–65, 1967, and 1968," *Survey of Current Business* (October 1970): 18–20.

8. Devlin and Kruer, pp. 34 and 37.

9. For a study of the experiences of U.S. companies with the U.S. government on transfer pricing, see Duerr, note 1, Chapter 4.

10. A range of plus or minus 20 percent was allowed on transfer prices on goods sold from one unit to another in the model. Although this range might be unrealistically high for some standardized goods, most sales between units of multinational systems in the real world do not involve sales of standardized goods, especially at volumes sold to the public. As a result, many disputes between U.S. companies and the IRS on transfer pricing of goods have involved a price range greater than plus or minus 20 percent. See Duerr, note 1, Chapter 4.

SIX

1. We estimated that current assets of overseas holdings of U.S. foreign direct investors consist of 6 percent cash and marketable securities, 42 percent accounts receivable, and 52 percent inventories. These percentages were derived from Tables 6–1, 6–2, and 6–3 and obviously are only crude approximations; the total of current assets came from Table 1–1.

2. U.S. Department of Commerce, Office of Foreign Direct Investments, *Foreign Direct Investment Program—Selected Statistics* (Washington: Government Printing Office, July 1971), p. 6.

3. See John M. Stopford and Louis T. Wells, Jr., *Managing the Multinational Enterprise: Organization of the Firm and Ownership of the Subsidiaries* (New York: Basic Books, 1972), Chapter 7.

4. John H. Dunning, "U.S. Subsidiaries in Britain and Their U.K. Competitors," *Business Ratios* (Autumn 1966): 15.

SEVEN

1. Amounts are from Chapter 1.

2. This and a number of our other findings are confirmed by a study of the actions that U.S. multinational enterprises took in protecting against devaluation of the pound sterling prior to the 1967 devaluation. See Hassanand T. Jadwani, "Some Aspects of the Multinational Corporations' Exposure to the Exchange Rate Risk," unpublished D.B.A. thesis, Harvard Business School (March 1972), p. ii–10.

3. Jadwani found that only 16 percent of the enterprises reduced their levels of cash and marketable securities to an "absolute minimum" prior to the 1967 sterling devaluation, but that 43 percent of the enterprises whose U.K. subsidiaries had prof-

its increased or speeded up their dividend payments. See Jadwani, pp. IV–33 and IV–50.

4. Jadwani estimated an annual cost of 17 percent for the United Kingdom. Jadwani, p. IV–26.

5. Jadwani reports that some subsidiaries in the United Kingdom prepaid dollar obligations or delayed collections from subsidiaries in other countries. Jadwani, pp. IV-33–34.

6. Only one out of twenty-five U.S. subsidiaries in the United Kingdom stocked increased inventories prior to the 1967 sterling devaluation. See Jadwani, IV–45.

7. None of the twenty-five U.S. firms in the United Kingdom attempted to delay payment on accounts payable prior to the 1967 sterling devaluation. Jadwani estimates the gross cost of increasing accounts payable by foreign discounts to be about 17 percent in the United Kingdom. Jadwani, p. IV–43.

8. Ernst and Ernst, *Financial Aspects of Foreign Currency Devaluation and Revaluation,* Special Report No. 3 (December 1969). A foreign branch of a domestic corporation may be permitted to deduct translation losses for U.S. tax purposes. Moreover, under special rules for the computation of earnings and profits adopted pursuant to the Revenue Act of 1962, a controlled foreign subsidiary of a U.S. parent corporation may be required to reflect translation gains and losses as well as exchange conversion losses, and such gains and losses may directly affect the amount of income required for inclusion in the income of the U.S. shareholder pursuant to the provision of subpart F. See articles by Ravenscroft and Korbel, note 2, Chapter 2.

9. Jadwani found that this was the case in the United Kingdom for the 2¾ years prior to the 1967 sterling devaluation, *provided* that the forward exchange was not purchased at a time when the rumors about devaluation became very strong. Jadwani, p. III–18.

10. Alan R. Holmes and Francis H. Schott, *The New York Foreign Exchange Market* (New York: Federal Reserve Bank of New York, 1965), pp. 44–45.

11. Jadwani's findings on the propensity of various types of firms to purchase forward exchange were similar to our findings. Small enterprises were less likely to purchase forward exchange than were larger ones. The lack of purchase of forward exchange by a small firm was the result of their not having given enough thought to the study. In contrast, when a large firm refrained from purchasing forward exchange, it was the result of a planned program.

12. Holmes and Schott, pp. 48–49.

13. Most decision makers when given the choice between two risky alternatives both yielding the same average returns but with different dispersions of returns will generally prefer the alternative with the lower dispersion of returns. For a comprehensive exposition of procedures for decision making under uncertainty, see Howard Raiffa, *Decision Analysis: Introductory Lectures on Choices under Uncertainty* (Reading, Mass.: Addison-Wesley, 1967). For an example of a computer model to protect one subsidiary against exchange risk, see Bernard A. Lietaer, "Managing Risks in Foreign Exchange," *Harvard Business Review,* 48 (September–October 1970): 113–25. For a description of "scenario programming," which permits one to construct a linear programming equivalent to any decision tree with discrete events, see G. B. Dantzig, *Linear Programming and Extensions* (Princeton, N.J.: Princeton University Press, 1963), p. 511.

EIGHT

1. It is possible to have the model solve for an optimal profit given the constraint of maintaining a specified ratio of debt to equity in the overall system; in this way,

there would be no increase in risk due to borrowing. For further discussions of risk and stock market valuations, see J. E. Stiglitz, "A Re-Examination of the Modigliani-Miller Theorem," *The American Economic Review,* 59 (December 1969): 784–93.

2. Robert B. Stobaugh, "How to Analyze Foreign Investment Climates," *Harvard Business Review,* 16 (September–October 1969): 100--108.

3. Joseph L. Bower, *Managing the Resource Allocation Process* (Boston: Division of Research, Harvard University Graduate School of Business Administration, 1970).

4. There have been few comparisons of actual experiences of subsidiaries with the estimates contained in the original requests for funds. However, our interviews plus other available data suggest that there are great variations between expected and actual results. See Stobaugh and Associates, note 2, Chapter 1. Even the technical methods used to calculate return on investment for the investment decision often are different from that used for the profit measurement system; see Edward C. Bursk, John Dearden, David F. Hawkins, and Victor M. Longstreet, *Financial Control of Multinational Operations* (New York: Financial Executives Research Foundation, 1971), p. 109.

5. For examples, see "Foreign Profit Performance," *Business International* (July 2, 1971): 214; and R. David Belli and Julius N. Freidlin, "U.S. Direct Investments Abroad in 1970," *Survey of Current Business* (October 1971): 31.

NINE

1. According to our estimates, the average worldwide sales of multinational enterprises in 1968 were $400 million, $900 million and $5,500 million for Small, Medium, and Large enterprises, respectively. We estimated an after-tax earnings of 7 percent of sales, or $28 million, $63 million, and $385 million, respectively. We had no data on profitability of U.S. operations, but earnings abroad were about 7 percent of sales in 1969; see U.S. Department of Commerce, Office of Foreign Direct Investments, *Foreign Direct Investment Program,* July 1971. Since earnings reported from abroad have been on the average about the same return on sales as those reported for U.S. operations, we use 7 percent of worldwide sales as an estimate of worldwide profits. For an example of a comparison of foreign with U.S. profits, see the series published annually in *Business International* (e.g., August 27, 1971, page 279).

2. This estimate of total profits for all U.S. foreign direct investors was more readily made from *foreign* earnings than domestic earnings, for an estimate of the latter is not available. The potential gains of the Small enterprises—16 percent of worldwide profits—and the potential gains of the Large enterprises—8 percent of worldwide profits—are more than 25 percent of foreign profits. However, our estimate of potential saving was reduced to this 25 percent level because some Small enterprises already have captured part of the potential gain of 16 percent, and the Medium enterprises—operating closer to an optimum than the others—would bring the average of all enterprises below that of the Small and Large.

3. In fact, in April 1972, one Large multinational enterprise had just completed a model similar in principle to our model. This incorporated its fifteen most important subsidiaries.

TEN

1. *Wall Street Journal* (July 22, 1971): 17.
2. See *Business International* (August 13, 1971): 257.

3. *Wall Street Journal* (August 30, 1971): 3.

4. *Wall Street Journal* (September 13, 1971): 8.

5. *Wall Street Journal* (October 5, 1971): 4.

6. "New Ground Rules for Luring Investment," *Fortune* (July 1971): 39.

7. Our basic data for these estimates are from *Annual Reports* and note 13, Chapter 4.

8. Estimated by assuming normal growth in the "liabilities to U.S. entities" shown in Table 1–1.

9. This area is treated more fully in another book in this series, Raymond Vernon, *Sovereignty at Bay: The Multinational Spread of U.S. Enterprises* (New York: Basic Books, 1971).

10. For fuller discussions of factors affecting the growth and decline of multinational enterprises, refer to Vernon's *Sovereignty at Bay* and Stobaugh and Associates, note 2, Chapter 1.

11. Raymond Vernon and Charles P. Kindleberger are two such authors; see Vernon's *Sovereignty at Bay,* Chapter 8, and Charles P. Kindleberger, *American Business Abroad: Six Lectures on Direct Investment* (New Haven: Yale University Press, 1969), Lecture no. 6.

12. Company interview.

13. *Systek International (D),* Harvard Business School case no. 9–371–425, ICR 463, 1971.

14. *Wall Street Journal* (September 17, 1971): 1; and *Wall Street Journal* (March 13, 1972): 14.

15. Lacy H. Hunt, "Recurrent Crises Plague World Monetary System," *Federal Reserve Bank of Dallas Business Review* (September 1971): 1.

16. Since the summer of 1971, when we initially wrote this sentence, exchange controls have proliferated; for examples, see "The Year of the Barriers," Survey in *The Economist* (January 27, 1973).

APPENDIX B

1. Michael G. Duerr, *Tax Allocations and International Business* (New York: The Conference Board, Inc., 1972).

INDEX

ACCOUNTING SYSTEMS (principles, policies, practices): for measuring effects of devaluation or revaluation, 24–26; reconciling differences in U.S. and foreign, 31; effect of variations in, on performance evaluation, 147

Accounts payable: payment for interest on, 13; and devaluation of local currency, 125

Accounts receivable: intercompany, 53–57, 107, 111, 124–125; and withdrawing funds from abroad, 75–76; as element of current assets, 97; from outside customers, 107–110, 123–124; prospects for change in policy of, 118; protection of, against exchange risks, 123–125

Africa, crude oil from, 160

Age (of foreign affiliate), effect of, on dividend payments, 85

American Institute of Certified Public Accountants (AICPA), 25; Accounting Principles Board of, 23, 24

Argentina: interest rates in, 26, 109; use of management fee in, to avoid dividend tax, 89; import restrictions in, 113; performance schedules in, 114

Arm's-length financial policy (prices), 45, 93; defined, 16; and the use of royalties and management fees, 88–89, 185; impact of, on profits, 165–171 *passim;* and government revenue, 176–178; effect of, on balance of payments, 180

Assets, current: types of, 97–98; held abroad by U.S. foreign direct in-

vestors (1970), 98–99, 120; pattern and trend of, 116–118; protection of, against devaluation, 121–125; ratio of, to current liabilities, 127; high ratio of, to total assets, 169. *See also* Accounts receivable; Cash; Inventories

Australia: General Motors' subsidiary in, 59; dividend payments in, 86; protection against devaluation in, 124–125

BALANCE OF PAYMENTS, effect on, of financial policies of multinational enterprise, 178–183, 186

Banks: widespread use of local, 66–69; handling of cash by, 101–102; as source of information concerning exchange risk, 134; and interest rates, 174

Barlow, E. R., 59

Belgium, multinational enterprises of, 3

Bonds, *see* Eurobond market

Borrowing, local, 63–71; and interest-rate differentials, 26–27; to protect against exchange risks, 125–127; and forward exchange market, 130. *See also* Equity and credit; Interest rates; Loans

Brazil: dividend payments in, 86; banking system in, 102; interest rates in, 109; import restrictions in, 113; performance schedules in, 114; weak currency market of, 115; devaluation of cruzeiros in, 119, 120; U.S. investment in, based on used equipment, 158–159, 160

Britain, currency reserves of, effect